PATAGONIA

Landscapes of the Imagination

PATAGONIA

A CULTURAL HISTORY

Chris Moss

OXFORD
UNIVERSITY PRESS

2008

OXFORD
UNIVERSITY PRESS

Oxford University Press, Inc., publishes works that further
Oxford University's objective of excellence
in research, scholarship, and education.

Oxford   New York
Auckland   Cape Town   Dar es Salaam   Hong Kong   Karachi
Kuala Lumpur   Madrid   Melbourne   Mexico City   Nairobi
New Delhi   Shanghai   Taipei   Toronto

With offices in
Argentina   Austria   Brazil   Chile   Czech Republic   France   Greece
Guatemala   Hungary   Italy   Japan Poland   Portugal   Singapore
South Korea   Switzerland   Thailand   Turkey   Ukraine   Vietnam

Copyright © 2008 by Chris Moss

Published by Oxford University Press, Inc.
198 Madison Avenue, New York, New York 10016

www.oup.com

Oxford is a registered trademark of Oxford University Press

Co-published in Great Britain by Signal Books

Library of Congress Cataloging-in-Publication Data
Moss, Chris.
    Patagonia : a cultural history / Chris Moss.
        p.   cm.—(Landscapes of the imagination)
    Includes bibliographical references and index.
    ISBN 978-0-19-534249-9
    1. Patagonia (Argentina and Chile)—Description and travel.   2. Patagonia
    (Argentina and Chile)—History.   I. Title.
    F2936.M88   2008
    918.2'7—dc22   2008023576

Images: p.xv John Snelgrove/istockphoto; p.34 Arne Thaysen/istockphoto; p.40 Hans Schachtschabel/
istockphoto; p.47 Alejandro Soto/istockphoto; p.54 Alexander Hafemann/istockphoto; p.65 Maria
Veras/istockphoto; p.73 Marcelo Silva/istockphoto; p.79 Bruce Block/istockphoto; p.212 Max-Steven
Grossman/istockphoto; p.222 Eva Ritchie/istockphoto; p.282 Laura Gugliermetti/istockphoto; Walter
Spina/istockphoto. All others images: Chris Moss, Archivo General de la Nación and Archivo Roil

Contents

Preface

I first went to Patagonia as a tourist. After moving to Buenos Aires in 1991 I soon felt a need to escape from it. Not that the city wasn't a wonderful place to live; it was dynamic, surprising, fascinatingly damaged. But it was also full of the usual urban clutter—cars, fumes, crowds, more cars—and there was no space to think.

I made my first getaway by flying to San Carlos de Bariloche, the ersatz Alpine town that sits beside Lake Nahuel Huapi's huge blue eye. I wasn't overly impressed by the Saint Bernard dogs or the local chocolate, but the air was bracing, rhythms were slow, and on the scruffy edge of the town I spied the beginning of Patagonia's monotonous steppe. This was space in abundance. Space and, it seemed, nothing else.

Subsequent journeys took me to rain-drenched Chiloé and the Chilean fjords, lonely Ushuaia shivering on the north bank of the Beagle Channel, and the stranded ports of Deseado and San Julián. The rail network was still alive in the 1990s and I took a diesel train down to Ingeniero Jacobacci to jump on *La Trochita* to Esquel, with rheas skipping across the line faster than the steam engine could chug along it. These overland trips tried my patience, as did the incessant westerlies, but they meant I saw the less obvious hubs and junctions: oil-capital Comodoro Rivadavia, convivial Viedma, the forlorn coal-mining town of Río Turbio. I always took a tent. I always made friends.

So there was "my" Patagonia: big skies, few people, camping under the Southern Cross, and learning to wait.

There were no dedicated guidebooks to Patagonia, and the chapters on the region in guides to Chile and Argentina were brief and all about getting in and out of towns and seeing the occasional museum.

Like most innocent backpackers, I was exposed to Bruce Chatwin early on. A copy of *In Patagonia* was as *de rigueur* in the 1990s as it is now and, while I found the book's elliptical structure and condescending tone irritating, I was impressed by the deftness with which Chatwin wove together dozens of storylines and with the range of the travelogue's source material. When I took up a few of his leads and began to delve, I discovered that my favourite empty space was crammed with literature.

I was intrigued by the fact that the book did not reflect in any way the country I was learning to love. It was not only that I spoke Spanish and so could engage with the "Patagonians" Chatwin had set out to caricature. There were other gaps. He had no time for the flora and fauna, for indigenous traditions, or for Argentinian and Chilean experiences of Patagonia. Those who live in Buenos Aires, Santiago de Chile, Córdoba and the other cramped cities of the temperate zone cherish a notion of the *sur* that is nothing like the myths Europeans spin about Patagonia. In place of Darwin and FitzRoy, Drake and Saint Exupéry, they have local heroes—Francisco Moreno, General Roca, W. H. Hudson—and instead of travel books and guidebooks that draw on a treasure trove of narratives written by past adventurers, they prefer to indulge in newly conceived films and fictions. Argentinians and Chileans live in Patagonia, they labour there and die there. They plant vineyards and raise children; they form hippie colonies and are sent to naval bases. Mapuches fight with governments over land rights; fifth-generation Welsh children try to learn the language of their pioneering forebears. For Chatwin and almost all visitors, Patagonia was "material" to be digested and reworked; for anyone born or living there, it is home.

There is also a glow in the Patagonian sky. The most inspired writers always discover something sublime down there and note, humbled, that it derives from some unnameable quality about the landscape. When you travel overland from east to west, at some point the Andes begin to emerge beyond the ochre grasslands. I have made that journey from Río Gallegos, from Playa Unión, and from Carmen de Patagones, and it has always been a revelation. Despite the richness and variety of the literature, nothing ever equals the experience of seeing such natural beauty. Many writers have seized upon the crude poetics of desolation, but in doing so perhaps they have missed the grandeur and exuberant beauty of Patagonia.

In his tango "Vuelvo al Sur", the writer Pino Solanas is thinking of the southside of Buenos Aires: the older, wiser, crumbling part of the city. But the longing felt in the song applies equally to the constant pull of Patagonia. Returning and returning again and again to Patagonia, both physically and through all the books that I had to open to research this book, has been a pleasurable journey. If I have learned that even the desert is never as barren as it first appears, I have also realized that Patagonia's human imprint is as marvellous as its wildernesses.

Yet Patagonia is changing. The "Uttermost Part of the Earth" is now only a fifteen-hour flight away from London or New York. Roads are paved, chic restaurants have opened, and many *estancias* have been given the boutique makeover. Even .thirty years ago southern South America was an out-there destination; now it is a standard finale to many a gap-year adventure.

We have become familiar with the region thanks to tourism and the power of hard currency. But paths to Patagonia were first opened by the texts that fill this book, all written by individuals who travelled there with causes they considered far nobler than tourism.

Some people pay lip service to the idea that once a place is discovered its mysteries wilt and die. Even so, tourism is better than many of the other alternatives that are available to Patagonia. Some would like to use this scarcely populated triangle as a vast dump for countries that have no room for their own waste. Others would fence it all off and sell it to expatriate millionaires. *Criollo* traditionalists, many of them non-resident, would farm it till the land was completely reduced to desert and then dig it all up and drill holes in it. Geographers, soldiers, dreamers, ethnographers, fossil-hunters, fortune-hunter, writers and photographers have all had their time in Patagonia, say the futurists, and now the land has to pay.

Perhaps tourism is just the latest, rather benign phase in Patagonia's history as a zone of pointless pursuits—a place for idling, daydreaming, walking and wonder. Having got lost for a time in the Patagonian library, I am looking forward more than ever to being back in the region with nothing more on my mind than the unfolding day and the cold, clear night.

Acknowledgements

Writing this kind of book is a fairly solitary act, but I have had help and support from friends and family, as well as newspaper and magazine editors. Since returning to London in 2001, I have revisited certain corners of Patagonia and found new ones, and the trips have served to remind me that it is the landscape that first stirred my imagination—and that the writings, however wonderful and beguiling, came second. For allowing me to write stories for them I would like to thank the editors at *Condé Nast Traveller* and *Wanderlust* magazines and the travel desks of the *Daily Telegraph*, the *Independent* and the *Guardian*. Writing and editing for *Time Out* guides permitted me to explore less obvious destinations while hunting down bus timetables, boat services and B&Bs. Also, warm thanks to Dafydd Tudur at Glaniad and Marcela Plust in Los Mimbres in Gaiman for help on the Welsh chapter and to the culture and tourism departments of Rawson, Trelew and Trevelin.

Thanks to Peter Hulme and Tomás Eloy Martínez for advice and suggestions. Ian Barnett in Buenos Aires helped with translations and Matt Chesterton and my wife Carolina Gryngarten read through the first drafts. The staff in the Science and Rare Books reading rooms at the British Library were helpful. Thanks to James Ferguson at Signal for his patient encouragement. As for the London-based burglars who stole the first draft of this book I only hope some ancient Tehuelche curse plunges them into an abyss of ice and fire.

Chris Moss
November 2007
Trevelin, Chubut province

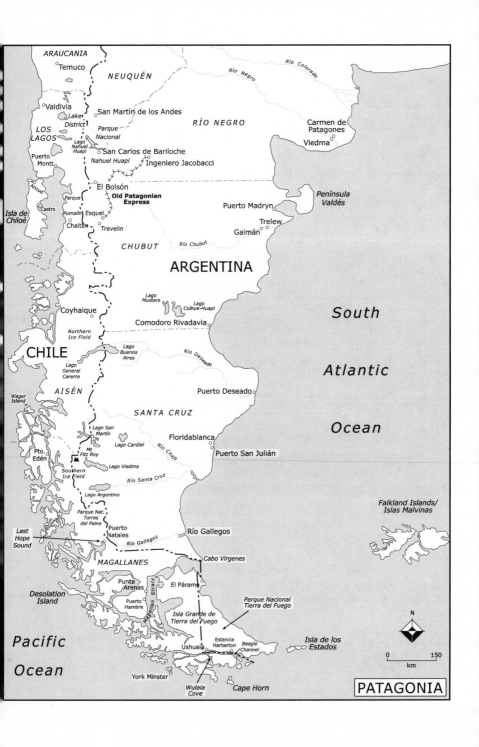

PATAGONIA

Introduction

"For visitors, Patagonia was first regarded as an obstacle, then it became a resource and it is now *un escenario*—a backdrop, scenery, a kind of theatre."

Pablo Antimi Rivera, tour guide, El Calafate

About the same size as Venezuela or three times that of Italy, Patagonia covers about 400,000 square miles. Its population of around 1.75 million souls—the same as Northern Ireland or Brussels—is largely settled in a few towns and small cities dotted along the Atlantic coast and in the fertile valleys abutting the Andean mountain range. The name, Patagonia, looks as confident as Catalonia or Transylvania, but this was never a nation or a country. For three hundred years it was largely ignored by the Spaniards and was the last frontier land to be claimed and colonized by Latin America's two southernmost republics. For Argentina and Chile, Patagonia is not a single province or county and only came to be regarded—tentatively—as a political region during the last century.

On a drive over the central plains of Patagonia on the Argentina side, you get the impression that no one lives there. In the huge province of Santa Cruz there is only one person for every 36 sheep and less than one person for every square mile of land. People who live in Ushuaia are farther from their Patagonian neighbours in San Carlos de Bariloche than Londoners are from the people of Warsaw.

In many parts of Chilean Patagonia the absence of people is rather more than an impression. The huge ice caps that stretch between latitudes 47 and 52 degrees south repel even the seabirds that battle with the winds off Antarctica. It is said that Chilean dictator Augusto Pinochet wanted to lay a highway across the ice fields, but for the time being this is a jagged, rain-soaked, empty place and one of the most remote corners of the planet. Even where the lonely Carretera Austral, or Southern Highway, has been cut through the dense beech and larch forests in Chile's Región de Aysén, human settlement is scant and sporadic.

From the sky you can take a view. Flying south in Argentinian Patagonia, the earth turns khaki, the oceans become turquoise, ice and granite dominate the high places, and the central plains are bereft of

native trees due to the ceaseless wind that whips up speed as it heads east. There is something distinctive about this landscape and even if you find individual elements of it elsewhere—in Greenland, Siberia, Canada— the precise arrangement of topographies is distinct and suggests that Patagonia might be a place after all.

But what gives the region a more exact unity is its cultural and historical reality. The far corners of Patagonia, and even those settlements separated by the Andes, are linked by maritime narratives, local legends and the stories of missionaries, military campaigns and pioneers.

The first notion of Patagonia was as a desolate shore. But with each sea-borne visitor the vista was widened and, gradually, as speculators, conquistadors and cartographers disembarked and rode their horses across the steppe, the interior became part of the definition. Many kept journals, and these were later added to by professional scribes and travel writers. Patagonia—as a construct, as an idea—evolved.

At the same time, people arrived with a desire to settle in the region. They built homes, chapels, farms, roads and eventually lives. They spun their own tales, real and fantastical, and they occasionally bartered and bred with the natives, who had their own long history and oral tradition. The people of Neuquén and Río Negro provinces in Argentina and Los Lagos in Chile are not only close to each other on the map, but they also have ties through the Jesuits who crossed the Andes to reach their churches on either side—paths used for generations before by the trans-Andean Mapuche tribes. Today they are also connected commercially, through trade and through the tourists who take the short cruises each day through the chain of lakes buried inside the mountains.

Geographical Patagonia: Between Extremes

Patagonia does not define a specific geography in the way, say, tundra, steppe and pampas do. But the region incorporates all these, as well as dense forests, white-sand beaches, chalky cliffs and flowery meadows. Sometimes, as in Chile's Parque Nacional Torres del Paine, all the topographies seem to be compacted into one relatively small space; a forbidding wall of glacial ice can be viewed from a balmy copse brightened by vermilion *notro* and yellow *amancay*.

The greater part of the southern tip of South America is a vast, scrub-covered, arid plain bordered by the Andean mountain range and Chilean ice fields to the west and the Atlantic coast to the east.

The plain looks flat but is in fact a series of gently rising tablelands, regularly riven by deep, multicoloured canyons and shallower river valleys. The vast majority of these last are ancient and dry but a half-dozen major waterways meander sluggishly down from the Andes to the Atlantic. On the eastern side of the cordillera, a small number of high-volume rivers flow in torrents down to the Pacific.

If the landscape is varied and the biodiversity impressive, the sky is the perfect mirror. Cigar-shaped lenticular forms, eerie mushrooms and vaulting cirrus clouds swirl surreally over the Andes, while the vast dome of the sky above the lowlands is often busy with flocks of cumulus clouds that seem to drift far more slowly than the dust-devils below. Great storms rise in the mountains, on the plains and, most famously, in the southern oceans, looming over ships and over *estancias* like super-natural beings.

The extreme geography has determined the history and culture of the region. For Argentina, with its rich farmlands in the region between Bahía Blanca in the south and Santa Fe in the north, Patagonia was for a long time considered useless, barren and best left to the savages. Slender Chile had more need of land, but needed to wage wars for centuries to win over what was in any case a region unsuited to settlement. Thus, over the years Patagonia's political borders have changed, depending on who was drawing the maps, the extent of conquests and, more recently, the requirements of tourism. For the purposes of this book, Patagonia refers to the land south of the Río Colorado in Argentina and south of the Río Biobío in Chile, and also encompasses Tierra del Fuego, the archipelago shared by the two nations.

European Patagonia: A Tall Story

Patagonia was mysterious even before it came into being. In the late fifteenth century Europeans spoke of a *Terra Australis que incognita est*, located somewhere between the legendary Cipango (Japan) and Cathay (China). Early mariners thought hell was somewhere in the far south, and the icy wastes of Antarctica did little to persuade them otherwise.

The name of Patagonia has several, equally improbable, etymologies, but most likely it alludes to a mariner's distorted perception of native footprints. The *patagones* or "big feet"—or, more likely, the expansive, if basic, winter footwear that made those feet seem outlandish—belonged to the Tehuelche nomads who lived in Patagonia in the sixteenth century when the first Iberian adventurers made landfall. These noble-looking savages were tall, but they were not giants. Still, the name coined by Magellan's diarist, Pigafetta, endures. Maps of the New World labelled Patagonia as a *regio gigantum*, region of giants, and included illustrations of nine-foot men ramming arrows down their throats and looking down from an implausible height on their European counterparts.

Conquering Europeans shunned the hostile plains for they had neither silver nor sources of slave labour. Absence of human settlement gave rise to fantasies and fears. On returning home sailors recounted stories of cannibals and murderous tribal rituals, and of huge waves in the cold oceans that were made all the more fearsome by the infernal creatures that lurked below. They told also of secret kingdoms ruled over by native chiefs, and of shipwrecked Europeans who had made their homes there.

Like the Sahara, Siberia and Outer Mongolia, there is a cartoon-like quality to our perception of Patagonia. It is one of the magical regions, the empty places. This impression has survived into modern times, as Hank Wangford admits: "[Patagonia] sounded mythological, the Furthest Place, the point beyond which you cannot go; a land of the imagination, like Ruritania."

Even so, the Patagonian library is full of books that seek to impose science on Patagonia. The first records are mainly dry accounts of soundings and shorelines by mariners. Darwin geologized the coast and river valleys and classified the beetles and birds; FitzRoy mapped the perilous bays and channels of Tierra del Fuego. Then came industry. Settlers from Spain, the British Isles, Italy, Germany and Yugoslavia came to be shepherds and dock labourers. Saint-Exupéry, undaunted by the wind and the wild weather systems, delivered the post to Comodoro Rivadavia and Punta Arenas. Religious people sought refuge in Patagonia, or came to evangelize to the pagan natives. Others preferred to slaughter them to show they had the newest corner of the New World under their control.

Other texts suggest a mythical region, even when that was not their author's original intention. The French "King of Patagonia", Orllie Antoine de Tounens, is perhaps the best example of the eccentric European travelling as far as possible from home—not so much in knots or miles as in cultural distance and political reality—in order to conjure up his own world. But writers have played a key role in the spinning of legends. Just thirty years ago British author Bruce Chatwin used Patagonia as a vehicle to find a fictional voice without taking all the risks of the novelist. His literary stunt paid off, handsomely, but Patagonia was re-mythologized, hyper-mythologized. Even as tourists fly into Patagonia from all over the world, the European gaze remains infected by magic realism. The mental map, at least, is still bordered with sea monsters and serpents, and there are all manner of giants—people, moods, weather systems and wild places—to give a poetic turn to the postcards people send home.

Argentinian and Chilean Patagonia

Are there such things as Patagonians? Have the descendants of the Europeans who settled here in the last three centuries shaken off the foreigners' fictions? Are all the real Patagonians dead and buried under the dry stones of the steppe?

For hundreds of centuries, only a handful of scattered nomads with neither knowledge nor memory of better climes wanted Patagonia. Small populations of indigenous tribes—the Halakwalup, the Selknam, the Yahgan—lived on its fierce southern coasts, while larger groups such as the nomadic Tehuelche and Mapuche ruled the northern plains. These distinct native peoples each evolved their own oral traditions that only became known to outsiders as the southern sun set on the civilizations that dreamed them up.

Anthropology came into fashion too late to have any moral influence, but we know something of the ritual dances in fearsome feathered costumes, the vision-inducing trances, and the feats of incredible human endurance that were the round of daily life for the original "Patagonians". In such a harsh climate, on barren lands, there were no Incas or Aztecs to build temples and, when the last white men came with their Remingtons there was no warm jungle or ice-free high peak to provide refuge.

In the skin tones and faces of some of the residents of modern-day cities like Río Gallegos, Punta Arenas, Comodoro Rivadavia and Bariloche—and in the shanty towns of the capital, nearly 2,000 miles to the north—vestiges of a tribal ancestry can be discerned, but the blood of warriors and hunters has been watered down, and their cultures vanquished.

Political Patagonia is associated with a handful of military men. In Argentina General Julio A. Roca was the creole hero who, through his brief but bloody *conquista del desierto*, crushed the savages and reined in Patagonia. In Chile, Lieutenant Colonel Cornelio Saavedra Rodríguez, stunned by the audacity of the French impostor Orllie Antoine, pushed the Mapuche south and rounded them up onto badlands and into reservations. European scientists came and went. In their wake followed Francisco Moreno, Clemente Onelli, Bernardo Philippi and Padre Alberto de Agostini. These stayed put, climbing mountains, finding passes, declaring national parks. Their missions mixed hard science and manly adventures with the practical concerns of defining frontiers and founding villages, but for Argentinians and Chileans, their journals and reports have added a patriotic dimension to the Patagonian catalogue of legends of conquest and human endeavour.

Literary Patagonia

The great steppe of central Patagonia easily seduces the mind as a sort of *tabula rasa*, an invitation to drift and dream. In their rutters, verses and travelogues, mariners and professional poets alike have struggled to describe the emptiness of the plains and the unearthly drama of the sheer cliffs and the thousands of uninhabited islands, the deadly waters off Cape Horn. But the attempts to capture the unspeakable in writing have often been memorable, for the pressures this exerts on language and the intensity of the human response to a stark, repellent landscape. So masterly when relating his palaeontological discoveries in his *Beagle* voyage journal, Darwin strains to convey the impression left on him by a "wretched and useless" place, which "can be described only by negative characters."

Theroux picks up on this "nothingness" in his otherwise lightweight long-haul narrative *The Old Patagonian Express* and Baudrillard gives it a moral twist in an essay that deconstructs the European fiction of the empty place. Neruda provides a rare counterpoint to the poetics of absence, celebrating in rich, rhythmic language the teeming, cosmic, often violent life of ice and forest and fjord, untouched by men and cities. William Henry Hudson sees an infinity of small lives hidden among the brush and scrub—birds, insects, rodents and foxes—and emerges with a newfound pantheism.

To this fantasia, Argentinian and Chilean authors have occasionally brought some sense of perspective. Journalists such as Roberto Payró, at the beginning of the twentieth century, and Germán Sopeña, at the end of the same, worked hard to reveal to educated *porteños*—the vivacious but often parochial residents of Buenos Aires—that the south had much to offer. A new generation of photographers has gone beyond coffee-table renditions of pristine perfection to show ecological damage or to suggest Patagonia has a meaning as well as a mythic beauty, while filmmakers have embraced the straight roads and big landscapes to tell stories about "Patagonians" who are rather less than giants.

Chileans and Argentinians are also great readers. In the branches of the Boutique del Libro bookstore in El Calafate, dozens of shelves are burdened with the ever-expanding library of Patagonian narratives. If a new King of Patagonia were to be declared tomorrow, he could look for a constitution in the massive library that now exists. It would be a constitution informed mainly by the thoughts and feelings of people passing through, and by the impressions of each new generation of natives, whether Spanish creoles, Chileans, Argentinians, or the grandchildren of Shetland islanders who came by way of the Falklands.

This book reads the texts of Patagonia in roughly chronological order. As well as tracing the history proper—with its Welsh colonists, French monarch, gold hunters, cowboys and penal colonies—it also surveys the historical evolution of the texts that have recorded it, from oral traditions, poems and memoirs to diaries, guidebooks and films.

Tourism's New Fictions

Tourism delineates new frontiers, creates new centres of command and control. Where converted *estancias* have not provided enough luxury, hotels have been built with views of peak and glacier, beside dolphin-dotted rivers and inside guanaco farms. Tourists are herded to photogenic marquee sites, while backpackers and "soft adventure tourists" jump off their buses to camp in La Esperanza or abandon the boat in road-less Puerto Edén to meet the natives. But only the very bravest reject the unremitting desire to move forward by pulling over off the forlorn dirt roads to hop over a barbed wire fence and head inwards—there is still much to fear out there in the Tehuelche lands.

Early editions of the *South American Handbook* offered just a page or two on Patagonia, and the section appeared separately from the rest of the country. Forage, sheep breeds, weather and commercial prospects were the concerns of the entries, and there was no mention of glaciers, fjord cruises or treks through the woods. Now there are guidebooks galore, hundreds of local tour agencies, a veritable highway of trekkers doing well-trodden circuits in the national parks. Peculiarly fashionable among travellers at the present time, Patagonia is a kind of well-known unknown, a faraway world we have easy access to and where the wilderness is dotted with European-style comforts.

Most of the ideas we inherit about Patagonia are suddenly at odds with the fact that thousands of people go there each year on holiday. In the 1740s John Byron almost died as he rowed his way through the Chilean fjords. Nowadays, cruise passengers are served Scotch whisky cooled by chunks of ice hacked off the surrounding glaciers. What was sublime for the Victorians is now commonplace for the world's global tourist. There is no need to suffer when you can stay in the Explora hotel in Torres del Paine.

The horn-shaped granite mountains of the Paine Massif at the centre of this reserve, and the pinnacles of Argentina's Fitz Roy, Torre and Saint- Exupéry mountains have become talismanic. They draw people in the way Mont Blanc used to draw Europeans. But talismans become brands and logos, and Patagonia is now full of stock shots: the dusty, open, empty Ruta 40 in Argentina; the great wall of blue ice at the Perito Moreno Glacier; the handsome Patagonian gaucho, the "Welsh tea" in Gaiman. These are the new fictions, the stories travellers tell when they get home to their warmer worlds.

Chapter One

THE LAST DAYS OF SHORR: PATAGONIA'S INDIGENOUS MYTHS

The history of Patagonia is a classic colonial enterprise of exploration, invasion, evangelization and ethnic cleansing, recast by the victors as a tale of heroes overcoming obstacles. This narrative has sought to supplant anything that went before, and has treated past peoples as lesser mortals and their culture as so much scrubland to be burned away.

A Fuegian myth refers back to a land bridge across the Magellan Strait—before the rise in sea level at the end of the Pleistocene period, some 10,000 years ago. This myth certainly fits the geology and it is generally thought that the ancestors of southern South America's indigenous peoples arrived in Patagonia and Tierra del Fuego some 14,000 to 10,000 years ago. This was the last stage of an epic migration of mongoloid peoples from East Asia across the frozen Bering Strait, and was the last great migration in history. Pottery was appearing in Japan and agriculture was already practised in Asia Minor; but the newly-arrived Fuegians were living in Stone-Age societies, and they would not move on significantly in the millennia to come.

Just as there are topographical symmetries at the extreme tips of the Americas—Canadians often liken the rugged coast of southern Chile to that of British Columbia—the groups who had forged south had come all that way only to find themselves in an inhospitable environment akin to that inhabited by their Innuit brothers. These days the remaining vestiges of the Ice Age are safely located far from the main rivers and passable routes, but when the first bands of hunter-gatherers were moving south the ice-caps and glaciers were retreating before them. On their way they encountered the last remnants of the large mammals of the Pleistocene age, and would have hunted mastodons, glyptodons, sabre-toothed cats and giant sloths.

The topographic and climatic extremes were not conducive to social and cultural life. Whereas the settled civilizations of the American tropics evolved into relatively sophisticated societies, the communities that settled

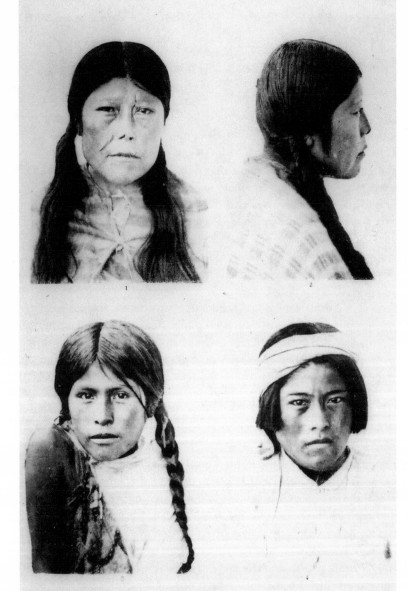

1 y 3. Margarita, hija del cacique Foyel; 2. hija del cacique Inakayal; 4. Trakel, hijo del cacique Sayeweke

the plains and deserts were largely nomadic, eking out a primitive existence hunting rhea and guanaco and living in makeshift tents of animal skin. Like other American indigenous groups, the original Patagonians lacked the art of writing. Unlike the Incas and Aztecs, they left no great temples or stone pathways to guide us towards an understanding of their cultures. They had no pottery, no wheel, and little in the way of textiles or clothing. The only animal the natives of the far south ever domesticated was the dog—and no one has proved conclusively that there were dogs before the Spaniards arrived. All the tribes were hunter-gatherers, and none practised any kind of agriculture except the Chonos of the Chilean fjords, who may have planted a few potatoes. Only the Mapuche eventually developed into a stable society, with fixed agricultural settlements at the foot of the densely forested mountains of north-western Patagonia; this may account, at least in part, for the fact that they are the only indigenous group to have survived to this day.

Nonetheless, there is evidence across the region that the indigenous imagination was fired by the environment. At the Cueva de las Manos at Río Pinturas in the upper part of the Deseado basin are the stencilled images of hundreds of hands, as well as cartoons of guanacos, human figures and what may be representations of *boleadoras* (stone-weighted lassos used for hunting rheas). This abstract artwork was composed some 8,000 years ago. Later textiles pick up on the browns, purples and creams of the landscape, and what we know of Patagonian music—whether field recordings from Chubut and Santa Cruz, the two Argentine provinces that occupy most of Patagonia, or modern ethnic fusions by Chilean *mestizo* artists—reflects the importance of the elements and of tribal identity.

Between the sixteenth and nineteenth centuries many Europeans came into contact with one or more of these native cultures, creating encounters that would produce no end of myths for the Old World. But it is the native oral tradition that communicates the essence of Patagonian prehistory, a strange, beguiling treasure trove of legends, rules, dreams, promises and wisdom sayings, only recently recorded and analysed by anthropologists. Praising the UCLA series of volumes on native lore that have been used as the source for much of what follows, Claude Lévi-Strauss wrote that "South American mythology belongs to the spiritual inheritance of mankind on a par with the great masterpieces of Greek and Roman antiquity and of the Near and Far East."

These peoples—Tehuelche, Mapuche, Chonos, Selknam, Yahgan and Halakwalup—struggled for millennia to survive in inhospitable climes, developing a rudimentary folk culture. During the last five centuries five of these groups have been wiped out—most of them during the past 150 years—and the Mapuche, despite resistance and some successes, have largely been forced into reservations and onto poor land with no tribal or agricultural value. All we have left are the faded, scattered fragments of their stories.

THE STEPPE LANDS: THE TEHUELCHE

> "'Where did the evil giants come from, grandmother Tama?' asked Tankelou.
> …The old woman replied: 'They were brothers, sons of the darkness.'"
> Tehuelche legend

The Tehuelche are the archetypal Patagonians. These tall nomads were the first natives encountered by Europeans and were the tribe the Italian

Antonio Pigafetta's log described as "giants"; he christened them the *pathagoni*, whence the name Patagonia. In fact, the two southern tribes who lived in the Argentinian plains were called the Güna-këne (occupying the northern sector between the Colorado and Chubut rivers and probably into the adjacent pampas region) and the Aónikenk (distributed between the Chubut river and the Magellan Strait). Tehuelche is simply a name used by another tribe, the Mapuche, to mean "southerners". Like *pathagoni*, it is an invading conqueror's nickname, but it has stuck.

As plains dwellers, the Tehuelche were hardy drifters who wandered across the barren steppe dressed in the skins of the guanaco, the pretty, rust-coloured relative of the llama that inhabits the southern reaches of the Americas. Their communal *toldos* or tents, made from the same hides stretched over wooden posts, provided meagre shelter and offered little resistance to the unrelenting wind that blasts across the steppe for most of the year. Pigafetta noted that the *pathagoni* "go hither and thither in boats... as the Egyptians do," and archaeology shows that they crossed the sometimes swift-moving rivers aboard primitive coracles not unlike the bull-boats of North America.

Though mass tourism has highlighted Patagonia's more photogenic topographies of glaciers, peaks and lakes, steppe is the dominant landscape. There are vast steppe lands in the modern Argentinian provinces of Chubut and Santa Cruz, and smaller tracts around Coihaique and Punta Arenas in Chile. The steppe is not a level plain, but tilts gently upwards towards the Andes and undulates along the way, sometimes breaking up into ridges and tablelands. At ground level, the yellowish blur breaks into distinct species of grass, dominated by tufts of *coirón* and stubby, spiky *mata negra* and *mata verde* bushes. These help hold in place the fragile dust and shell particles of what is essentially a beach on which the tide went out millions of years ago.

Paintings and sketches from the colonial period and photographs taken when their culture was almost extinct show the Tehuelche to be long-limbed and long-haired, with the strong, slightly gaunt facial features of North American Indians. In the photographs the subjects often seem to be scowling and group shots give an impression of a tough, down-at-heel tribespeople made miserable by a harsh environment and unforgiving climate.

Yet in the UCLA collection *Folk Literature of the Tehuelche Indians*, based on the work of a small number of keen Argentinian anthropologists, in particular Alejandra Siffredi and Marcelo Bórmida, and on the writings of Salesian missionary Maggiorino Borgatello (1857-1929) and acclaimed naturalist and explorer Ramón Lista (1856-97), are dozens of richly detailed myths dreamed up by the Tehuelche in their wide-open, tree-less moonscape.

CREATION MYTHS

The Tehuelche creation story is known as the Elal Cycle, after a heroic man-god who arrives in Patagonia from a "Big Island" on the back of a swan. He lands on the summit of Chaltén Mountain (now known as Fitz Roy) and surveys Patagonia, resisting the ice and snow by rubbing stones together to make fire. From the magical island Elal brings all the animals that will become his "faithful friends" in the new world. Elal wrestles with pumas, is swallowed by a whale, fights with his father (who tried to kill him in the womb), resists the sexual advances of his grandmother (and turns her into a field mouse), courts and marries a daughter of the sun and prevails over all the other daily trials and tribulations that would have beset the average Tehuelche man. Night and the monsters in the mountains were the source of some of the tribe's deepest fears, according to a narrative recorded by ethno-historian Manuel Llarás Samitier in 1950:

Night (Tons) is the legendary mother of the evil spirits, although nobody knows who engendered these gods in her. When Sun and Moon came together, Night rushed promptly to cover the earth, experiencing amorous desires herself as she watched the lovers in the blue space. When the two separated, Night withdrew from earth (so that apparently only Time [Shorr] could have been Night's lover). And that is how Axshem, Máip, and Kélenken came about, the three loved ones of darkness, who, respectively, represent the bringer of pain in humans and animals, the bearer of anxiety and bad luck, and the spectre of pestilence and affliction.

Later, Night gave birth to the Hol-Gok, the giants, of the island. But all these monsters of Darkness were ignored by the other gods, and their names rarely mentioned. Their mother had hardly given birth to her offspring when she deposited them in the mountains. Here, each one of them occupied his cave. The mountains were giant women themselves who had been either stillborn or born in a very sickly state. Some of them vomited fire during the night and trembled because Kélenken had entered them. But there was no shaman who would have attempted to cure them.

Unsurprisingly, sky also dominates the Tehuelche universe. According to their cosmology, Kóoch, the "sky" or creator god, lived alone on the eastern fringes of the world. Weeping bitterly in his abject solitude, he made *arrok*, the primordial sea. When he saw the waters were rising he sighed, and this wind parted the clouds and a dim light shone on the waters. Eager to behold his handiwork, Kóoch made the Sun-man and Moon-woman, who made love behind the mountains and gave birth to a daughter, the evening star. The people of the moon, the evil ones, take the forms of a male guanaco, a rhea and a rock-hurling mountain. In contrast, the stars are images of the souls of deceased Tehuelche and the night sky is paradise.

DEATH AND DANGER
Death shadowed the Tehuelche on their wanderings. When captured or injured, panic-stricken guanacos often kick out with incredible force and ferocity, and a hoof to the head would fell the tallest Tehuelche. Rhea, the flightless *choique* or Patagonian ostrich, are less dangerous, but are so fleet of foot that they often left the hunters and their *bolas* helplessly behind. Across the plains of Patagonia and the pampas, all the native tribes—and, after them, the gauchos and even Anglo and Scots cowboys—used *boleadoras* to hunt. These are usually three medium-sized stones wrapped in rawhide and tied to each other with three long strips of hide. As the hunter runs—or, as is now more commonly the case, rides—towards his prey, he spins the balls around his head to build up speed before unleashing the whole like a lasso. On impact the ropes wind violently around the rhea's legs and stop it dead in its tracks.

As hunters the Tehuelche spent much of their time pursuing, killing, skinning and cooking animals and birds. Most of the oral narratives are filled with creatures native to the Patagonian plains and peaks: the condor, the flamingo, the guanaco, the skunk. Imaginary animals contained in the Tehuelche bestiary are Okpe, a pig made of solid rock, and Oóuk'en, a man who walks on all fours with a shell on his back. Similarly maligned were the Tchóion, women who lived without men. While the weird mammals abducted children, the spinsters/lesbians stole rhea meat when the men's backs were turned. The Tehuelche heroically conquered these evils by being honest, by being brave and by employing the arts of seduction.

The image of the mountain, like the dark forest in European folk culture, is always the most ominous. The act of hurling rocks that features in a wide number of legends alludes to volcanic eruptions and landslides, but it may well be a general metaphor for the Andes, and the constant danger faced by any Tehuelche who strayed too high and deep into the mountain range. The steppe might be barren and either baking hot or freezing cold, but it was more predictable than the violent storms and avalanches that lay hidden in the dark recesses of the cordillera.

NATURE AND NURTURE

Most Tehuelche myths have passed into extinction with the tribe. But one has endured and become something of a cliché: travellers to Patagonia are always told that whoever eats the berries of the Calafate (box-leaved barberry) bush will return. The myth's source is a story about an old sorceress, Koonek, who was too weak to migrate north when the weather began to change. She sat out the winter alone in her *toldo*; when the first snows fell, even the birds abandoned her. Though she had abundant food, Koonek detested this season of solitude, and when the swallows and snipes began to return, she rebuked them for leaving her so alone for so long.

When the birds explained that they migrated because there was no food or protection, Koonek transformed herself into a beautiful thorny bush with yellow sweet-smelling flowers. The birds and the returning tribespeople ate the purple fruit and so the seeds were spread far and wide. Many birds never left again and in later years those that did choose to migrate always longed for the tasty fruit—thus, he who eats fruit from the Calafate bush will always return.

Nature morphs into humanity and vice versa in Tehuelche stories. There is also a notable absence of absolutes: there is twilight before creation rather than total darkness; before Elal created the world "there existed very little"; Elal's father "was also like a god but of less power." Perhaps the Tehuelche experience of reality had no need of extremes, or even of a remote mythological divinity. Living on the eerie, wind-blasted plains with only firelight, the moon and stars after dark, they were always intimately connected with their mysteries.

Apart from the myths, scant evidence of artistic endeavour remains, but Tehuelche belts, bags, tapestries and furniture pieces display considerable flair for abstraction. Rhombuses, crosses, linear designs and checks, often in rust and blue-greys were the tribe's response to an environment devoid of symmetries, notable order or vivid colour. There was also song and dance; in 1960 the musicologist Oscar Giménez recorded a Tehuelche ancient explaining the *kaani*, a ritual in which performers wore a feather headdress and chanted a simple melody to welcome visitors. But Giménez was hearing an old man's memories. A census of indigenous people in Argentina less than a decade later found only 210 Tehuelche, and in the 1980s only around one hundred were extant, many of them crossed with whites or Mapuche. We cannot know how many Tehuelche inhabited the plains before the conquest, but documents left by European explorers refer to 1,500 or 2,000 individuals across the continent, suggesting that the group was never numerous. Between 1520 and 1670, at least eight European expeditions made contact with the Tehuelche, but little can be gleaned from the archives. After this period the low-plains drifters adopted the horse and other innovations of Spanish or Mapuche origin and so abandoned their traditions as foot Indians to become mounted hunters. Towards the end of the eighteenth century the Mapuche began to make inroads into the plains and completely subjugated the northern Tehuelche; subsequent Argentine military campaigns in the 1870s and 1880s rounded up or killed the few, scattered remaining tribes.

The Tehuelche have their epitaph in place-names throughout Chile and Argentina that have retained the Aónikenk language, as at Chabunco (smelly water), Orkenaike (good place to camp) and Güer Aike (story place). Some are Spanish but with native associations: Laguna Casimiro (Casimiro's Lagoon, after a legendary *cacique* or chief who led negotiations with Chilean and Argentinian provincial governors in the 1870s); Cueva del Gualicho (cave wherein dwelt a *gualicho*, or much-feared deity, near the modern town of El Calafate); and the Charcamata canyon, which takes its name from the Tehuelche word for a native woodpecker.

It is ironic that one of the most common indigenous words to appear across Patagonia is *aike*, the Tehuelche word for "place", often used in the names of *estancias*. As nomads the Tehuelche had a fluid idea of home, moving in the direction indicated by the seasons and the elements—especially the wind and the cold—and by the trails that led them to guanaco

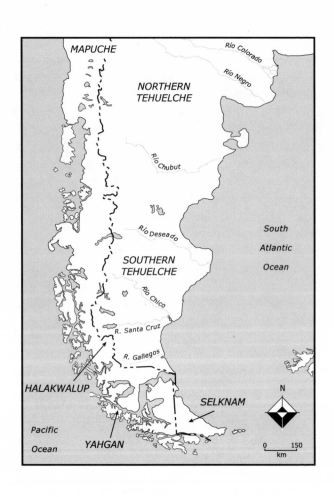

breeding grounds or to burial sites. They wandered the plains and coasts protecting only their extended family, but by the early twentieth century every *aike* was fenced in and occupied by a sheep, a ranch or a belligerent Scot with a rifle, and they had nowhere else to go.

ICE AND FIRE: THE NATIVES OF TIERRA DEL FUEGO

> "Viewing such men, one can hardly make oneself believe they are fellow-creatures, and inhabitants of the same world."
>
> Charles Darwin, *Beagle Diary*

Tierra del Fuego and its adjacent islands are the southernmost inhabited landmasses in the world. One of the harshest environments on the planet, the whole region is at the mercy of biting winds and sudden blasts of rain and snow. Dense forests of *nothofagus* beech hug steep mountains that plummet down to a jagged coastline where the icy waters of two great oceans crash and broil in a maelstrom that has sunk countless ships.

South of the main island, sometimes called Isla Grande but more commonly just Tierra del Fuego, are three large islands (Gordon, Hoste, Navarino) and a large number of smaller ones (Gable, Picton, Lennox, etc). Farther to the south are the Wollaston Islands, the southernmost of which is Horn Island and the infamous false cape that represents the limit between the Americas and Antarctica.

Discovered in 1520, Tierra del Fuego remained free of colonization until the late nineteenth century, with contact between Europeans and natives limited to encounters on the shoreline or on the storm-tossed seas.

Magellan and his fellow mariners were the first Europeans to set eyes on the Fuegian coast. On entering the strait that now bears his captain's name, Pigafetta noted how the natives they saw on the southern shore rubbed pointed sticks together to make fire. Later mariners observed the many campfires that glowed along the shores, giving rise to the name Tierra del Fuego. One version of the Magellan voyage tells how he christened the land Tierra del Humo (Land of Smoke) but that Charles V changed it to Land of Fire, on the well-founded principle that "where there's smoke…" Until the Horn and its islands were properly mapped cartographers showed Tierra del Fuego to be at the edge of some great Antarctic continent, a Terra Australis wherein dwelt the Antipodes who sheltered underneath upside-down trees from the rising snow and rain. Theologians from the Middle Ages onwards banned the postulated continent, but Dante placed his "Hill of Purgatory" in a southern land, and the infernal associations persisted into maps from the sixteenth, seventeenth and even eighteenth centuries, which show active volcanoes where there are none.

Religiosity and colourful fictions may well have inflamed mariners' imaginations, but for the inhabitants of Tierra del Fuego daily life was pretty hellish. The main tribes were the Selknam and Haush, who were foot natives, and the Yahgan and Halakwalup, who used canoes. Further north in the Chilean fjords were the Chonos, whose dominion in the waterways may have overlapped with that claimed by the Halakwalup. For all these groups, hunger was a constant challenge. Foraging on the shores and land produced shellfish, herbs, berries such as the barberry, and about ten types of fungi. Edible mammals included marine otter and fox in the west and guanaco in the east, as well as the occasional rat. Birdlife was abundant, and goose, penguin and cormorant supplied meat, feathers and eggs. Rowing against the violent williwaws that hurtle down from the glacial valleys, the canoers would occasionally catch seal and porpoise; whales were something of a delicacy. In this harsh environment survival left little time or energy for craft and culture. None of the Fuegian tribes practised weaving, pottery, tanning techniques, sculpture, painting or other visual arts. They had no fishing hooks, and no cooking pots till Europeans arrived, but archaeologists have found anklets made from grass, cradles using guanaco skin, windbreaks, and harnesses for carrying backpacks.

In the Frozen Forests

For all Fuegians, animistic forces were constantly at play in the angry natural world around them. American anthropologist Samuel Kirkland Lothrop visited the region in 1924-25 and summed it up as follows:

> The Yahgan world was peopled by innumerable unseen beings: ghosts (*kushpig*) of departed shamans, spirits of the sea, the rocks, and the trees. These people, for the greater part, were malicious by nature, resentful of intrusion on their privacy, and, when seen by man, terrifying in aspect. Solitary travellers might suddenly find themselves facing a fierce spirit across the light of his camp-fire, and might be seized and done to death.

However, the shaman usually had power over demons of this type and could give protection.

Europeans often found the natives of Tierra del Fuego terrifying in aspect. Perhaps the Fuegians, with their scant resources and island mentalities, also resented intrusion and when they began to understand that the white men on ships who repeatedly made incursions into their territories were not going to go away, they invoked and sought to embody these ancestral spirits.

Martin Gusinde, a German priest of the Roman Catholic Order of the Divine Word, was 32 years old in 1918 when he made his first trip to Tierra del Fuego. It is thanks to his detailed observations and interviews, collected in the monumental three-volume *Die Feuerland-Indianer* (1931-74), that we now have access to indigenous lives and legends. Basing himself at Punta Remolino on Lago Fagnano, he worked closely with a Yahgan woman and her white husband, establishing a rapport with the natives, especially the Yahgan, during the first visit and then returning to the region on three further expeditions.

It was almost too late. There are no accurate censuses, but there were probably no more than 4,000 individuals in any of the tribes by the 1850s. At the time of Gusinde's first visit fewer than 300 Selknam, 80 Halakwalup and about 70 Yahgan had survived. In 1924 he wrote: "It is a sad fact that at the present time no remedy can be found that could prevent the impending and complete extinction of these tribes. Hardly more than twenty-five years will pass before the last of these Fuegians will have been lowered into the grave." Regrettably, his prophecy was proven true and by the 1950s Europeans had completely obliterated the Fuegian natives through epidemics, territorial displacement and murder.

On Shore: the Selknam

Looking south from the steppe, the Tehuelche viewed the Fuegians as a single group, direct descendants of a Tehuelche "daughter of the Sun and Moon" called Airra. They shared a common language and certain customs with the Selknam tribe, and anthropological records indicate that they were of similar stature. Their other neighbours, the Yahgan, moved around the southern bays and islands in boats. When asked by Spanish seamen who lived in the north, they replied *ona*, meaning "men". The Selknam tribe is still often referred to as the Ona.

Like all the Fuegians, the Selknam were nomadic, roaming the northern and eastern portions of what is now the Isla Grande de Tierra del Fuego between the Magellan Strait, the north shore of Lago Fagnano and Bahía Thetis. Selknam myths also refer to Staten Island, visible on a clear day from the southern tip of Tierra del Fuego, to the depressions at Cabo María and Cabo Peñas (which they believed had been dug by a woodpecker to sneak up on a stingy old woman) and to the hills near Bahía Policarpo. The tribe knew its tiny kingdom well, and central to many of their myths is a belief that humans must learn to share land with the native fauna; for the Selknam, everything and everyone comes from and eventually returns to the land, even if the outward form changes.

The oral tradition played a key role in the daily cycle of Selknam life. After dark people would sit around the fire in their huts and allow themselves to be drawn into meandering tales, told usually by the older men. Young men never opened their mouths to tell stories when the elders were present, and women were always passive, not even telling stories to their own children.

Selknam mythological heroes are ever-present in the stories. Kenos, for instance, determined every aspect of life, from creating and managing the weather to parcelling out land into districts controlled by families and fauna. Swamps, matted roots, grass tufts and dark earth feature in the creation stories, reflecting the topographies of the Selknam domain, and human genitalia are formed from the very mud, thus explaining the Selknam's swarthy skin colour. The snowstorms sent up from Antarctica were known as *xoše*, personified by a marching army of strong men sent by the south wind.

FAMILY TIES

Mighty shamans, night spirits called *yóši*, the sun and the moon and the cycles of birth and death are prominent in Selknam folklore, as are legends and beliefs about family members. The ancestors were often invoked to legitimate myths with the words "That is how the Selknam told it," and the tribe believed that on death, their ancestors' spirits passed into the surrounding landscape of mountains, lakes and rivers, or into the bodies of wild creatures. Gusinde recorded folk tales about the animals and birds that shared the seas and shores with the Selknam—whales, albatrosses, sea lions, cormorants—and a large number of tales feature guanacos, often emphasizing the prowess needed to hunt them.

In Selknam lore women were regularly taught lessons by men. An archetypal myth tells of a sun-man who finds out that his wife, the moon, has devised sham spirit appearances to trick her male ancestors and legitimize a social order in which women rule. Naturally the sun-man warns his fellow men about the scheme and so prevents a crisis.

KLOKETEN MYTHS

This basic fable in support of patriarchy was reworked into elaborate stories called the *kloketen* myths, which were employed at the exclusively male puberty rite. Details were added such as how women were turned into animals (hence the showy feathers and fur of the Fuegian avifauna and fauna) and how the moon-woman's scars, caused by a burning brand, can still be seen on her face.

In one of the central *klokoten* stories, which elaborates the theme of punishing the women, all the men gather at a mountainous area called Máustas (near the site of what is now Estancia Blanca, south of the Península Mitre) and perform the very first puberty rite. The men are in the form of beasts—there is a sperm whale, a dolphin, a seal and birds of every size—all under the tutelage of Kran, the sun-man. But after the ceremony all are transformed into rocks, hills and peaks—the only landscape the Selknam knew. Just as their animal souls were set in stone, so the procedures, and roles of the *kloketen* were established for all time at that first gathering of the men.

During the recounting of these richly detailed and powerful myths all the men adopted a squatting position as a sign of respect (standing and lying down were not permitted), and those who had been cooking or eating laid aside their food and concentrated on the ceremony. A large conical hut was used, perhaps mirroring the form of the nearby volcanoes and mountain peaks. During the ceremonial period, which lasted for months at a time, an adolescent boy would be initiated into manhood through intensive instruction while being deprived of food, sleep and comfort—thus making him liable to trances and the reception of esoteric truths. Those males observing would in turn don bark masks and perform stage shows featuring spirit apparitions, all designed to impress—and subjugate—the women, thus further advancing the males' (and the sun-man's) cause against their wives and daughters.

The Selknam lands bore the names of families, topographical features and wild animals, and though few of their original place names have survived, we know that many had symbolic value. The third biggest town in Tierra del Fuego after Ushuaia and Río Grande, Tolhuin, was only founded in 1972; it takes its name from the Selknam word for "heart". In Río Grande itself the Angela Loij state school honours a native Selknam woman, and the name of the Iyú school means "he who leaves a trail."

A smaller tribe, sometimes referred to as the Haush, was part of the same ethnic group as the Selknam. With their territory restricted to the western limits of the Isla Grande—a region now known as the Península Mitre—the Haush may well have made greater use of canoes. By the 1920s there were perhaps two or three pure blood Haush remaining.

Towards Cape Horn: the Yahgan

Living between the Beagle Channel and Cape Horn, the Yahgan were the poor relations of Tierra del Fuego, foraging and making their homes wherever the other groups had not bothered to establish settlements. If the Isla Grande was hostile, the craggy islands, gloomy bays and rocky straits around Islas Navarino and Hoste and the Wollaston Islands were positively forbidding. Their name comes down to us from Thomas Bridges, who says that Yahgan was the native name for the Murray Narrows, which were near to his own mission. The other commonly used name, "Yamana", says Bridges, was simply the Yahgan word for "man" or "person" or "alive".

On what passed for dry land, nature was ranked against the Yahgan, forcing them to take to the seas. Dark, dense forests cloak the hills at this extreme southern point, the snowline descends to around 1,500 feet and great glaciers disgorge directly into the sea. Wherever the Yahgan moved they were subject to the full force of the Antarctic winds, rains, sleet, hail and snowstorms. Using fragile bark canoes and wigwams covered in scraps of loose hide, they led an existence whose misery was mitigated only by warming fires and by the abundance of fish, shellfish and marine mammals found in the icy waters. Water features in Yahgan legends as a threat and an element demanding respect: every time a Yahgan man sees a flat stone at the bottom of a river he is seeing the water spirits of those who have been slain by other men. But the dead are safe. Those stones that are less stable and jagged are still living, and will often drag a man under the water.

Gusinde collected a variety of fascinating myths during his sojourns.

Many relate to autochthonous fauna, especially birds—cormorants, woodpeckers, gerfalcons, ibises—while others give guidance on the resolution of family issues. Alongside stories about glaciation and floods are narratives about the discovery of those items essential for survival in the icy wastes: arrowheads, harpoon points, fire, whale oil (for food) and the sole luxury item, sexual intercourse. In one story nature and sexuality are linked through a scene of incest and transformation: a son fondles and then sleeps with his mother, after which they turn into wild geese and fly away to remain together forever.

Intriguingly, a pair of Yahgan myths about cannibals seems to identify the neighbouring tribe of Halakwalup whose "custom [it was] to eat everybody who came from the east. In order to kill them with ease they would permit only one stranger to enter a hut and stay there overnight, for each family could easily overpower one stranger in their hut and quickly kill them." The cannibals' children, who sit in a basket hanging in the hut, even jump around singing *Yárum hapánana, yárum hapánana*, meaning "Today we'd like to eat a man."

Yahgan dance masks, made of either bark or seal hide, were a cross between those worn by the Ku Klux Klan and those used in the *Scream* movie. Eye and mouth slots were made in long pointed steeple-shaped headgear, not unlike those donned by strawboys in Ireland, and painted with vertical or horizontal stripes. Gusinde's photographs show that the body would be decorated in similar fashion.

The Yahgan also had "Kina" myths and rites associated with puberty, based on ancient tales of conflict between men and women and very similar to the Selknam narrative. In the Kina ceremony feather headdresses were worn, the initiate would wear a headband and there were scratching sticks and painted wands that were waved to the rhythm of the chanting, and even a thong, provided to tie up any participant who became unruly.

A fascinating glimpse into Yahgan culture is provided by Thomas Bridges' 32,000-word *Yamana-English Dictionary*, compiled in the 1880s and 1890s. It is the compound verbs that are most striking, with any number of ways of cutting a tree, of fishing, of being cold and of searching for, catching and gnashing scraps of meat "as a dog". Some of Bridges' locutions suggest a people always on the lookout for the main chance, though any kind of interpretation must take into account the author's role as missionary and the fact that the dictionary is a highly personal, unscientific interpretation of a complex indigenous society.

Mamihlapinatapai: to look at each other, hoping that either will offer to do something, which both parties much desire but are unwilling to do;
Aguri: to go, with the hope of getting a present;
Linganana: to fain distress for the sake of charity.

But the Yahgan were occasionally generous to each other:

Tugait-owomutu: to sit close up against a weak and sick person in order to prop him up.

The Yahgan also left us the beautiful word Ushuaia, which translates prosaically as "the bay penetrating the west". This bay of Ushuaia would provide safe harbour for ships in the era of great maritime expeditions to Tierra del Fuego, and would also become the chosen locale for a Christian mission in the nineteenth century.

FJORDS AND SOUNDS: THE HALAKWALUP AND THE CHONOS

One of the most magical places in southern Chile is Puerto Edén. Shrouded in swirling mist, hemmed in by Isla Wellington's impassable rainforest and drenched by the torrential rain that the Pacific dumps on the fjords of central Patagonia, it is only accessible from the mainland by boat. The thirty or so residents of this tiny hamlet are the last of the canoe peoples who once plied Patagonia's channels and fjords. Archaeological evidence shows that the Halakwalup (sometimes written Alacaluf) rowed their small wooden vessels around the channels west of Dawson Island and Cape Froward, sharing many of the bays and channels with the Yahgan, and as far north as the Golfo de Peñas. From this point north the channels belonged to the Chonos, whose territory in turn bordered Mapuche lands.

Halakwalup mythology revolved around the cold, the rain and the storms, all part of the handiwork of Xolas, the supreme creator who lived in the sky. Little is known about their ceremonial practices, but according to José de Vargas Ponce's account of the voyage of the *Santa María de la Cabeza* to the Magellan Strait in the late eighteenth century, the Halakwalup employed monotonous chants in a rite at which only men were present. One of the stages of the ceremony was to place pieces of meat over a fire—which the Spaniard immediately took to be human flesh.

From the animal kingdom, the fox had cultic significance, but destiny was ultimately in the hands of an all-powerful triad: Ayayema, a foul-smelling spirit whose winds could blast the canoes out of control; Kawtcho, a giant who roamed at night; and Mwono, a spirit of the glaciers who would only harm those who penetrated his dominion.

As well as birds, seals, shellfish, fish and porpoises, the Halakwalup ate whales. Five or six canoes would go out into the deeper channels and shoot arrows at a whale until it was mortally wounded. The beast would then be abandoned and left to die slowly, while the tide—with any luck—caused it to drift towards the shore. The first to see the dead whale beached would light a fire to inform all the others that it was feasting time. Seals were used for their meat and oil, but also for their skins and, following a successful hunt, some seal meat was stored in trees or placed on the rooftops of huts for a lean period. The offal was thrown away, but seal tongue and seal brain were considered delicacies. Occasionally the meat was smoked, but the Halakwalup usually preferred raw flesh and even meat that was in the later stages of putrefaction. The livers and sweetbreads of penguins and cormorants were also popular, though were barbecued for a longer period than plain muscle.

Though elusive to historians and ethnologists, the Halakwulup and Chonos had regular contact with sailors. In the eighteenth century John Byron and other survivors from the shipwreck of the *Wager* used their navigational know-how and intimate knowledge of the landscape to help them find a passage north through the labyrinth of channels. By the 1920s the Halakwalup were reduced to a handful of families scattered along the shores of the Smyth channel. The islands and waterways used by the Chonos are known in Chile today as the "archipiélago de los Chonos".

UNDER THE VOLCANOES: THE MAPUCHE NATION

Feulá korn mapu choli̇̃	At this hour all the sons of the earth
Llellipua fili̇̃ la chau ngünechen	Pray for the god of life
Taiñ mogerlerpual ka entuafiel	So that we the Huilliche survive,
Winka wekufe kake mapu küpalu	And the foreign demon from
Pu lamgen	Other lands vanishes
Winka inchiñ	Foreign brother we shall stay
Tañl mapu meu meleaiñ.	On our land till the end of the world.

Contemporary Huilliche poem recorded by Armazón

The great survivors of South America, the Mapuche are the only indigenous group from the Patagonian region to have made it into the twenty-first century. They were called *los Araucanos* (the Araucanians) by the conquistadors, in reference to the araucaria or monkey-puzzle tree which grows throughout the lake district region and which provides edible cones. Books and maps from the early colonial period show that there were a number of sub-groups, including the Pehuenche or "pine-cone eaters", the Picunche, the northern tribes, and the Huilliche, or southern tribes—the latter term is still used for the descendants of those tribes on the island of Chiloé.

Before the Spanish arrived, the Mapuche occupied a vast territory straddling the Andes but are now confined to a few towns and cities mainly around the lake districts. Their numbers are still significant, with some

930,000 Mapuche in Chile and anything between 90,000 and 200,000 in Argentina, though many of these will also have Spanish blood flowing in their veins. A symbolic frontier is the Río Biobío: it was here that Spanish forces attempted no fewer than 35 invasions of Mapuche territory over the 300-year colonial period. But the proud tribes fiercely resisted Spanish rule, and the would-be conquerors were forced to build a line of forts along the Biobío to demarcate the region of Chile they had under control. The Treaty of Quillín of 1641, which defined the frontier, was a tacit admission that the natives south of here were indomitable and beyond any kind of enslavement into the *encomienda* system. Smallpox, however, affected the Mapuche, and a number of major volcanic eruptions caused the mountain tribes to flee towards the lower plains and lakes—the main reason why the present-day national parks around Lago Llanquihue remain so beautiful and untamed.

Until the mid-nineteenth century this stand-off was the status quo, but in 1862, following reports that a Frenchman had declared himself King of Patagonia and was allying himself with the *caciques*, Colonel Cornelio Saavedra began to push his Chilean forces south. Over the next two decades the Mapuche were finally, bloodily, subjugated. Chilean historians refer to the period of trading and cultural interchange as one of "Araucanization" and the 1860-80 battles as the "Pacification", but for militant Mapuches these were invasions and massacres. The logging of forests forced many natives into the newly founded urban centres and Temuco, the largest town in the region, is regarded as a kind of Mapuche capital.

Mapuche means "people of the earth", and there are still a handful of rural communities, in small villages and in reservations, where they continue to sow wheat, potatoes and other crops, as well as raise sheep, cattle and horses around their *rucas* (huts made from mud and branches) and homesteads. The damming of the Biobío in 1994, attacked by whites as an ecological disaster, can also be seen as a final insult to the Mapuche; now even the waters of the ancient frontier are no longer wild and free-flowing.

AT PEACE ONLY WITH THE LAND

While more than willing to chop conquistadors' heads off when pressed, the Mapuche maintain the belief that "the whole earth is a single soul and we are all part of it" and that nature must be treated with reverence and sensitivity. The hierarchy of Mapuche deities is believed to have at least some of its roots in Incan beliefs, with food supply, divination and curing illness at the centre of spiritual life, and there is also the concept of an earth-mother or ñuque Mapu, equivalent to the Inca Pachamama.

The most important festival, the Nguillatun, is an opportunity to give thanks to the Mapuche gods—invisible old people with limited powers—for the goodness of the past year and to pray for abundant blessings for the year to come. There is always a Nguillatun ceremony at harvest time, and also during periods of great strife or on the occasion of an important military victory. Key figures in the Mapuche pantheon are: Ñenechen, an active god who intercedes on behalf of men, rather like Viracocha, the Inca creator of all men and supernatural beings; Pillan, the god of thunder or volcanoes, who was viewed by Christian missionaries as a surrogate Satan; and Ñenemapun, creator and ruler of earth. A number of minor gods control the sea, the sun, the moon and the wind, but the Mapuche look to the lakes, the mountains and earth for guidance and governance.

BOGEY-MEN, BOATS AND BATTLES

While Fuegian folklore is the preserve of specialists and a handful of local historians in the far south, some Mapuche ideas are well-known outside native communities. The Trauco, the Mapuche bogey-man, is a familiar figure among those of European descent who live in the south (and there are many exiles from Santiago and Buenos Aires in the lake regions, as well as Germans and Anglo-Argentinians). One account describes him as the biggest and strongest member in a pack of naked, monstrous-looking giants, who burst forth out of the icy volcanoes: he is "the lord of the mountains who still walks—for he is immortal—in the high peaks, leaning on his massive crook."

Also popular is the myth of the Caleuche or "boat of spirits". In one version the animals beside Lago Lácar begin to panic, and a vessel appears carrying two rowers heading for the south. They pass slowly, silently, and seem to stop when suddenly, "the boat seemed to be getting bigger and seemed to want to climb into the air above, like a pale cloud." Those on board can become gulls, steamer-ducks and other life forms, and they hide gold and the most beautiful women at their port at the bottom of the lake. The idea of the Caleuche is central to the Mapuche belief that their ancestors' spirits remain active in the relationships of the living. Argentinian director Ricardo Wullicher used the idea of the mythical ship in his film

1995 *La nave de los locos* (see p.236).

An oral narrative recorded in 1950 preserves the rhythms and cadences of the Mapuche story teller, Gervasio Paila Cura, of Catán Lil, Neuquén, even when rendered in English:

When the wind blows strong, the "puelche" (easterly) wind which is very strong, you know that a troop of horses is being rounded up. Many people hear this. That is the enchantment of a city that is lost. That's what they say, that there is a lost city, how many years is it now that it has been lost. It is in the mountains, in their middle. You see people, but they look different from the people nowadays, holding their heads, sometimes they are like skeletons. Sometimes they say other things have happened. They say that there were some women going around gathering pine cones. They have left the pine cones, mountains of pine cones. And they have returned. Afterwards the pine cones never appeared again.

…That must be a city that is over there. By day, quiet, you hear nothing. As it went dark, the same. You hear voices and songs and whistling.

…That story was told by an old neighbour, I barely remember him, Manuel Cayleuf. He has said that there is a lost people, over there. Old, so old, with many people who are lost, that cannot come out until the end of the world. They say they speak Spanish, that they don't speak the common tongue in the mountains.

For a record of Mapuches at war we have a unique European source. In 1597, only 56 years after the founding of Santiago de Chile by Pedro de Valdivia, Alonso de Ercilla y Zúñiga published his verse epic, *La Araucana*, dedicated to King Phillip II of Spain. It interweaves a narrative of conquest with the personal life of the author (who was in the army sent south to subdue the natives) and observations about the tribes encountered in what was to be the last undiscovered corner of the New World. Over 37 cantos Ercilla recalls ambushes, battles, vengeance, fiestas and games, the deaths of Valdivia and other conquistadors and the capture of their Mapuche arch-enemies Lautaro and Caupolicán.

Though the purpose of his poem is to sing the praises of Spain and its "just war" on a heathen nation, Ercilla cannot disguise his admiration for Mapuche courage and conviction.

Out of the troop advance
The noblest of the Barbarians
Imperious masters of heaven and earth
Eager to display their courage
Dragging their spears,
Striking different attitudes
Saying: "If there be any brave Christian
Let him come forward hand to hand."

Even as he witnessed the capture and execution of Caupolicán, Ercilla showed prescience in his assessment of the Mapuche's capacity for resistance: "Don't think that because I die here at your hands/the State will lack a leader/For afterwards will come a thousand more Caupolicans/But unlike me none of them wretched."

Ercilla alludes to the Araucanos' self-healing body politic; severing a single head merely leaves room for another to come forward. Four centuries later, Latin American leftists would look to the Mapuche model of non-hierarchical inspiration in their manifestos of guerrilla warfare.

In the last few decades the Mapuche have become increasingly politicized, forging links with international labour movements and environmental organizations and reclaiming cultural as well as land rights. In 1991 the Coordinación de Organizaciones Mapuche presented a proposal to the Argentinian state, demanding rights to administer all natural resources found in Mapuche territory. This spirited appeal is couched in Mapuche terminology and ends with an impassioned cry for self-determination and the freedom to exist:

We come to speak on behalf of the *newen* [spiritual power] of fecundity, of abundance, of good health, of the forces that supported and still support the life of all these woods, lakes, rivers, and lagoons of our Wajmapu [the Mapuche people's territory] that today are under siege.

Yet we also come to speak on behalf of our ceremonial centres, which have been locked behind wire fences; of our cemeteries that have been desecrated; of our woods, plants, and species that disappear and do not blossom again. We also speak in the name of our children, who see their

Wajmapu hurt by the scars that come from the proliferation of wire fences that crush Mapuche community life.

That is why we prefer to conclude here, to start walking right now.

Essential to the campaign for indigenous land rights has been the preservation of the Mapuche language, Mapundungun. It is taught in schools, dictionaries are widely available and there is even a version of Microsoft Windows for Mapundungun speakers.

Though the usual Catholic saints and Chilean and Argentinian national heroes have been imported into most of the place-names of northern Patagonia, many Mapuche names have survived. Bariloche is a corruption of the Mapuche word *vuriloche* and means "people behind the mountains", an indication that is has long been a tribal settlement (and not the great town "discovered" and founded by Argentina's much-loved scientific pioneer, Francisco "Perito" Moreno); Piltriquitron, the jagged mountain looming over El Bolsón, means "hanging from the clouds"; Rucapillan is a house of spirits—as in the title of Isabel Allende's novel about ancestors—and the tongue-twisting Curarrehue (Ku-ra-rray-way) means "stone altar". Even the name of Chile may come from Mapuche *Chilli* or "where the land ends".

Postscript: Genocide

In Ushuaia's main plaza is a little monument *al indio*. You find these statues all across Patagonia, tributes to fallen peoples erected late in the day. They are prettified tombstones, attempts to cleanse the past as ethnicity was once cleansed. There is something tragic about the way in which the sculptors always give these dead natives the rippling muscles of warriors; you always find yourself looking for the scars, the gashes, the bullet-wounds.

While the history of the annihilation of the Aztec and Inca peoples is considered colourful enough to enter primary school syllabuses, the eradication of the Patagonian tribes is met with denial both at home in Latin America and around the world. Throughout this book members of all these tribes figure in the conquest narratives as guides, trophies, victims and ghosts. Some accounts merely reflect the prejudices of their times. Captain Cook, during a three-day visit, complained that he found no religion among the Fuegians, while Charles Darwin—probably unaware of the impact three centuries of contact with whalers and sealers had already had on them—thought them the "most miserable wretches on earth". Sensitive, searching portrayals by Thomas Falkner in the eighteenth century and explorer Bailey Willis in the nineteenth gave a more balanced view, but the champions were always in the minority.

In 1904 geographer W. S. Barclay wrote that the Yahgan marked "the limit to which a man may strip himself of all aid and comfort and yet survive and perpetuate his kind." Even anthropologist Kirkland Lothrop, writing in the 1920s, could make unfavourable comparisons between Tierra del Fuego and Magdalenian Europe. After pointing to the Fuegian natives' artistic limitations—their lack of polished stone, in particular—and to their perceived lethargy and small, stunted bodies, he sums up: "Although the Fuegians had partly attained the technological plane called Neolithic in the Old World, nevertheless in most respects they were scarcely better off than the semi-simian Neanderthal man of Europe. Clearly then they were laggards or backsliders in the development of mankind."

At the present time, while between fifty and sixty per cent of Bolivia's population is indigenous, 97 per cent of Argentinians are of European descent. The last Selknam, Virginia Choinquitel, died in 1999. There are no pure-blood natives in southern Patagonia or Tierra del Fuego.

Chapter Two
THE INVENTION OF PATAGONIA:
MAGELLAN AND DRAKE

"And this is to be taken for a warning, that he that commeth neere this Cape, and passeth by it as I have said with the wind at Northeast, or any other off the sea inclining to the Southeast, must not come to anker, but presently be sure to pass by; because in Sommer this place is much subject to Southwest winds, which blow right in: and they put a man from his tackle, & make him to loose his voyage... And if you see beds of weeds, take heed of them... But men must beware and not trust the Indians of this Cape: for they be subtill and will betray a man."
Description of the Magellan Strait in *The Principal Navigations, Voyages, Traffics, and Discoveries of the English Nation*, edited by Richard Hakluyt (1589)

For European mariners, Patagonia would come into existence first as an unknown coast at the far edge of a stormy ocean. The first man to see that coast probably didn't. In his *Mundus Novus* (1502), a letter to Lorenzo

Pietro di Medici, the Florentine navigator Amerigo Vespucci claims to have sailed into the "torrid zone" beyond the equator, where he and his crew found "a multitude of people (as we read in the Apocalypse), a race I say gentle and amenable. All of both sexes go about naked, covering no part of their bodies; and just as they spring from their mothers' wombs so they go until death. They have indeed large square-built bodies, well formed and proportioned..."

Vespucci's colourful account asserts that the women are "very libidinous" and that the members of the tribe "eat one another... the father has already been seen to eat children and wife, and I knew a man whom I also spoke to who was reputed to have eaten more than three hundred human bodies." He gives a vivid description of the natives' numerous body piercings, and reports that the women, "being very lustful, cause the private parts of their husbands to swell up to such a huge size that they appear deformed and disgusting; and this is accomplished by a certain device of theirs, the biting of poisonous animals. And in consequence of this many lose their organs which break off through lack of attention, and they remain eunuchs."

The degree of embellishment applied here matters little, nor the fact that that Vespucci probably never got anywhere near Patagonia; his reports in *Mundus Novus* and in the *Letter to Piero Soderini* (1504) make no mention of sighting the River Plate estuary or of any recognizable landmark on the Argentinian coast. The important contribution from the man who gave his name to America is that he gave later sailors the expectation of seeing naked, wild, cannibalistic and, most pointedly, "large" people in the far south.

Others successfully voyaged beyond the Tropic of Capricorn. The Andalucian pilot-major Juan Díaz de Solís was sent by King Ferdinand of Spain to take possession of the southern territories. He may also have been under orders to look for a route to Asia. He sailed into the River Plate in 1516, and arrived near the junction of the Uruguay and Paraná rivers, where he was murdered by the native Charrúa tribe. Two years later King Charles I of Spain (afterwards the Emperor Charles V) made the experienced but somewhat idle Portuguese navigator Hernão de Magalhaes (Magellan) commander of a fleet of five vessels and commissioned him to find a new western route to the Moluccas and, on arrival, to claim the islands for Spain.

FERDINAND MAGELLAN: PUERTO SAN JULIÁN

"His art is of such power,
It would control my dam's god Setebos
And make a vassal of him."

Caliban in *The Tempest* Act I, Scene 2

On a raised platform close to the beach at Puerto San Julián is a simple altar commemorating the first ever mass celebrated in what is now Argentina, on 31 March 1520. Finding relief from the swell of the South Atlantic in this well-protected harbour, Magellan christened the bay San Julián after the patron saint of wanderers and seekers of shelter. As the chronicle kept by Antonio Pigafetta, a young Italian nobleman who was a volunteer member of Magellan's crew, tells us, he also baptized other topographical features including the vast Gulf of San Matías and the Cape of 11,000 Virgins (now Cabo Vírgenes). Some names have been changed—Cabo Deseado, or Cape Desired, is now Cabo Pilar—and some have been lost altogether, such as the quaintly named (in Portuguese) River of Sardines.

A diligent record of naval manoeuvres, Pigafetta's log is also a book full of natural wonders and astonishing native customs. It tells, in the words of Gabriel García Márquez, "of hogs with navels on their haunches, clawless birds whose hens laid eggs on the backs of their mates, and others still, resembling tongueless pelicans, with beaks like spoons" and "of a misbegotten creature with the head and ears of a mule, a camel's body, the legs of a deer and the whinny of a horse." Published in 1524, it was to become a fountainhead of myths and revelations on which later voyagers would base their preconceptions and flights of fancy. For García Márquez it provided inspiration as the first work of "magic realism".

Magellan and his men were on the lookout for strange and fearsome natives at every stage of their New World voyage. Pigafetta had marvelled at the clothing of the natives of Verzin (Brazil) and reported that the River Plate, discovered by Solís just four years earlier, was full of "men of the kind called Canibali, who eat human flesh." Pigafetta relates that Solís and his sixty sailors had trusted the locals far too much, and so had been eaten.

But cannibalism was neither unknown nor particularly shocking to mariners. There is far greater drama and far more space given over to the next group of natives, encountered, says Pigafetta, at "forty-nine and a half degrees toward the Antarctic Pole" when the ships were anchored off San Julián for the winter. They had been two whole months without seeing a soul.

But one day (without anyone expecting it) we saw a giant who was on the shore, quite naked, and who danced, leaped, and sang, and while he sang he threw sand and dust on his head. Our captain sent one of his men toward him, charging him to leap and sing like the other in order to reassure him and show him friendship. Which he did.

Immediately the man of the ship, dancing, led the giant to a small island where the captain awaited him. And when he was before us, he began to marvel and to be afraid, and he raised one finger upward, believing that we came from heaven. And he was so tall that the tallest of us only came up to his waist. He had a very large face, painted round with red, and his eyes were painted round with yellow, and in the middle of the cheeks he had two hearts painted. He had hardly any hairs on his head, and they were painted white.

When he was brought to the captain, he was clad in the skin of a certain animal, which skin was very skilfully sewn together. And this animal has the head and ears as large as a mule's, and a neck and body like that of a camel, a stag's legs, and a tail like that of a horse.

This last section has been cited by scholars to call into question the veracity of Pigafetta's report about the size of the natives, who must have been Tehuelche nomads. What were probably oversized garments made of guanaco skin—patched together in Pigafetta's imagination like a centaur—may well have made a "giant" of a man: loose flaps of skin, long ears for epaulets, perhaps a guanaco's head for a hat. Pigafetta says that the women were also big, and "had teats half a cubit long" but, unlike the men, wore a patch of skin to cover their private parts. The women did all the carrying ("loaded like asses") and while slightly smaller than their male counterparts, they were somewhat fatter.

One of the natives seemed amenable to being "civilized":

This giant was of better disposition than the others, and was very graceful and amiable, loving to dance and leap. And when dancing he depressed the earth to a palm's depth in the spot where his feet touched. He was with us for a long time, and in the end we baptized him.

The captain and crew proceeded to teach the tame Tehuelche how to say the name Jesus, and made him repeat the *Pater Noster*, the *Ave Maria* and his own new name. They also dressed him in European clothes and in exchange for a guanaco gave him a mirror, a comb, bells and other trinkets.

After these promising developments, Magellan came across four Tehuelche men and decided to take the two youngest back to Spain to add to a collection of weird specimens to present to the king. Offering temptations in the form of the usual trinkets, he made sure of his plan by having the two natives' feet placed in iron fetters, which were bolted shut with a hammer. Pigafetta notes how the captain was intelligent enough to load up the natives' arms with all the gifts they could bear so that he could place irons onto their ankles without resistance. Angered by such trickery, the giants called to their god Setebos ("that is, the great devil") for help. Their collars ruffled, the Iberians decided to tie the hands of the other two Tehuelche.

After one of the prisoners managed to escape, the other began to struggle, and was struck on the head and seriously wounded. When, the next morning, the giant returned with a band of rebels wielding bows and arrows, chaos ensued. A European was killed, but Pigafetta does not seem outraged and hints that a pilot, João Carvalho, had spent the night with the wife of one of the ensnared giants: "And verily these giants run straighter than a horse, and are very jealous of their wives."

The narrator does, however, protest at the heathen ceremonies the Tehuelche perform at funerals, claiming to have some understanding of their language:

> When one of them dies, twelve devils appear, and dance around the dead man. And it seems they are painted. And one of these devils is taller than the others, and makes much more noise, and rejoices much more than the others. And from this the giants took the fashion of painting themselves on the face and body, as has been said. And in their language they called these devils Setebos and Cheleule. Besides the things aforesaid, he who was in the ship told us by signs that he had seen devils with

two horns on their head, and with long hair down to their feet, and through their mouth and backside they belched fire.

NAMING THE GIANTS

Just as the conquistadors in Mexico and Peru hacked their way through jungles and crossed deserts, their minds busy with chivalrous tales and romances, so the sailors who voyaged to Patagonia carried with them a back catalogue of fantasies and fables. The third and final book of a chivalric romance entitled *Primaleon et Polendos*, published in Spain in 1512 (and translated into English in the early seventeenth century as *Primaleon of Greece*), refers to a character called *el gran patagón* or "the great Patagón". On an island are wild men who:

> ...live like animals and are very fierce and wild and eat raw meat, which they obtain by hunting in the mountains. They are like savages and are dressed only in the skins of the animals they have killed... But this is nothing compared with a man who now lives among them and is called Patagón. They say that this Patagón was born of an animal that lives in the mountains and is the most monstrous being on earth; he is very intelligent, however, and loves women very much. He looks like a dog, with big ears that reach down to his shoulders and with very long, pointed teeth which stick like carved fangs out of his mouth. His feet look like a stag's and he runs so fast that nobody can keep up with him.

In this tale of dwarves, necromancers, damsels in distress and knights (which inspired Cervantes' famous parody, *Don Quixote*), the hero Primaleón must, of course, fight the foul dog-man. But the Patagón exhibits certain positive qualities, too: he walks into Constantinople leading a lion on a chain, and is reported to be but one of several giants, and a rather tame one at that.

Bruce Chatwin makes much of this in his *In Patagonia* (1977), writing that one Professor Gonzáles Díaz drew his attention to the source. It is likely that the said academic knew of Argentinian scholar Lida de Malkiel's comprehensive account of the Primaleón-Patagonia connection in a paper published in 1952. While some historians dispute the theory, it is far more colourful than the theory that "Patagon" was merely a superlative of the Portuguese word for foot, *pata*; Pigafetta only ever uses the term *pathag-*

oni and gives no etymology or other explanation. Another, more remote, possibility is that Patagonia comes from *Patac-Hunia*, which in Quechua—the language of the Incas—means "mountain regions".

Giants were just part of the picture. Everything Pigafetta sees is utterly new to him and, like any innocent abroad, he gawps goggle-eyed at all the oddities. While jaguars in Brazil had seemed to the Italian urbanite "pretty little cats", of "sea wolves" (seals) he says: "They have feet, nails on their feet, and skin between the toes like goslings. And if these animals could run, they would be very fierce and cruel. But they do not leave the water, where they swim and live on fish."

Before sailing on south to find a route to the Pacific, Magellan erected a cross at the summit of Monte Cristo, four miles north-west of the anchorage—it can be seen in the background of a watercolour by Conrad Martens, FitzRoy's artist on board the *Beagle*. In his journal of 14 January 1834 Charles Darwin mentions a "small wooden cross" on a hill, which could well be the one left by Magellan.

In the spirit of the Inquisition, where masses were celebrated stakes and gibbets soon followed. After Luis de Mendoza and Gaspar de Quesada led an unsuccessful revolt against Magellan, they were executed and their dismembered bodies left on the shores.

Magellan was killed in Mactan in the Philippines in April 1521. The single ship that returned to Spain, the *Victoria*, was captained by Juan Sebastián del Cano, originally master of the *Concepción*. He, along with 17 others, had become, quite inadvertently, the first man to circumnavigate the world. Ironically, del Cano had played a part in the rebellion led by Mendoza and Quesada, but had been spared by Magellan.

Maximilian Transylvanus, secretary to Charles V, the Holy Roman Emperor, interviewed the survivors and reported his findings in a letter:

> One night a great number of fires were seen, mostly on their left hand, from which they guessed that they had been seen by natives of the region. But Magellan, seeing that the country was rocky, and also stark with eternal cold, thought it useless to waste many days in examining it; and so with only three ships, he continued on his course along the channel, until, on the twenty-second day after he had entered it, he sailed out upon another wide and vast sea.

Thus, in passing, Tierra del Fuego was baptized.

Pigafetta was among the survivors, and his legacy endured. Vespucci may have thought he saw giants, but he omitted to name their homeland. Pigafetta's story immortalized the meeting between Europeans and a newly-christened ethnic group—the Patagonians—which would soon designate an entire region.

In his Nobel Prize lecture of 1982 Gabriel García Márquez says that Pigafetta's log "contained the seeds of our present novels." In the magical realist school which Márquez more or less invented the absolutely natural and real is met with wonder, and every outing from the village is a voyage of discovery. But the Colombian author also draws attention to the scene in which the native Patagonian, like Caliban, was "confronted with a mirror, whereupon that impassioned giant lost his senses to the terror of his own image." Latin Americans, he argues, have been doing the same ever since, notwithstanding the slaying of the indigenous peoples and independence from Spain. Theirs is the solitude and madness of the giant.

If Pigafetta gave the world "Patagonia" and his diary, Magellan gave mariners his Strait. He and his crew had been expecting an open passageway, perhaps a narrower version of an opening like the Strait of Gibraltar. But Magellan was prepared for a "well-hidden strait" and that is certainly what he found. In his Pulitzer Prize-winning history of exploration, *The Discovers* (1991), Daniel Boorstin sums it up neatly:

> The Strait of Magellan—the narrowest, most devious, most circuitous of all the straits connecting two bodies of water—was a wonderful ironic prop for a seafaring melodrama. This meandering narrow maze debouched unexpectedly into the most open, most vast of all the seas. We must view on a modern map the tortuous passage, the angular disorder of small islands, the countless unexpected slots of water, to grasp the full measure of expertise, the persistence, the courage—and luck—required to find the way... To sail the three hundred thirty-four miles between the oceans took Magellan thirty-eight days... others would take more than three months, many would simply give up.

SAN JULIÁN REVISITED: FRANCIS DRAKE

For a pirate used to rough seas and stormy relations with his many foes, the voyage south had been a breeze. Apart from occasional skirmishes with Moors and the usual run-ins with Spaniards while stealing their fishing boats and caravels, the crossing went well. At Cape Blanco, in Mauritania, Sir Francis Drake had turned to the west with the firm belief that on this voyage he would make it to the farthest horizon.

Anchoring off a promontory six or seven leagues up the River Plate in April 1578, Drake's ship, the *Pelican*, rendezvoused with the *Christopher*, thought lost in a storm off the Brazilian coast. Drake christened the spot Cape Joy. According to the main source on Drake's circumnavigation, *The World Encompassed*, the two crews were able to feast on "sea wolves" (seals), drink their fill of fresh water and repair their ships. The journal notes on 16 April 1578: "The country hereabout is of a temperate and sweet air, very fair and pleasant to behold, and besides the exceeding fruitfulness of the soil, its stored with plenty of large and mighty deer."

Drake had sailed out of Plymouth on 15 November 1577. A born mariner, he had already visited the West Indies several times and in 1572 commanded a voyage to Nombre de Dios, during which he was able to explore the narrow Isthmus of Panama. Seeing the Pacific fired his imagination, and in 1577 he won the support of Queen Elizabeth to attempt a voyage round the globe. As captain-general, Drake sailed on the *Pelican* (later renamed the *Golden Hinde* in honour of his patron Sir Christopher

Hatton's family shield), heading a squadron made up of four light ships, the *Elizabeth*, the *Marigold*, the *Swan* and the *Christopher*.

The fullest account of this landmark voyage, *The World Encompassed*, is based on the notes of Francis Fletcher, chaplain to the expedition. It was edited by Drake's nephew and published in 1628. A "Gentleman at Arms" on board, Francis Petty, also left a narrative. The British Museum has what appears to be a literal copy of the first part of Fletcher's notes, preserved in the Sloane MSS collection, probably published in 1677, and a further document relating to the latter part of the voyage known as the "Anonymous Narrative", and dated 1580. At the time of the voyage, the details of Drake's activities and discoveries—and his looting of Spanish ships—were too sensitive to be made public and so further strain Anglo-Spanish relations. Indeed, Drake had kept the full purpose of his voyage secret from his crew, only giving his officer-colleagues on board the absolute minimum of information necessary to steer the ship to the next port.

But from 1589 onwards, in the wake of the defeat of the Spanish Armada, Richard Hakluyt, using Fletcher and other sources, began to publish his *Traffiques and Discoveries*, turning Drake into a national hero.

To the South

In May the four ships sailed south along the storm-blasted, rock-strewn coast between the River Plate estuary and the "land of Giants" Fletcher and other literate members of the crew had read about in accounts of Magellan's voyage. Begrudgingly, *The World Encompassed* informs us:

> Magellan was not altogether deceived in naming them giants, for they differ from the common sort of men, both in stature, bigness, and strength of body, as also in the hideousness of their voice; but yet they are nothing so monstrous or giantlike as they were reported, there being some English men as tall as the highest of any that we could see, but peradventure the Spaniards did not think that ever any Englishman would come thither to reprove them, and therefore might presume more boldly to lie; the name Pentagones, Five cubits, viz, 7 foot and a half, describing the full height (if not somewhat more) of the highest of them.

Drake and his crew made contact on several occasions with natives along the coast. They observed how the Indians dressed in feathers to deceive and catch the fleet-footed rheas, and exchanged gifts of glass-beaded bracelets and knives in return for these feathers and for arrows. The jingoistic narrator of *The World Encompassed* notes that mistreatment at the hands of the Spanish has made the natives "more monstrous in mind" and "inhospitable to strangers".

Far greater attention is reserved for the "strange birds, which could not fly at all, nor yet run so fast as they could escape us with their lives." On coming across a colony on two small islands near a larger one that Drake names "Elizabeth Island", the writer strains to compare and contrast the penguins' physical features with those of mallards, geese, conies and crows of England. He is particularly impressed by the penguins' agility once in the water and remarks on the sheer number of birds he sees and their usefulness to the crew: "such was the infinite resort of these birds to these Islands, that in the space of one day we killed no less than 3000... they are a very good and wholesome victual."

At San Julián Drake's men found a gibbet which they believed to have been erected by Magellan "for the execution of John Carthagene, the Bishop of Burgos' cousin". The crew buried the human bones they discovered beneath the structure and made a makeshift tomb from rocks shaped with a "grinding stone". A memorial was also placed bearing Drake's name in Latin, the lingua franca of the Elizabethan maritime world. Relations between the sailors and the Tehuelche were on the whole amiable, but two of the crew were killed when some natives perceived their bow-practice to be a threat. Drake shot the killer and the Patagonians fled into the woods along the coast.

Throughout the first phase of the voyage, Drake's main problem was neither the ocean nor the natives, but one of his crewmen, Thomas Doughty. The sources vary in their accounts but Drake accused Doughty of conspiracy, mutiny and witchcraft, and offered him three options: to remain stranded in San Julián, to be taken back to England for trial, or to be executed on the spot. Living up to his name, Doughty chose the latter, and after dining with Drake and receiving the sacrament, submitted his neck to the executioner.

To keep his flotilla lean and swift Drake had the *Mary*, a ship stolen en route from the Portuguese, broken up and, after careening the hulls of the remaining three ships, sailed out of the "port accursed" on 17 August and headed south. The expedition's crew saw fires burning along the Strait and were struck by the "huge and mountainous" landscape bordering the channel. Clouds floated through the high valleys between the ranges, snow was visible on the slopes and the trees "seem[ed] to stoop with the burden of the weather." Drake's ships made haste through the Strait, but the *Marigold* was lost in a gale, followed shortly after by the *Elizabeth*. The latter managed to sail back through the Strait and on to England, its crew claiming later that they had never intended to abandon Drake.

While the *Hinde* (newly baptized on entering the South Seas) was struggling to make way in a storm that blew it back into the islands south of Tierra del Fuego, a small shallop was also lost. Its crew made their way back to San Julián and then the River Plate, where one survivor, Peter Cardew, managed to escape the belligerent natives and spent the next eight years roaming the wilderness between the Plate and Bahia in Brazil.

Drake later told his kinsman Sir Richard Hawkins that "at the end of the great storm, he found himself at 50 deg S," indicating that he had anchored somewhere off the "southernmost point of land in the world" and making Drake the first European to visit Cape Horn. Drake christened the islands the Elizabethides (now called the Wollaston Islands) in honour of his royal mistress. Fletcher's account corroborates this: the *Terra Incognita* of the Spanish geographers thus became the *Terra australis bene nunc cognita* of the chaplain. A 1598 map by Cornelius Clarz of Amsterdam incorporates Drake's discovery.

But the captain had other things on his mind. With a fair wind from the south, he sailed north-west for the island of Mocha off the coast if Chile and onwards to circle the globe.

The significance of Drake's circumnavigation goes far beyond its adventure story quality; it had a profound cultural and historical significance. The English navy had come late into the fray, but Drake's exploits sowed the seeds for its future domination of the world's oceans. As Peter Hulme and Tim Youngs point out in their introduction to *The Cambridge Companion to Travel Writing*, "The English did not have a figure to set alongside Columbus in the national imagination until 1580, when Francis Drake returned from his three-year voyage around the world... In the wake of Drake's voyage a wide range of texts and images were produced to celebrate his achievements: they display a new sense that the English could play a role in the apprehension of the wider world—and of the globe itself."

In an emblem designed by Geoffrey Whitney in 1596, Drake was shown sitting on top of the world with God steering the bow of his ship with a bridle. In the accompanying legend Drake is compared to Jason, returning with the Golden Fleece. We have to bear in mind that at this time the English had only made sporadic voyages to the Caribbean, Brazil, Newfoundland and northern Russia, while Spain and Portugal dominated all the fastest, most profitable sea routes. Consequently, the reading public in England (still very small at this time) had access mainly to translated accounts.

This was all about to change, and Drake's circumnavigation provided the impetus. From 1589 onwards Richard Hakluyt began compiling sea voyages, showing that the English were "men full of activity, stirrers abroad, and searchers of the remote parts of the world." Hakluyt, who had begun with translations and whose *Divers Voyages Concerning the Discovery of America* (1582) dealt mainly with non-English sources, possessed in Drake a figure who could justify recounting all the previous—and subsequent—voyages taken by English sailors. The resulting work, *Principal Navigations, Voyages, Traffics, and Discoveries of the English Nation* (1589), contained 93 voyages and spanned 1,500 years of English maritime history. The second edition, published in three volumes between 1598 and 1600, contained double the number of voyages and pages. The books would make travel writing a popular genre and turn Drake into an icon.

As for Patagonia, it would no longer seem quite so exotic or alien. It had been seen by an Englishman, and a great national hero. Moreover, he had managed to sail through it, breaking a physical as well as a metaphorical barrier. Drake opened up the southern oceans for hundreds of captains who would follow in his wake, and he opened up the southern lands to the imaginations of millions of people in the English-speaking world. He was also a pirate and a slave trader whose wanderlust was fuelled by greed as much as curiosity, a man whose death from dysentery in 1596 was as gleefully celebrated by the Spanish as it was solemnly mourned by the English. In other words he was the quintessential Elizabethan, and the myth of Drake is, at least in England, richer and more complex even than that of Patagonia.

Chapter Three

PORT FAMINE:
SARMIENTO DE GAMBOA

"In some places we found so many pearls in the shells that we regretted
we could not eat the molluscs, for it would have been like eating gravel."
Sarmiento de Gamboa

News of Drake's voyage through the Straits came to the attention of Don
Francisco de Toledo, the viceroy of Peru. Since 1513, when Vasco Núñez
de Balboa had waded sword in hand into the Pacific Ocean and claimed
the whole vast ocean for the sovereign, the Pacific had been regarded as the
exclusive preserve of Spain. The arrival of "Francisco Drac"—as they called
the English pirate, his name suggesting *draque* or "dragon" to the Castilian ear—was akin to the Devil himself washing up on these shores.

Then on 13 February 1579 Drake's men sailed directly into the port
of Callao—at the time the most important Spanish port in South
America—and slipped through a cordon of nine Spanish ships. Toledo
raised the alarm but Drake was able to escape, though on this occasion

without any significant treasure. The viceroy dispatched one of his captains, Diego de Frías Tiejo, in command of 300 men—among them the navigator Pedro Sarmiento de Gamboa—to give chase. But the men had been sent out without provisions or ballast and were ill-prepared for a drawn-out pursuit. Sarmiento wanted to continue, but Frías Tiejo broke off the chase.

A second expedition was mustered, this time with the viceroy's kinsman Luis de Toledo in command; once again Sarmiento was among the officers, as *sargento mayor*, and fourth in rank—but by then Drake had two weeks' start on his pursuers. Sarmiento proposed that the Spanish ships set course for Nicaragua or Mexico, there to intercept Drake who was bound to be sailing north in search of a north-west passage to England. But Luis de Toledo insisted on hugging the coast around Panama, where he discovered that Drake had already made off with a treasure ship loaded with some 400,000 pesos. Drake had sailed into the sunset to complete his circumnavigation; a dejected Luis de Toledo disembarked in Panama, with plans to return to Spain. Sarmiento seethed. "God pardon the man who made us turn back the first time and would not cross the gulf the second," he wrote, "for had we pressed on in either of these expeditions we should have brought the famous robber to book."

The viceroy decided that, since the chances of catching Drake were so slender, the least that could be done was to find a way of preventing other adventurers from following in his stead. The whereabouts of two ships that had sailed out of England with Drake, the *Elizabeth* and the *Marigold*, were not known to the Spaniards. Perhaps they were about to make further assaults on the Chilean and Peruvian coasts. It was deemed necessary to send an expedition to survey and, ultimately, fortify the only obvious entrance into these western reaches of the empire: the Straits of Madre de Dios, a.k.a. the Magellan Strait. Sarmiento de Gamboa was the obvious man for the job.

Sarmiento, the son of a Galician father and a Biscayan mother, was born at Alcalá de Henares in 1532. He entered military service at the age of 18 and served as a soldier between 1550 and 1555, before leaving to seek his fortune in Mexico and Guatemala. In 1557 he arrived in Peru, where he spent seven years researching the history of the Incas. Sarmiento appears to have been on intimate terms with the viceregal authorities but was persecuted by the Holy Office of the Inquisition for claiming to have possession of a magical ink which could be used in love letters to seduce women.

His sentence was to hear mass in the cathedral at Lima, to be stripped naked with a candle in his hand and then to be banished from the Indies. But while being held at the Monastery of Santo Domingo Sarmiento appealed to the Pope and obtained a commutation of the banishment. He was given permission to reside in Cuzco and elsewhere in Peru until 1567.

During his investigations into the Incas Sarmiento claimed to have been told by the Inca Tupac Yupanqui of two islands to the westward. This led, in 1567, to a major expedition, supported by the governor of the time, Lope García de Castro, during which Sarmiento discovered the Solomon Islands. When the governor was replaced by a new viceroy, Don Francisco de Toledo, Sarmiento was taken into service and played a leading role in the persecution of the Incas. In 1571 he organized an expedition to penetrate into Vilcabamba, the river valley close to the site of Machu Picchu, to capture the young Inca Tupac Amaru. Sarmiento delivered the boy in triumph to Cuzco, where the viceroy had him executed in the main plaza.

For his efforts Sarmiento was praised by Toledo as "the most able man on this subject [the Incas] that I have found in this country." When the Inquisitors again condemned Sarmiento, first for necromancy and then for the "crime" of showing the lines in the palm of his hand to an old woman, Toledo placed him under special protection.

This was the state of affairs when the expedition to the Strait was being arranged. Sarmiento's second-in-command was to be Juan de Villalobos, and his force was further strengthened with Hernando Lamero, a chief pilot familiar with the maze of islands and fjords of southern Chile. The viceroy went down to Callao to select two of the fastest, strongest vessels available. The flagship was to be christened *Nuestra Señora de la Esperanza*; the second ship, with Villalobos as its *almirante*, was the *San Francisco*.

A thorough survey and fortification by means of a colony were the main aims of the expedition. Further instructions from the viceroy also ordered Sarmiento to offer gifts (combs, scissors, knives, fish-hooks, etc.) to the natives, with a view to employing them as interpreters. He was to take note of the religious beliefs of the indigenous tribes and to investigate if they used precious metals, herbs or spices. Above all, he was to ensure their allegiance as it could prove vital should there be some news of the presence of Drake or other pirates in the Strait.

On 11 October 1579 the ships weighed anchor and sailed south. En route, they explored the huge labyrinth of islets, channels, capes and ice fields around the 50th parallel and found an access to the continent through the Gulf of Trinidad. Sarmiento took formal possession of the towering walls of rock cloaked in impassable forest. They had no idea of where they were in relation to the entrance to the Strait so he and a small party of seamen climbed a steep hill to take in the view. The sharp rocks ripped into the men's feet and they had to scramble along clinging to the twisted branches of trees. Sarmiento's narrative tells us that the land looked as if it had been "torn to shreds" and he and his crew counted some 85 islands in the archipelago.

The men made voyages in long-boats, searching for a channel. Time and again they rowed into coves and bays that allowed no passage through to open waters. They were struck by the extreme humidity of the forest and the incessant rain. The cold was intense and there were mossy banks on the shores which, when stepped upon, sucked in a man to his armpits. They found shellfish crammed with pearls. In an ominously prescient moment, Sarmiento noted "how worthless a thing are riches, which cannot be eaten, when men are hungry." Several groups of natives were seen on the shore, but gave the men neither food nor directions; they captured one, perhaps in the hope that he could guide them or convince his tribesmen to come to their aid, but at the first opportunity he scrambled ashore and disappeared into the thick, soaking undergrowth. The men began to fear that they would never find a path out of the labyrinth when, on one of the voyages, they discovered an island which they called Madre de Dios. An island meant that not all the bays were dead-ends.

After further botched attempts to locate a passage through the continent, Sarmiento began to suspect that his *almirante* was planning a mutiny. It was resolved to attempt to go back out into the sea, which they knew meant tempests and huge breakers, and head south. A vicious gale took the *San Francisco* perhaps as far as Cape Horn, whence Villalobos, egged on by a mutinous crew, decided to make for a port on the Chilean coast.

On 21 January 1580 Sarmiento de Gamboa sailed into the Magellan Strait. As well as Magellan and Drake, two Spanish captains—García Jofre de Loyosa, in 1425, and Simon de Alcazava, in 1535—had previously sailed through the Strait. But Sarmiento made the first eastbound crossing of the Strait and his accounts, published in 1579 and 1580, provide the most detailed picture of its physical geography. In the eastern sections of the Strait Sarmiento discovered a number of bays that he thought suitable for his putative colony and his record suggests a change in mood:

> The days that we were in this port of the Río de la Posesión were warm, with a fresh south wind from eight in the morning to five in the afternoon, when it fell calm, and was calm all night. The nights are very fine, with clear sky, the stars shining brightly, and the air healthful. Here parakeets and catalines, another species of parakeets, with half the head of a red colour, were seen. We heard linnets and other singing birds, which is a sign of fair weather, and saw the tracks of lions and tigers... The county is plain and without hills, and well peopled with these natives, so far as we could see. Our men who went on shore found the ground burrowed with rabbit holes, the rabbits being like those in Castile, and the natives wore cloaks of the skins of vicuñas, the same as those of Peru... this region is warmer and has a better climate than those we had passed. Moreover, it is pleasant to look upon, is capable of sustaining a large population, and wild and tame flocks, and would yield grain. According to Felipe, the big native, the land yields cotton, which is the best proof of a mild climate, and cinnamon they call cabca.

Eleven days later the *Nuestra Señora de la Esperanza* left the Strait and was blown out into the Atlantic by a following wind that rose sharply to gale force. Having traversed the Magellan Strait with unusually fair weather on several star-lit nights and having found the promised land he had sought, Sarmiento decided to sail on to Spain. There he tried to persuade King Philip to colonize and fortify the passage, an argument bolstered by the fact that Portugal held sway over the Cape of Good Hope.

Only a handful of men and equipment had been granted to Cortés for his conquest of the Aztecs. Twenty-three ships were commissioned and around 3,500 men recruited for this far less strategically vital expedition. To Sarmiento de Gamboa's chagrin, Diego Flores de Valdés was placed in command of the vessels; the relegated visionary was appeased with the title of governor-to-be of the proposed settlements. Alonso de Sotomayor was the third captain, of equal rank and similarly authoritarian character as the other two, and he had at his command 600 soldiers. He had been appointed governor of Chile and was to proceed to Santiago following the establishment of the colonies in the Strait.

On 27 September 1581 the fleet set sail from Sanlúcar de Barrameda. From start to finish, the voyage was a catastrophe. Sarmiento and Flores de Valdés were at permanent loggerheads. Five ships were dashed against the rocks off Cádiz. Fever struck many of the sailors shortly after leaving Cabo Verde, 150 men dying after suffering agonizing bowel pains.

The fleet wintered in Rio de Janeiro to avoid the worst of the weather, but a new and virulent fever struck and caused another 140 deaths, including a number of Sarmiento's colonists and two natives whom Sarmiento had picked up when traversing the Strait.

When the fleet, now made up of 16 ships, did eventually head south in the spring, the disasters multiplied. One ship sprang a leak and sank, all hands perishing with her. Flores de Valdés decided that the ships should seek refuge in the estuary of the River Plate. En route, he was informed by some friars that two English ships—one of them captained by the privateer Edward Fenton—were bound for the Strait, making the voyage all the more urgent. After sending three of the least seaworthy ships laden with all the women and sick men back to Rio de Janeiro, Flores de Valdés apportioned a further three vessels to Sotomayor, who had resolved to make a land crossing to Chile. They lost another vessel, this time a supply ship, and with it considerable stores and munitions.

Flores and Sarmiento and their remaining five ships sailed on south. On reaching the mouth of the Strait, Flores de Valdés' ship was prevented from entering by adverse winds and tides. He decided enough was enough. He had obeyed the royal commands in reaching these latitudes, and that would suffice. He sailed for Rio; Sarmiento had no choice but to go with him, and from there Flores de Valdés continued home to Spain.

Sarmiento's account portrays both Sotomayor and Flores de Valdés as cowards, but his own stubbornness probably played a role in losing so many ships and in the general breakdown of communications. Once again he was incensed by what he believed to be erroneous decisions taken by commanders unfit for their posts.

NOMBRE DE JESÚS AND REY FELIPE

Strengthened by reinforcements from Spain, the expedition that left Rio in December 1583 numbered 529 soldiers, seamen and colonists, and their

wives and children, on five ships. After less than two months of relatively fair sailing they entered the Straits. Here they anchored, but powerful tides and winds threatened to tear the boats from their moorings. Unable to penetrate further, the colonists disembarked on Cabo Virgenes, which offered only scant shelter.

On this lonely beach, peopled only by a handful of tribesmen, the governor-designate of the Straits colonies decided to found his first settlement. His account records the landing:

> Pedro Sarmiento went on shore with Captain Gregorio de las Alas and Anton Pablos. Sarmiento carried a great cross on his shoulder, with which, in the name of the most Holy Trinity, he jumped on land, and the others after him, with eight arquebusiers. With the cross on high they went on their knees and recited *Te Deum laudamus*. Coming to a large plain clothed with odiferous and consoling herbs, and putting his hand on his sword, he solemnly took possession for your Majesty and your heirs and successors to the crowns of Castile and León, in the name of the most Holy Trinity, Father, Son and Holy Ghost. In sign of possession he cut the grass, moved stones, and made a great heap of stones with his hands, the others helping.

With the cross and the cairn, Sarmiento wished into being the settlement of Nombre de Jesús on 11 February 1584, at present-day Punta Dungeness, a slender, pointed cape where the north shore of the Magellan Strait meets the Atlantic Ocean.

On the following day "a strong breeze with the current" obliged the ships to weigh anchor and run out for three days. Sarmiento believed they had deserted and gone to Brazil, but as captain-general and governor of the new lands he encouraged the settlers to take in the impressive sweep of all this new land they had acquired and to consider that they had all the resources they needed—and plenty of hard work to occupy them. They set about building huts and foraging for provisions. With only some biscuit and flour from Brazil, perhaps enough for four days, the men went in search of roots and found "some that were sweet and well flavoured like turnips, which, when roasted or boiled, might serve as bread; and also some very small roots as sweet and pleasant as conserved pine nuts." Sarmiento traced out a town, including a plaza, houses with gardens and a church and store house. Municipal officers were named and seeds were planted on the treeless wastes.

Sarmiento appointed Andrés de Biedma, a veteran artillery office, to be commander of Nombre de Jesús. Meanwhile, he marched a forward party of settlers inside the Strait following the jagged coast, thus necessitating long treks just to cover what were only a few nautical miles. At the same time, the *Santa María*, under the command of his nephew, Juárez de Quiroga, sailed on to wait for him in the region of the Santa Ana point and the San Juan river. With no fresh water and few supplies, the men were soon faint with hunger and thirst. They scoured the spiky grass for rhea eggs and ate shellfish and seaweed. They killed two of their five dogs for food.

Sarmiento scanned the horizon in vain, unable to sight the *Santa María*. Then, suddenly, he spied one of the ship's boats and he and his men were able to obtain food and water from their fellow sailors. After fifteen days of hard walking on the windswept, sun-baked plains they had covered only eighty leagues (240 miles) and so, when he came to an area of level ground between two rivers—which he named San Juan and San Alfonso—he founded the second settlement.

On 25 March 1584 the city of Rey Felipe was established. It was sited some 25 miles south of Punta Arenas, on the eastern shore of what is now the Península Brunswick, overlooking the Bahía San Blas. In Peru Sarmiento had seen the lofty peaks of the Andes, rising high above the great Incan citadels. Here the new "town" was also in the shadow of the rain-drenched foothills of that impressive range. Perhaps Sarmiento sensed a connection with the great metropolises of the north. But at Rey Felipe the mountains were low and freezing and they plunged directly into the broiling waters of the Straits; no native tribe had ever built anything more than a primitive hut.

His narrative is upbeat: "A perpetual festival was instituted, to be held every year on that day, with vespers and a mass, in honour of the Annunciation and in memory of the founding of the city." The settlers built a church "of very fine timber", as well as carpenters' and blacksmiths' shops around the town square. A royal store house, a hundred paces long, was commenced, using beech wood, clay and straw. A hospital was erected and then the men concentrated on building their homes.

Suddenly the winter descended and "during fifteen days it never ceased to snow." But Sarmiento had promised the citizens of Nombre de Jesús that he would visit them after founding the second settlement. He also hoped to begin making plans for the building of a fortress on the banks of the Strait. At just before daylight on 25 May, at the moment when a total eclipse of the moon occurred, he weighed anchor off Rey Felipe.

A dreadful storm tore the anchor off the only vessel remaining. The ship, at the mercy of the prevailing westerlies which "blew furiously for upwards of twenty days," was flung out of the Strait and Sarmiento had no choice but to sail on to Rio de Janeiro where he began to muster support for a rescue mission.

In August 1586, on his way to Spain, he was captured by vessels under the command of Richard Grenville, who took him to England where he appeared before Queen Elizabeth at Windsor. They had a conversation in Latin, their only common language. The queen presented him with a "Letter of Peace" to be carried to King Philip II of Spain. Sarmiento left England but on his way back to Spain was detained by French Huguenots, who kept him prisoner at Mont-de-Marsan until 1590. In the intervening period the *Grande y Felicísima Armada* attacked the English fleet, and historians have speculated that if Sarmiento had arrived home to deliver his letter there might never have been a war. After his liberation, Sarmiento de Gamboa gave an account of his experience to the Spanish court and made a complaint against Flores to Philip II, but it appears his calls for justice were ignored. He spent the rest of his life dedicating himself to his writings and worked as an editor of poetry. On his last naval mission in the service of the king he was made admiral of an armada of galleons en route to the Indies. He died on board ship, off the coast of Lisbon.

Nombre de Jesús would only ever be a metropolis for penguins. But in 2005 four skeletons were found by a team of archaeologists from the University of Buenos Aires and the National Institute for Scientific Investigation (CONICET). One of the skeletons was of a child between 10 and 14, and the others belonged to a woman and two men, all aged between 16 and 24. They archaeologists calculated that the settlers may have been stranded on this lonely shore between four or five years, and concluded that the bones indicate the subjects died from malnutrition.

PORT FAMINE

Rey Felipe was visited by mariners over the following centuries. In January 1587 English privateer Thomas Cavendish picked up Tomé Hernández, the sole survivor of the Rey Felipe settlement, at Bahía Munición in Primera Angostura. In a declaration to a Spanish judge Hernández explained how all the settlers came together at Rey Felipe: "Two months after Pedro Sarmiento had sailed from the second settlement… the people who had remained in the first settlement arrived, and all were collected in the second settlement. This was in August, which was winter, and they came by land."

With no sign of Sarmiento's return, Biedma—sometimes written Viedma—took charge and sent 200 soldiers to Nombre de Jesús to pick up shellfish and gather whatever food they could. They were also to look out for any ship seen entering the Straits. These men never came back. Nor did Sarmiento, and when the next winter came round, Biedma, on seeing so many of the settlers dying of hunger, proposed to build two boats and sail up the Straits. One boat, carrying no sailors on board, foundered upon rocks and dumped its passengers on the beach. Biedma instructed these to scatter themselves along the shore and live off shellfish. He returned with the remaining boat and 22 others to Rey Felipe. By December 1586 there were only fifteen men and three women left. "All the rest had died of hunger and sickness," Hernández tells us, "which supervened through the sterility and rugged characteristic of the land. These survivors agreed to go to the first settlement, and were journeying with this intention by land… Along the coast they found many dead bodies, being those of the soldiers sent by Viedma."

The road between Nombre de Jesús and Rey Felipe was well-trodden by January 1587. If the latter location was an improvement on the former, it was still no southern Cuzco. Hernández' chilling account of being stranded in the Strait led to Cavendish renaming the stillborn city Port Famine (or Puerto del Hambre in Spanish).

On 23 May 1843 the Chilean government of President Manuel Bulnes sent a schooner called the *Ancud* south on a colonizing expedition. After four months the ship arrived at Puerto del Hambre, where a fort—Fuerte Bulnes—was built. This was the first Chilean settlement on the Magellan Strait. Neither the setting—on a rocky outcrop surrounded by dense forest—nor the location was suited to a future city, and in 1848 the governor of the fort removed the population to a site known to English mariners as Sandy Point—re-baptized in Spanish as Punta Arenas. In 1964 Chilean writer Reinaldo Lomboy reworked the drama of Sarmiento's Port

Famine as a narrative of heroic failure—and as a stage on the way to nationhood—in his plodding novel *Puerto del Hambre*.

Sarmiento de Gamboa's long life was rich in adventure and misadventure. As well as discovering the Solomon Islands, crossing Peru in the viceroy's suite to compile his history, and taking on the Inquisitors, he waged war against cannibal tribes, studied maths and classics, became an admiral and even had a spell as a poetry editor, before rotting for four years in the dungeons of his French Huguenot enemies. In Spain, *el conquistador* Don Pedro Sarmiento de Gamboa is remembered as a navigator, admiral, astronomer, soldier, explorer, colonizer, scholar, historian, man of letters, diplomat and necromancer—in other words, a Renaissance man in the truest sense. In Chile and Argentina, and especially in Patagonia, he is the man who failed to catch Drake, who founded one city where he was washed up by a storm and another because he could not walk any further, and who left his men to starve on the world's bleakest shore.

Chapter Four

THE ENGLISH MARINERS:
CAVENDISH, DAVIS, BYRON

From the late sixteenth century right thorough to the early twentieth, the southern oceans were something of a distraction for English sailors. Like other colonial powers, the British were bent on finding a north-west passage that would allow a speedy route through the Arctic and down to the west coast of America. In the 1570s and 1580s Martin Frobisher and Sir Humphrey Gilbert made significant explorations and claims on behalf of the English crown, while John Davis, who would also come to be associated with the southern seas and the Falkland Islands, was the first Englishman to enter Cumberland Sound at Baffin Island.

But the chimerical passage was not to be conquered by sea until 1906, when Roald Amundsen completed a three-year voyage aboard the *Gjøa*, and strolled into the town of Eagle, Alaska. For those unwilling, or unable, to make an overland crossing of North America, the only route to California or westward to Asia was through the Magellan Strait or by rounding Cape Horn. Though the Iberian empires—and, from the early nineteenth century, the newly independent Latin American nations—controlled almost the whole of the South American coastline, Patagonia remained a no-man's land.

For the Spanish authorities, the possibility of English pirates following in the wake of Sir Francis Drake was a constant dread. But for the mariners, Patagonia, with its wild, rock-strewn coastal waters, its giants and its savages, presented a hell of its own.

THOMAS CAVENDISH AND JOHN DAVIS

The third man to sail around the world, Thomas Cavendish has been awarded relatively scant attention by biographers and historians. Little is known about the personal life of this East Anglian aristocrat prior to becoming a privateer, but he is known to have squandered his inheritance before working his way into the inner circle of Elizabethan patrons.

After accompanying Sir Richard Grenville's expedition to Virginia in 1585, Thomas Cavendish hoped to emulate Drake and complete a voyage around the world. But where del Cano and Drake had circumnavigated owing to a series of accidents, Cavendish set out with that specific ambition in mind—his was the first attempt to conquer the globe by sailing ship. On 21 July 1586 he sailed out of Plymouth aboard the *Desire*, a 120-ton vessel, taking her first to Sierra Leone and then across to Brazil, which he sighted on 25 October. Two smaller ships, the *Content* and the *Hugh Gallant*, made up the fleet, the three ships carrying between them around 120 men.

Cavendish's log, contained in Hakluyt's oeuvre, tells us that the ships anchored in Port Desire (some sources erroneously claim he christened the bay after his ship, but it had been named Cabo Deseado, or Cape Desire, by Magellan). Cavendish found seals and, on a small island in the bay, huge numbers of penguins. As well as providing the men with a source of food, the relatively wind-free bay provided an opportunity for cleaning the ships and obtaining fresh water.

While scrubbing the linen, a man called John Garge and his young companion, Lutch, were shot at (presumably with a slingshot) by natives. After pursuing the Tehuelche, the crew managed to measure an individual's foot, and recorded it as "18 inches long". (Pigafetta's report had obviously circulated in the English court and satisfying the foot fetish was by now established as an essential duty for Patagonia-bound mariners.)

After killing several thousand penguins for salting Cavendish sailed on to Cape Virgins or Cabo Virgenes (which, on passing on 6 January 1587, he says he renamed Cape Joy) and put into the Magellan Strait. As he sailed through the outer narrows of the Strait, he came upon a party of 23 Spaniards, the remnants of Sarmiento's Rey Felipe colony. One of them, Tomé Hernandez, was taken on board and accompanied them through the second strait. There they came upon another penguin-infested isle before sailing into Rey Felipe itself, where more than 350 Spanish settlers had perished.

Hakluyt's record points out for the benefit of his English readers that the Spaniards had put a fort there solely to stop other nations passing through, and that this was clearly not God's will. We are told that, at first, the miserable *hidalgos* had eaten mussels and limpets from the sea and occasionally even enjoyed the meat of a native deer that came down from the mountains to drink from the rivers. (These were almost certainly *huemul*, a small deer now in danger of extinction.) But the natives repeatedly attacked the Spanish colony, limiting food supplies and causing the men to die of hunger, "like dogs in their houses", or to flee. Failing to found their city, they had left only a gibbet and the ruins of their churches and houses, from which emanated "the smell and savour of dead people". The last survivors had made it through a year eating roots, leaves and an occasional fowl. Picking at the remains of Gamboa's fortress, Cavendish requisitioned half a dozen great guns that had been abandoned and christened the spot Port Famine. He did not, however, offer to take any more survivors with him. It is possible that the wind changed and he wanted to make speed; it is equally possible that he did not want waste time, effort or provisions on a band of starving, desperate Spaniards.

Hakluyt's description of the Strait, as seen through Cavendish's eyes, is a picture of horror. Amid the "craggy rocks and monstrous high hills and mountains" dwelt tribes of savages who "were men eaters, and fed altogether upon raw flesh, and other filthy food." They had, the narrative claims, eaten the Spaniards who had tried to create a colony and "used all the means they could possibly to have allured us farther into the river, of purpose to have betrayed us, which being espied by our General, he caused us to shoot at them with our harquebuses, whereby we killed many of them."

The *Desire* made good progress through Froward Reach and into Long Reach and after sailing for days in "vile and filthy foul weather" came to the western outlet of the Straits: "a fair high Cape with a low point adjoining unto it" (Cape Pilar and Cape Deseado). On 24 February 1587 Cavendish and his crew entered the "Mare Pacificum" and began a slow haul up the coast of South and Central America. Passing through the waters off southern Chile with his ships leaking, Cavendish was forced to go onshore somewhere along the coast of the Chilean lake district. Here he learned of the "great place called Arauco", where the local natives were even more ferocious enemies of the invading Spanish. The Hakluyt text describes it thus:

> The place which is called Arauco is wonderfully rich, and full of gold mines, and yet could it not be subdued at the time by the Spaniards, but they always returned with the greatest loss of men. For these Indians are

marvellous desperate and careless of their lives to live at their own liberty and freedom.

Following the circumnavigation, Cavendish—true to form—is thought to have quickly spent his earnings at court. He then embarked on a second voyage to the Americas, leaving Plymouth on 26 August 1591. As admiral of the fleet, Cavendish now sailed aboard a galleon, the *Leicester*, with the *Desire* under the command of Captain John Davis, a pilot already famous for his voyages in the Arctic. They were joined by one Mr. Cook, on a third tall ship, the *Roebuck*, as well as two barks, the *Black Pinnace* and *Daintie*.

Notwithstanding a suffocating month in the doldrums and an outbreak of scurvy, the voyage got off to a good start. After raiding a Portuguese vessel, pillaging the port of Placenzia in Brazil, attacking Santos and sacking a town called San Vicente, they headed for the Magellan Strait. A violent gale led to the ships becoming separated but four crews regrouped in Port Desire on 7 March 1592, the men aboard the *Daintie* having absconded while in Brazil after stealing tons of sugar. They had left their captain with nothing but the clothes he had on and he was now sailing aboard the *Roebuck*.

As the weeks went by and the remaining ships travelled south, no doubt many of the other hands wished they had joined the sugar stealers. A fascinating first-hand account of what turned out to be a nightmare voyage is provided by Cavendish, in a personal testament first published in *Purchas His Pilgrimes* (based on Hakluyt's collections) in 1625. Worn out by a lengthy period of storms and squalls and beset by further inclement weather while in Port Desire, Cavendish's men became mutinous and he was forced to abandon the *Leicester* and join Davis on the *Desire*. The melancholic admiral relates how "we had been almost four months between the coast of Brazil and the Strait, being in distance not six hundred leagues, which is commonly run in twenty or thirty days; but such was the adverseness of our fortune, that in coming thither we spent the summer, and found the Strait, in the beginning of a most extreme winter, not durable for Christians." He writes that the cold led to the spiritual collapse of all the "weak men" on his ship. Another source, written by John Jane, a friend of Davis, relates that the hungry men had to fill their bellies with mussels, water and weeds.

Davis, who knew more about icy weather than any of the other officers, argued that they must press forward as conditions could only improve. For his part Cavendish wanted to give up the planned route altogether, recommending a hasty retreat and a trip to China via the Cape of Good Hope. But Davis persisted, and the two navigators reached a compromise, agreeing to return first to Brazil to obtain supplies and then to make another assault on the Strait once the worst of the winter was over.

Cavendish returned to the *Leicester*, but shortly after setting sail his galleon was separated from the *Desire* and the *Black Pinnace*. Cavendish would later claim that Davis wilfully abandoned him. Fleeing the southern winter, the *Leicester* was beset by storms, while tides prevented it from entering Port Desire or Port San Julián. A terrible gale and further tempests led to the loss of an entire set of sails. The ship, its crew now ravaged by scurvy and utterly worn out by bailing and pumping water, was blown out to sea.

Cavendish's narrative is less a ship's log than an outpouring of despair and paranoia:

> The Roebuck left me in the most desolatest case that ever man was left in. What is become of her I can not imagine, but if she returned to England it is a most admirable matter... And now come to that villain that hath been the death of me and the decay of this whole action, I mean Davis, whose only treachery in running from me hath been an utter ruin of all.

In his descriptions of the Strait in late autumn Cavendish's record takes us into the soul of a stricken mariner. His syntax is shattered, its flow broken by verb-less parentheses and clauses that trail off; in the facsimile of the account there is barely punctuation to hold the sense together. His prose is an evocation of the weather and land that, conspiring with Davis, seemed to be willing the worst for him:

> In despite of all storms and tempests, so long as we had ground to anchor in and tides to help us we beat into the Straits some 50 leagues, having for the most part the winds contrary. At length being forced by the extremity of storms and the narrowness of the strait, being not able to turn to windward no longer, we got into a harbour where we rid from

the eighteenth day of April till the tenth of May, in all which time we never had other than most furious contrary winds, and after that the month of May was come in nothing but such flights of snow and extremity of frosts as in all the time of my life I never seen none to be compared with them. The extremity cause the weak men, in my ship only, to decay, for in seven or eight days in this extremity there died forty men and sickened seventy, so that there was not fifty men that were able to stand upon the hatches.

Davis' defenders insist that he went in search of Cavendish and remained in Port Desire, keeping watch for the galleon and for the *Roebuck*, which had also been lost, and foraging for food and refitting his own ship. Once in the Strait, Davis and his men continued to look out for Cavendish, but on 7 August they decided to press on. After obtaining a sighting of the Pacific, they were forced back and driven in "among certain islands never before discovered by any known relation, lying fifty leagues or better off the shore, east and northerly from the Strait." These were the Falkland Islands, and Davis is credited with their discovery. James Burney, sailing on Cook's third voyage (1776-80), recorded their name as Davis' Southern Islands but an earlier voyager had baptized the passage between the two main islands the Falkland Sound, after Viscount Falkland, and the name stuck. (Spanish speakers use the name Malvinas, from the French name *Malouines*, after the St. Malo seal-hunters who visited the islands regularly during the eighteenth century.)

Attacking the Strait once more, Davis got through to the Pacific on 2 October 1592, but found himself once again at the mercy of a maelstrom. As the vessel cast about on a massive sea, a gale blasted, blowing away the pinnace and splitting the fore-sail. The storm became furious and the clouds black and evil as wintry hail and snow lashed the deck. After resigning himself to the worst, Davis was finally relieved to see the sun break through and on 11 October they at last put back into the Strait, "their sinews stiff, their flesh dead". This was their third attempt at making their way into the Pacific. But after being forced to rest in a cove along the Strait, hunger drove them back on to Port Desire, where they obtained wood, water and birds. The last straw was when a gang of natives, leaping and running and wearing dog masks, came onto the shore and began to set fire to the bushes.

Before sailing for Brazil at the end of December, Davis' men slaughtered 14,000 penguins. Conscious that this might make for a monotonous diet, the *Desire*'s crew paused to plunder the island of Placenzia once more, but combined Indian and Portuguese resistance forced them back, with the loss of thirteen sailors. Just 27 of the original company of seventy now remained. When ill winds overtook them in warm latitudes, Davis' crew lost their bearings and their water supplies began to dwindle. The penguin carcasses, almost their only source of nourishment, began to rot and "ugly loathsome worms an inch long were bred in them." Having eaten and ruined all their victuals, the worms then proceeded to eat all clothes, hats, boots and stockings. When the worms were about to feast on the very timbers of the hull, the men attacked them, only to be turned on by the worms, which "would eat out flesh like mosquitoes." The men "fell into strange and horrible diseases." Some went completely mad and a further eleven souls perished en route to Ireland. If Cavendish had indeed been betrayed by Davis, it seems that his God was watching and exacting hasty and severe retribution.

Cavendish, for his part, died aboard the *Leicester* near Ascension Island, assailed by "bitter torments" from within and without. He may have taken his own life. In his own account of the voyage, Davis, who would go on to enjoy an esteemed career as a navigator and author, admits that he was "only induced to go with M. Candish [Cavendish]… upon his constant promise unto me, that… I should have his Pinnace and my own Bark… to search that North-west discovery upon the back parts of America."

CALAMITY IN THE CHILEAN ARCHIPELAGO: JOHN BYRON

"The shore look'd wild, without a trace of man,
And girt by formidable waves; but they
Were mad for land, and thus their course they ran,
Though right ahead the roaring breakers lay:
A reef between them also now began
To show its boiling surf and bounding spray,
But finding no place for their landing better,
They ran the boat for shore, and overset her."

Lord Byron, *Don Juan*, canto II, stanza 104

The *South American Pilot*, the mariner's bible, quietly bypasses the dramas of the past in its description of a small island off the Chilean coast somewhere around 47° south, and some 500 miles north of Cape Horn. It tells us that "Isla Wager lies close E of Isla Byron; it can be identified by Monte Anson... also by Monte Wager." The *Pilot* goes on to mention Bahía Speedwell, Canal Cheap and a host of other small islands with very English names. These exiled names hark back to an eighteenth-century story as melodramatic as any fictionalized romance to come out of England.

In September 1740 Commodore George Anson led six warships and two victualling-ships on an epic voyage to destroy Spanish settlements on the Pacific coast. Undermanned, the squadron carried 1,900 men, including 210 untrained marines, hastily recruited when the original crew— 260 invalids from Chelsea Hospital—deserted. Anson, on HMS *Centurion*, would go on to complete the mission himself, successfully capturing the Acapulco treasure galleon and becoming an exceedingly rich man in the process.

For the rest, the voyage was as ill-fated as it was ambitious, as the ships sailed off on their own tragic plot lines. Most dramatic was the destiny of the store ship, the *Wager*, which was wrecked off the coast of southern Chile on 14 May 1741. Her captain was Dandy Kidd, a gloomy man beset by fears of "Poverty, Vermin, Famine, Death, and Destruction" and in particular of his own death, which in fact took place a few weeks into the voyage. Afterwards George Murray took the helm but when he was promoted to command the 40-gun *Pearl*, the *Wager* was passed to David Cheap, a courageous but belligerent type. At the moment that the inevitable disaster struck Cheap was in an opium dream, convalescing after falling from a ladder during the early phase of the storm, while his lieutenant, Robert Baynes, nominally in charge, was drunk.

We have three first-hand accounts of the event; none is entirely reliable, but all give a keen sense of the scale of the disaster and the dire consequences for the crew.

THE MUTINEERS

In 1743 gunner John Bulkeley and carpenter John Cummins published their *Voyage to the South Seas*, telling how they and several other seamen had decided to abandon another group of survivors, who proposed to head north towards Santiago de Chile, and sail westward. The book, dedicated to Vice-Admiral Edward Vernon, seeks to show that "Captain David Cheap, our commander… never consulted any of his officers for the safety and preservation of the said ship" and that losing contact with Anson led to "general disorder and confusion".

At San Julián, the first rendezvous point in Patagonia, the squadron had had a brush with five large Spanish men-of-war but managed to escape by throwing water, long-boats, oars, and just about everything else that might prove useful on a voyage, overboard. There follows a sorry tale of broken masts, incessant gales and the break-up of the squadron, including, for those on the *Wager*, a terrible passage through Le Maire Strait and a near-miss off the rocks around Staten Island. When the ship lost its mizzen–mast, Bulkeley and Cummins started to quarrel with Cheap, who, they report, refused to accept their claims that land was in sight.

Having watched her sister ships disappear into the tumult of the storm, the *Wager* became isolated and was unable to tack westward. On the morning of 14 May 1741 her rudder broke when the she struck a reef in the Gulf of Peñas and she was instantly "bilged, and grounded, between two small islands." The small, barren rock they landed on—christened Wager Island—was to be their home for the following five months. One of the wettest places in the Americas, whatever the season, it becomes all but uninhabitable in the winter months, which were looming at the time of the accident.

Throughout, Cheap insisted that the only solution was to forge ahead to Socorro (Juan Fernández Island) in order to rejoin Anson and so finish the job in hand. In his own account Bulkeley comes across as a loquacious, somewhat legalistic seaman, not prone to feigning respect for supernumeraries or those who had achieved rank and influence through family connections. The text of the *Voyage* may have been polished by a Grub Street hack, but he did not do a very good job and certainly the work was no bestseller. The book comes over as a sailor's personal defence, packed with lists of those who sided with Bulkeley and of the obstacles faced by all the sailors in the wilderness of southern Chile.

Shortly after landing on the island, a group of five men ("the Deserters" in Bulkeley's narrative) split from the main group. Despite this mutinous act and notwithstanding the continuing storms and torrential rain, the captain, having taken up residence in an empty hut found on shore, tried to impose order. Using the small boats, the crew were able to live off the wreck for a time, rowing out to bring wine, brandy and rum ashore, as well as food and some basic tools. While some simply ignored Cheap's instructions and the deserters were left in relative peace, Bulkeley and his faction began to assert their independence. The major point of contention was whether to follow Cheap's plan and try to overpower an unwary Spanish merchantman and so continue the voyage north, or, as proposed by Bulkeley, attempt to return home via the Strait of Magellan. While they debated the pros and cons of these equally problematic courses of action they remained stranded on their inhospitable rock.

Captain Cheap's fatal shooting in the cheek of midshipman Henry Cozens, following a dispute over wine, is viewed as a decisive "Act of Inhumanity", and on 14 October 1741 Bulkeley left aboard a schooner, the *Speedwell*, captained by breakaway Lieutenant Robert Beans. He claimed that the plan was originally to take Cheap on board as a prisoner, but that it was agreed to leave him behind to rot on the island for fear of riots during the long voyage back to Rio de Janeiro.

The ship's cooper John Young, who sailed aboard the *Speedwell*, published his own version of the events in 1751. Known as the *Affecting Narrative*, his account gives further insight into the breakdown of order from a less senior and therefore probably less prejudiced position. Young's narrative suggests that Bulkeley was right in his estimation of Cheap as a second-rate leader. Following the collision with the reef, he records, "Oaths and Execrations greatly prevailed" among the sailors. But the crew managed to rescue a yawl, a barge and a cutter. To the horror of those left on board the *Wager*, the mate in charge of the barge sent off to reconnoitre the surrounding shores decided not to return to pick them up. The lieutenant was sent on the yawl to rectify the situation, but when this boat came back, the crew were told he had stayed on land.

The captain then left the ship. As soon as he had boarded the yawl those remaining on board turned to the wine and broke open their superior officers' wardrobes to dress up in their finery. The next day they also went onto dry land, still in the stolen clothes. When some natives, probably Halakwalups, appeared, there was hope of obtaining food and the crew feasted on "sea-weed, fryed with the Grease of Candles. Pick'd up along Shore, [it] was esteemed a dainty Repast." As if this desperate dinner was not bad enough, the anonymous narrator tells us, Bulkeley and his mates stole a "mangey Dog" from two natives for their dinner.

BYRON'S DISTRESSES

Midshipman John Byron was one of the men who chose to remain loyal to Cheap. His *Narrative of Great Distresses on the Shores of Patagonia*, published in 1768, provides further memorable images. One group of men is portrayed diving on vultures as they fed on the carrion of drowned men, in order to roast them, while a small boy is caught eating a dead man's liver. Wading out to the wreck through the icy waters was made troublesome, Byron reports, by the sheer number of "mangled" corpses floating on the shore. There were also robberies and murders though, according to Byron, Cheap only took the decision to shoot Cozens because he thought he had "come to mutiny."

While it goes over some of the ground of Bulkeley's text, Byron's account hastens forward to the drama of the escape. As well as providing a far more vivid read than other sources, it is also the first detailed account of the fjords, islands and ice caps of the still unpopulated and barely accessible Chonos Archipelago between the Gulf of Peñas and Chiloé.

With Bulkeley out of the way, a plan of action was decided; the remaining men were to proceed north through the channels towards the island of Chiloé—an important Spanish settlement—in the hope of continuing on to Santiago de Chile. Byron and Cheap had stayed behind with three loyal mariners, but were soon joined by the five deserters as well as ten men sent back by the *Speedwell* to collect canvas, and who decided to remain. During the journey their hardships were numerous. The best of their diet was berries, but they had also to obtain protein from boiled seals and shags, which they learned how to club to death by copying the natives.

The weather was always awful and the terrain a "morass". Attempting to fulfil at least the basic duties of a captain, Cheap christened certain landmarks as they travelled north. One hill was given the name Mount Misery. One night, in addition to the rain and wind and cold, there was an earthquake. Many of the men fell ill and died of hunger, exposure or by drowning.

Visitors to the icy inlets of southern Chile are often struck by the seeming absence of wildlife. In the preface to his account, Byron, having lamented the absence of fruits, grains and roots on terra firma, stresses to his readers:

...and what is still more rare, the very sea, which yields a plentiful support to many a barren coast, on this tempestuous and inhospitable shore is found to be almost as barren as the land; and it must be confessed that, to those who cannot interest themselves with seeing human labouring, from day to day, to preserve its existence under the continual want of such real necessaries as food and shelter from the most rigorous climate, the following sheets will afford little entertainment.

Yet, after all, it must be allowed there can be no other way of ascertaining the geography and natural history of a country which is altogether morass and rock, incapable of products and culture, than by setting down every minute circumstance which was observed in traversing it. The same may be said of the inhabitants, their manners, religion, and language. What fruits could an European reap from a more intimate acquaintance with them, than that he will find in the following accidental observations? We saw the most unprofitable spot on the globe of the earth, and such it is described and ascertained to be.

The only support encountered by the men during the early days, both while on Wager Island and as they attempted to row through the channels and fjords towards the north, came from the local indigenous tribes. They bartered and received mussels, dogs and, on one occasion, three sheep.

> Wild sellery [sic] was all we could procure, which racked our stomachs instead of assuaging our hunger. That dreadful and last resource of men, in not much worse circumstances than ours, of consigning one man to death for the support of the rest, began to be mentioned in whispers; and indeed there were some among us who, by eating what they found raw, were become little better than cannibals.

A *cacique* and his wife helped the survivors, sharing their wigwams and showing them how to gather shellfish. Only thirteen men made it through the Chonos Archipelago to Chiloé, where they were passed on to another group of natives. These tribesmen agreed to guide them up the coast on the promise of keeping the boat on arrival. Two men died shortly after, and after burying them, six men rowed off in the boat.

Cheap, Byron, midshipman Alexander Campbell, Lt. Hamilton, and surgeon Walter Elliot, now dying, were left abandoned on the shore scratching around for food. After Elliot died, the native chief offered to transport them in his canoe in return for their one remaining valuable, a musket.

Byron was (and remains) one of very few Europeans to have had contact with the indigenous peoples of the western islands off Patagonia—and long before the Christian settlements that augured their demise. His accounts of their hunting practices, religious observances, dress codes and burial rituals continue to be used by ethnographers. Yet those parts of the narrative that deal with native habits also serve to compound the narrative's horror and sense of melodrama. Byron's intentions were not overtly negative nor, for their day, unusually prejudiced. But there is an exclamatory zeal to the account that rises in a crescendo as the survivors are forced to depend on their guide-captors. The "despotic" and "cruel" males, the "orgies" of eating till they "foam at the mouth" and the "dismal groans" they emit to their idols are of the same substance as the "incessant tempests", "hard gales" and "overgrown seas". One scene is clearly intended to shock the reader into judgment:

Here I must relate a little anecdote of our Christian cacique. He and his wife had gone off, at some distance from the shore, in their canoe, when she dived for sea-eggs; but not meeting with great success, they returned a good deal out of humour. A little boy of theirs, whom they appeared to be doating [sic] fond of, watching his father's and mother's return, ran into the surf to meet them: the father handed a basket of sea-eggs to the child, which being too heavy to carry, he let it fall; upon which the father jumped out of the canoe, and catching the boy up in his arms, dashed him with the utmost violence against the stones. The poor little creature lay motionless and bleeding, and in that condition was taken up by the mother, but died soon after. She appeared inconsolable for some time; but the brute his father showed little concern about it.

In an earlier book (about a later voyage), Byron had claimed to have seen the Patagonian giants, and was widely viewed as a dubious narrator. The above paragraph, which applies all the rules of sensationalist journalism—an eye for detail, measured sympathy, moral outrage—may have been given its dramatic finale just to remind readers that Byron was superior to the class of men to which the cacique belonged and, also to point out that even the native women were more human than the men. Nonetheless, the episode was later quoted by John Millar in his *The Origin of the Distinction of Ranks* (1779) "to show the spirit with which the savages of South America are apt to govern the members of their family." There were so few accounts of the region where Byron had spent so much time that perhaps it was inevitable that singular events would be used to make generalizations.

The climax of the drawn-out encounter between white, "civilized" seaman and savage host comes when Byron is thrashed by the natives for throwing empty limpet shells over the side of the canoe. He attributes it to a superstition, but there may be a more intelligent reasoning here: a half-eaten or uneaten, open shell could be fished up again and have its rotten contents consumed. The natives also prevent Byron from eating a bunch of berries, which he concedes might have been poisonous.

Shortly after this episode, Byron and Campbell, having suffered months of near-starvation in the grim channels, are required to row hard while the cacique sits in the boat, haughty and imperious:

This was dreadful hard work to such starved wretches as we were, to be slaving at the oar all day long in such a heavy boat; and this inhuman fellow would never give us a scrap to eat, excepting when he took so much seal that he could not contrive to carry it all away with him, which happened very seldom... It is impossible for me to describe the miserable state that we were reduced to: our bodies were so emaciated, that we hardly appeared the figures of men. It has often happened to me in the coldest night, both in hail and snow, where we had nothing but an open beach to lay down upon, in order to procure a little rest, that I have been obliged to pull off the few rags I had on, as it was impossible to get a moment's sleep with them on for the vermin that swarmed about them; though I used, as often as I had time, to take my clothes off, and putting them upon a large stone, beat them with another, in hopes of killing hundreds at once.

He describes Cheap's body as "nothing but an ant hill, with thousands of these insects crawling over it"—though he, at least, was often treated by the natives as a cacique, and so was provided with food. Byron is at pains to stress the extent to which relentless privations and sheer proximity to the natives dragged the men down. He writes of a dying seaman's pleas for food: "But we were become so hardened against the impressions of others suffering by our own; so familiarised to scenes of this and every other kind of misery, that the poor man's dying entreaties were vain."

Of the twenty men who set out from Wager Island only four survived: Cheap, Byron, Hamilton and Campbell, who later wrote his own account of the disaster. On arrival in Santiago in January 1743, they were taken prisoner and only allowed to sail to England in March 1745. Campbell took a mule over the Andes and continued overland to the River Plate. By July 1746 all were back in England. A court martial was limited to investigating the loss of the *Wager*, for which Baynes—nominally in charge—was acquitted but reprimanded for failing to fulfil his duties.

Between June 1764 and May 1766, Byron completed a circumnavigation as captain of the 508-ton frigate the *Dolphin*, the first vessel to complete the voyage in under two years and the fastest to date. His *Voyage Round the World in His Majesty's Ship the Dolphin*, published in 1767, reminds us of the territorial ambitions behind any English "voyage of discovery" and the fact that Patagonia was considered a viable location for the British flag: "If this country was properly examined, many valuable discoveries might be made with respect to its vegetables and minerals: for upon a slight examination of the hills we found a kind of iron ore, and had some reason to believe, that if a more exact scrutiny was made, other ores might be found of greater value." Much of the *Dolphin* log has this mercantile tone. All these riches, he believes, should by divine right be garnered for England and, in addition to casting aspersions on the Portuguese, Spanish and Dutch colonials he encounters, the author is careful not to give the coordinates of seven newly discovered islands in the South Pacific.

In an appendix, the *Voyage* revisits the subject of the "gigantic race of Patagonians", pointing out that Byron's experience is of significance for "putting an end to the dispute, which for two centuries has subsisted between geographers, in relation to the reality of their being a nation of people of such an amazing stature, of which the concurrent testimony of all on board the *Dolphin* and *Tamer* can now leave no room for doubt." The author of the appendix analyses Pigafetta's account, criticizing the Italian author for reporting colourful conversations between the Europeans and the natives when, he insists, there could have been no communication whatsoever.

Briefly summing up reports from the voyages of Cavendish (whom he credits with the naming of Patagonia), Van Noort, Spielbergen and Shevlock, Byron's text compares each captain's notes on the height of Patagonians. The tone is thoroughly scientific throughout and the author concludes that "this voyage has effectually established the testimony of these authors." With aplomb the narrator glances heavenward as he summarizes: "What use Divines may make of this, we know not; but it certainly proves what is recorded in scripture, and even in heathen authors, that there was, (and still is) a race of giants."

The *Voyage* became an instant bestseller largely due to the nine pages, in a 181-page book, that spun once again the tale of the Patagonian giants. The frontispiece of one edition shows an English sailor giving a biscuit to a nine-foot-tall Patagonian woman, while her husband looks on.

Byron's account of the *Wager* disaster was published a year later. Peter Hulme, in his essay "Abject in Patagonia: Stories from the *Wager*", argues that by this time the commodore could make good use of the degradations suffered on the Patagonian beach:

Only now, as an establishment figure, did Byron write his account of his experiences with the *Wager*, long after these events had been a matter of any public interest… Byron's Patagonian abjection must not only have been physically and mentally distressing, but also culturally and ideologically humiliating. Not only did Byron's structure of authority collapse after the shipwreck, only to survive in the parodic form of his vermin-laden captain, his whole worldview was also undermined on that Patagonian shore: an experience which must have destroyed his understanding of his place in the scale of human superiority. The second son of an English aristocrat had been treated as sub-human by savage Patagonians. He'd travelled to the outer edge of the known world only to find that in those southerly latitudes the world really did turn upside down. The deep trauma of that abjection could only be spoken once it was not the climax of his personal story.

It did not help him much, however. For his role in the *Wager* catastrophe and later frequent brushes with disaster, John Byron earned the nicknames "Foul-Weather Jack" and "The Jonah of the Wager". Later authors sought to rescue his name, most notably his grandson, George Gordon, Lord Byron, who reworked some of the raw material from the *Wager* narrative into the storm and shipwreck scenes in the second canto of *Don Juan*. To have survived an archetypal tempest gave his grandfather a heroic sheen and Lord Byron no doubt enjoyed pondering the fact that he had a propensity for disaster in his very lineage. Comparing his own trials and tribulations to those of his grandfather, he once remarked, "He had no peace at sea, nor I on land." Author Patrick O'Brian, without venturing anywhere near the region, successfully reworked the *Wager* story into his novel *The Unknown Shore* (1959), presenting Cheap as a weak-willed, pompous and selfish figure and Byron as an inspiring, energetic soul. He plays with the heredity, however, and his likeable Jack Byron is a closet poet.

FANTASY ISLANDS
In a heavily abridged edition of the log of Byron's *Dolphin* voyage, published in 1767 by one M. Cooper of Paternoster Row, London, is a bizarre footnote to the *Wager* episode. Stitched between pages 24 and 25 are twelve pages of pure fabrication about the Patagonians. The edition's fron-

tispiece claims it to be material provided by "a midshipman aboard the same ship". Unlike the text in the *Narrative*, it is all incredibly upbeat, and, after detailed remarks on how Patagonians raise children, how they enjoy "gymnastic" exercise, and how they employ wonderful farming techniques, the author tells us about urban life on the Argentinian steppe:

> The Patagonian metropolis is much more extensive than the greatest city in Europe, but not near so populous. A fine river divides it, with bridges of a great length, and prodigious elevation thrown over it… The houses are but one storey high, built separate, with a garden and park to each house. They build their houses with large beams of wood, notwithstanding they have plenty of stone quarries, but make use of stone only in building publick edifices… Some ignorant, but charitable Patagonian had built hospitals in different parts of the city, but finding the people more sickly in those quarters of town, the hospitals were removed without the walls… at the same time a regulation was made that every patient should have a bed to themselves.

In this wonderful place there are no beggars, no unemployment, no polygamy. No one dodges taxes and there are no wars. The author explains how the citizens of this ideal city only take wine as medicine, preferring milk, but do like to go to the circus and to wrestling contests. He reports that the operas are very low-key, with little action, but that their comedies are gentle and lack sarcasm—though dwarves are brought onto the stage for hilarious contrast. The comic moment arrives when a Patagonian damsel asks a midget to rescue her: "Ah my dear lover! cries the fair Patagonian, protect me!"

FILLING IN THE GAPS

Between the end of the sixteenth and the beginning of the nineteenth centuries Patagonia and its islands would be visited by ships from all the seagoing empires. Gradually ever cape and cove was given a name, each perilous fjord was roughly mapped, and the myths and illusions that inspired hardy mariners to risk passage through the Strait opened up a new dreamscape: Antarctica.

Major Dutch voyages were led by Sebald de Veert and Olivier de Bort in 1599 and by George Spillbergen in 1614. All three related encounters with the Patagonian giants. In 1616 Dutch merchant Jacob Le Maire and navigator Willem Schouten of Hoorn weathered the surf-ringed headland of a tiny island, which they named Kaap Hoorn or Cape Horn, before sailing onwards to the Pacific. They had thus also established that Tierra del Fuego was an island, a discovery that alarmed the Spanish crown as it effectively opened up a route to the Far East over which the Armada held no sway. In 1619 the García de Nodal brothers were despatched to survey the Horn and gather data for the government. They circumnavigated Tierra del Fuego without loss of a single life. In 1643 Dutch mariner Henry Brouwer sailed along the eastern and southern coast of Staten Island (Isla de los Estados) and proved that Antarctica was not connected to the smaller Fuegian islands. Notwithstanding, maps continued to show a land-bridge well into the eighteenth century. In 1671 Dutch explorer Henry Schouten published an account of an island populated by twelve-foot Patagonians covered from head to toe in coarse hair, complete with map, drawings and details about their form of government, religion and customs.

In mid-December 1774 Captain Cook's *Resolution* arrived at Tierra del Fuego. Near the western entrance to the Magellan Strait Cook passed a headland which he named Cape Gloucester. After a week scudding south-east before a westerly gale, Cook neared a black, 800-foot, castellated rocky promontory which he baptized York Minster after the imposing gothic cathedral in his home county of Yorkshire. Due to a stiff south-easterly, *Resolution* was anchored there over Christmas while Cook's crew surveyed and charted the coastline—the channel where they sought shelter was named Christmas Sound. Captain Robert FitzRoy was later to praise Cook's surveys in Tierra del Fuego, and the name York Minster would come to have a special significance for him.

Chapter Five

UNREAL CITIES:

FOUNDING FATHERS AND FANTASISTS

"It has always seemed significant to me that, in 1780, some Spanish wise men, setting sail from Angostura, should still embark on a quest for El Dorado, and that, at the time of the French Revolution—long live Reason and the Supreme Being!—Francisco Menéndez from Compostela should wander through Patagonia in search of the Enchanted City of the Caesars."

Alejo Carpentier, prologue to *The Kingdom of This World* (1949)

The sixteenth and seventeenth centuries were busy times for the Spanish crown. All commercial and military activity was taking place far north of Patagonia, with goods moving in and out of the lower reaches of the Americas via Callao, near Lima in Peru, and on to the ports of Veracruz (Mexico), Cartagena de Indias (Colombia) and Nombre de Dios or Puerto Bello in Panama.

In 1536 Emperor Charles V sent an *adelantado*, Pedro de Mendoza, to the south of the continent with eleven ships and over 1,200 soldiers and settlers. He founded Buenos Aires on the west bank of the River Plate, but repeated attacks by indigenous tribes and scarcity of food made the project unviable. Mendoza sailed for Spain the following year and died at sea. In 1541 Buenos Aires was abandoned and the colonists moved to Asunción. The city was founded again in 1580 by Juan de Garay. Far from the main shipping lines in the tropics, the newly established royal province of La Plata managed to generate wealth through bribes and smuggling operations, but it was in thrall to the viceroyalty of Peru and remained one of the backwaters of the empire.

Of course, neither Argentina nor Chile had ever had been able to boast a Tenochtitlán or a Cuzco, and Patagonia had no cities whatsoever. Perhaps it was beyond Spain to build a city where there were no temples to demolish or foundations to desecrate. But in the absence of any remains of great cities past, or scaffolding for grand urban projects for the future, those who did stray from the hubs of commerce to visit the southern plains were able to conjure up idealized metropolises of their own.

CITY OF THE CAESARS

Hakluyt records that in 1529 the Italian explorer Sebastian Caboto, based at the fort of Sancti Spiritus on the River Plate (now Gaboto in Santa Fe Province), sent fifteen men into the interior "to discover the gold and silver mines that there are in that land." After forty or fifty nights in the wilderness only six or seven survived, and were guided back to the settlement by one Francisco César. The men reported that there were precious metals and stones, as well as fine textiles and cattle.

César and the survivors may have penetrated as far inland as Córdoba or San Luis and been told stories by the natives—using whatever tools of interpretation they had to hand—which referred to the silver mines of Alto Perú. But César's name became associated with a legend about great riches yet to be plundered. Later it was used in the plural to designate the Spanish and indigenous residents of this wonderful place, and so César and Césares slipped easily into myth. The legend was compounded because the very name César hinted at some obscure link with the great Roman dynasty.

Once the germ of the story had been formed, it was free to flourish throughout South America.

In 1539 two ships sailing with Alonso de Camargo were wrecked off Cabo Vírgenes at the entrance to the Magellan Strait. Some of the men survived and made their way to shore. A rumour began to circulate in Spanish court circles that the survivors had joined with native women and exiled Incas and founded a city. A document dated 1601 in the Archivo de Indias asserts that these lost sailors, known as "Césares", still obeyed the Pope and professed submission to the king, and continued to "live in stone houses and are dressed and eat from dishes of silver and gold and are waited upon by some of the Indians... It is thought these were sent to the Magellan Strait by the Bishop of Plasencia [Camargo's sponsor]."

Eight years later, a Jesuit, Diego de Torres Bollo, reported that these same men had lost their faith and become barbarians, went about naked in summer, and in winter wore only a beaver skin, which "men and women took off while working, to be more efficient." Long haired, "like the other Indians", gold and ivory pendants hung from their pierced lower lips and nostrils.

In 1707 Silvestre Antonio de Roxas presented his *derrotero* (charts) of "a journey from Buenos Aires to the Césares" to the Spanish court. He claimed to have visited the city while being held captive for twelve years by the native Pehuenche—a branch of the Mapuche—describing it as spread out over a plain, close to mineral-rich mountains and beside a sea abundant in fish and seafood. "It possesses beautiful temples and well-made stone houses with roofs of the Spanish style... They lack wine and oil, as they have never had vineyards or olive trees." Roxas said that the natives were so healthy that the only illness was old age, adding, "it only lacks Spaniards to populate and exploit such great riches." In 1711 another Spaniard claimed that there were in fact three cities, and that they were located on the western flank of the cordillera; thus the Ciudad de los Césares jumped over the Andes and gained a new association with the regions of Aysén and Chiloé Continental, in Chilean Patagonia.

In 1746 José Cardiel, another Jesuit, wrote a letter to the governor and captain-general of Buenos Aires, reporting that he had met a man of mixed race who had been taken prisoner by the inhabitants of the Patagonian city of the Césares. He said that this man had seen with his own eyes one mountain made of gold and another of diamonds.

Witnesses began to proliferate. A woman swore that she had been taken prisoner by a race of white, blonde people who lived on an island city in a great lake. Peru's *corregidor* Don Alvaro de Quirós claimed to have visited an island off the coast of Patagonia, where he had been given a box full of pearls by the Césares. A prior in Valdivia insisted that he had seen a fair-haired man in European dress on the shore while sailing past in 1750; despite repeated offers of help to the man, whom they assumed to be a shipwrecked sailor, he failed to reply and was seen slipping away indifferently into the interior. Other navigators told of strange ships spied sailing off the coast of Patagonia.

In 1774 infantry captain Don Ignacio Pinuer wrote of a large Spanish city in the indigenous Mapuche territories south of Valdivia, whose existence he had been assured of by natives. Rounding off his description of a completely normal, civilized conurbation on a lakeside, where people sported hats, shoes and smart beards, Pinuer added that the Césares were "immortal, as in that land Spaniards did not die." Owing to the unrelenting increase in population, he said, a new city had been founded on the other side of the same lake, in the east.

The City of the Caesars would not stay put. One source had it that it was "between Chile and the North Sea and with its back to Arauco", another that it was "some 60 to 80 leagues from the [Argentinian] city of Córdoba". But more often than not it was sited in central Patagonia, in the Andes, or in the deep south, near to the Strait. A 1775 map of South America made by D. Anville points to a location in the cordillera at the latitude of San Julián, with the legend: "The Césares are placed about this Latitude who are mixt with and descended from the Spaniards being the People of 3 Ships that were wrecked on this Coast in 1540."

By the late eighteenth century official papers in Chile made reference to the existence of one or more Spanish cities in the southern Andes, in the Magellan Strait and in Cape Horn. Citing Cardiel, who had reminded sceptics that many had once doubted the existence of the Americas, the Pacific and the even Batuecas valley in Extremadura—all quite recently discovered—the colonial government warned against incredulity. Explorers and missionaries went out from Buenos Aires, Alto Perú and the Atlantic coast in search of the elusive city. Those who did not find it reported meeting Spaniards, native Indians, Incas or stranded sailors—all of whom were indiscriminately called "Césares".

THE EL DORADO COMPLEX

Truths and fiction swirled freely in the minds of the conquistadors, and the very real discoveries of great riches at places like Potosí in Alto Perú (now Bolivia) and in the Aztec cities of North and Central America inspired a relentless search for further treasures, not least among those who had missed out first time around. The motif of the lake may well have alluded to Titicaca, and the mountains of gold and silver to Potosí's Cerro Rico. The Inca element in the story may have its basis in the migration south of some Incas on being pursued by Pizarro's armies. Some scholars have linked the myth of the Caesars to the province of Telán in Peru, where Quechua fables tell of a mysterious kingdom hidden from white invaders where the brother of the Inca was rebuilding the empire. Others have alluded to a story told by the Guaraníes of northern Argentina and Paraguay about a *Mbaéberá-guazú* or "great, shining city" hidden in the jungle. Other names were used for the mythic settlement, including Lílín, the Province of Salt, Puytita, Manoa, and Trapalanda or Trapananda. This last name, of obscure origin, features in a map, produced to accompany the *Relation des voyages du sieur dans la rivière de la Plate, et de là par terre au Pérou* (1696) by the navigator Acarete du Biscay, who explored the pampas in 1657.

When ships were sunk off the eastern coast of Patagonia stories circulated among the natives that survivors had travelled up the course of the Río Negro and established a settlement on an island. The natives passed these stories onto other Spanish explorers and sailors, who had only the vaguest notion of the inland topography of the territory they were passing. Thus the tales were never anchored to a fixed place.

These manifold Césares stories travelled over the oceans and then back into the Americas, acquiring colour and distance, detail and drama. When conquistadors settled in central Chile they were told by Puelche natives that there were ships wrecked in the southern straits and fjords, and when ships were lost in the southern oceans, stories of survivors began to take shape. In some ships men and women did scramble to shore and some had contact with native tribes; given the extreme remoteness of these events, it took only a short flight of the imagination to envisage these marrying, having children and founding cities. Some, as in the case of Gamboa and his men, were rescued, proving that it was possible to survive for a time *in extremis*, and providing the rescuers and survivors with great yarns to spin in the inns and taverns of the Old World.

As recently as the 1930s the City of the Caesars was the subject of lively discussion among settlements in the more far-flung corners of Argentina and Chile. For the inhabitants of Chiloé, known for their fascination with magic and witchcraft, it was always "somewhere over there", in the mists that hover over the mountain-walled fjords of the mainland. It is a *chilote* who tells of the city in Manuel Rojas' 1937 novel, *La Ciudad de los Césares*, a clumsy attempt to wrap a piece of naturalistic fiction around a myth resistant to anything so prosaic.

Even rational minds have wondered at the city's existence, and in the 1920s the discovery of a skull and a high barricade near Lago Cardiel inspired one scientist to believe he had found the remains of the fabled city (he had actually found a head-shaped rock and a natural wall of basalt). Some myths argue that the city's very concealment is essential to its power and beauty and that, although visible on Good Fridays, its location must never be revealed as this would mean it would lose its ability to enchant and grant immortal life to its citizens. As the last enchanted city on earth, it is worth keeping secret.

Argentinian historian Enrique de Gandía captures the enigmatic character of the notion of an enchanted place: "An imaginary city which, like a wandering chimera, shifted its fantastic towers and the peel of its bells from the pampas of northern Argentina to the snowy peaks of Tierra del Fuego. This city of illusions was finally lost in the unknowable immensity of silent, tragic Patagonia, where there are still dreamers who, without admitting, search for it and dream of it."

Two other Argentinian authors, Jorge Lanata and Marco Denevi, have blamed the Trapalanda-fixation for some of Argentina's cyclical woes. It is the notion of an ideal city, they argue, that leads to a state of apathy when people are called upon to construct a real one and, ultimately, is the source of infinite melancholy.

THOMAS FALKNER

One legacy of the troubled Anson voyage was the English ambition to secure a safe harbour on the Falkland Islands. In the lengthy preface to his *A Description of Patagonia* (1774) the Jesuit priest Thomas Falkner alludes to this as sufficient reason for his own mapping of the mainland. "The settlements in Falkland's Islands [*sic*], in Florida, and on the River Mississippi may be looked upon as precautions against the too apparent intentions of the Family Compact, and the warlike preparations of the Court of Spain."

Not much is known about Falkner. Born in Manchester in 1707, the son of a Presbyterian apothecary, he was educated at Manchester Grammar School. Having studied physics and mathematics under Isaac Newton and medicine, he became a surgeon, working in his home city, but was advised to take a sea-voyage to improve his poor health. A colleague was ship's chaplain on the *Assiento*, a slave ship owned by the South Sea Company that plied the trading route between Britain and Guinea and took slaves on to Buenos Aires. In 1731 or thereabouts he decided to accompany the vessel to the Río de la Plata. On arriving in Buenos Aires he converted to Catholicism and in 1732 joined the Society of Jesus' Paraguayan province.

Falkner travelled south around 1740 and spent some thirty years on the border between the pampas and Patagonia. He was based for a time near Cabo San Antonio, from which he set out to explore Argentina's eastern seaboard. He gathered information from natives, naming as one of his key sources a *cacique* called Cangapol from Huichin near the Río Negro, and from Spanish settlers, including the son of one man "who was six years prisoner among the Tehuelhets." (The latter is Falkner's spelling for Tehuelche; he also uses the names Puelche and Patagonians for the natives.)

Editions of his book, a geographical and anthropological treatise detailing everything from soil types and flora and fauna to native customs, were printed with a meticulous map—based on at least four cartographical sources and "the latest discoveries" made by mariners from the Falkland Islands, and engraved by Thomas Kitchin, Hydrographer to His Majesty—of the whole of Patagonia, showing the limits of tribal regions, the main rivers and all the named settlements. On the island of Tierra del Fuego it shows a body of water traversing Isla Grande de Tierra del Fuego called the Channel of Sebastian—it could, by a slight stretch of the imagination, be the Beagle, supposedly discovered decades later by Philip Parker King and Robert FitzRoy. The map of the northern part of Patagonia depicts wide rivers flowing all the way to the Andes and beyond, suggesting that ships could sail inland and go right up to the foothills of the Andes, or even, on the Río Negro, beyond and into Chile.

Towards the latter part of the seventeenth century the Jesuits had discovered a series of low passes and navigable lakes that allowed a relatively safe and speedy crossing of the Andes between their mission at Calbuco in Chile and the settlements of the Vuriloche tribe (now San Carlos de Bariloche) on the Argentinian side. The leader of one of the earliest expeditions was the Italian Jesuit father Nicolás Mascardi, who was dispatched by the viceroy of Peru and Chile to found a mission in 1672.

Mascardi and his men were probably more interested in finding the City of the Caesars than in evangelizing, but they established a mission called Nahuelhuapi on the lakeside. They also planted apple trees (*manzanos* in Spanish) in the area; these proved so popular with the natives that one Mapuche tribe became known as the *manzaneros*. The Nahuelhuapi mission only survived until 1717, when it was raided by a band of natives, but there was still a significant Society of Jesus presence in the lake districts on both sides of the Andes when Falkner explored the region. Thanks to his local Jesuit connections, we have one of the first descriptions of the Argentinian lake district and Isla Victoria in Lago Nahuel Huapi:

> The Lake of Nahuelhuaupi is one of the greatest that is formed by the waters of the Cordillera and (according to the account of the Chilenian Missionaries) is near fifteen leagues in length. On one side if it, near it's [*sic*] bank, is a small, low island, called Nahuelhuaupi, or the Island of Tigers; nahuel signifying tigers, and huaupi an island. It is situated in a great plain, encompassed by hills, rocks, and mountains; from which it receives many brooks and springs, as well as water from the melted snows. A small river enters it on the south side, which comes from the country of Chonos, on the continent over against Chiloe.

Falkner goes on to describe the River of Wizards (an allusion to native shamans), the battlegrounds where one *cacique* Cacapol kept the Pehuenche at bay, and the rivers that run down from the Andes towards the Atlantic. His concise descriptions are the first to connect the varied landscapes of Patagonia and to explore the potential for settlement. He gives an account of an expedition undertaken in 1746 that explored the mouths of the main estuaries and rivers between the Plate and the Strait of Magellan. None is perfect for ships, he concludes, but the Bay of St. Matthias—also known as the "Bottomless Bay"—has practical advantages in its swift, silt-free tide and relatively deep bed. But he has a warning for any Britons planning to settle there:

> If any nation should think proper to people this country, it might be the cause of perpetual alarm to the Spaniards; as from hence ships might be sent into the South Seas, and their sea ports destroyed, before such a scheme or intention could be known in Spain, or even in Buenos-Ayres. And farther, a nearer way might be discovered, by navigating the river with barges near to Valdivia. Many troops of the Indians of the river, would enlist themselves for the sake of plunder; so that the important garrison of Valdivia might be taken; which would of course draw after it the taking of Valparaiso, a much weaker fortress; and the possession

of these two places would ensure the conquest of the fertile kingdom of Chili.

Perhaps with a view to providing prospective English armies with some knowledge of their likely allies, Falkner gives a vivid description of the Moluche (i.e. Mapuche) as warriors, bandits, savages and rebels, listing their long, bloody wars with the Spaniards "whom they almost drove out of Chili, destroyed the cities of Imperial, Osorno and Villarica, and killed two of their presidents, Valdivia and Don Martin de Loyola." He also writes of the smallpox that is devastating the Mapuche and the "pulcu, or chichi", a fire-water made from the aforementioned apples and which "has made the greatest havoc among them."

Falkner challenges the legend of a magical city where white men live in splendour: "The report that there is a nation in these parts descended from Europeans, or the remains of shipwrecks is, I verily believe, entirely false and groundless, and occasioned by misunderstanding the accounts of the Indians." He gives three good reasons for his assertion. First, he claims to have questioned natives in Chile about inland settlements and found them to have been in fact referring to Buenos Aires; secondly, he says survival in Patagonia would be impossible for Europeans isolated from civilization and that if there had been a settlement 200 years ago, they would have died from hunger or been enslaved or killed by the "warlike and numerous" indigenous nations; thirdly, "there is not a foot of this continent, that the wandering nations do not ramble over every year; for even the uninhabited desert, which is washed by the Atlantic Ocean, is travelled over every year, to bury the dry bones of the dead, and to look for salt."

Equally perceptive are Falkner's in-depth studies of native funeral rites and beliefs about the afterlife:

> They have formed a belief that some of them after death are to return to… divine caverns; and they say also that the stars are old Indians, that the milky way is the field where the old Indians hunt ostriches, and that the two southern clouds [presumably the Magellanic clouds of dwarf galaxies, conspicuous in the southern hemisphere's night sky] are the feathers of the ostriches which they kill. They have an opinion also that the creation is not yet exhausted, nor all of it come out to the daylight of this upperworld.

The detail and sense of drama in Falkner's book give his writing a vividness not found in earlier accounts of the indigenous peoples, nor in many of those that followed—and this despite the fact that his papers were edited and abridged by William Combe who, it was later reported, "extracted from them the whole spirit of the original" before publication.

Falkner's observations were, of course, not merely academic. He had in mind a Christian future for all Patagonia's warring clans, and his research is that of a highly educated Jesuit preparing the way for education and, later, conversion. He closes his book with a list of useful phrases in the Mapuche tongue, as well as a translation of the Lord's Prayer, which begins thus:

> Inchin in Chao,
> huenumeuta m'leymi,
> uschingepe mi wi;
> eymi mi toquin...

During his long stay in South America Falkner spread Enlightenment ideas among local congregations, introducing experiments in the natural sciences while studying at the Jesuit mission headquarters in the city of Córdoba. His fellow Jesuits recognized that Falkner's medical background would be useful in winning over the witchdoctors who enjoyed esteem in many of the native communities. But Falkner was always a student, and sought to learn from the Tehuelche and Mapuche tribesmen whom he met: he lived on horseflesh and used his hat as a plate. (The latter became so greasy that it was finally eaten by a pack of wild dogs while he slept.)

Yet Enlightenment ideas of an anti-religious hue were also spreading through the Iberian empires. The Jesuits were expelled from Argentina in 1767, and Falkner sailed to England via Cádiz and Sardinia. On his return to London, he moved in secular society and shared his experiences in Patagonia with curious Englishmen. His eye-witness reports of the Tehuelche began to circulate among scientists, including the eminent zoologist and naturalist Thomas Pennant, and went some way to correcting the widely-held view that the whole of southern South America was ruled over by a single race of mysterious giants. Shortly after its publication in Britain, Falkner's work was translated into German and French, and into Spanish by the state publishing department in Buenos Aires.

CARMEN DE PATAGONES

The myths of Trapalanda and the Ciudad de los Césares—and the related and enduring notion of Patagonia as a region somehow outside the realm of nationhood—owe much to Spain's failure to gain control over the region. After the second, definitive, founding of Buenos Aires in 1580, some two hundred years would pass before the colonial authorities decided to establish settlements in Patagonia.

At the close of the eighteenth century Friar Francisco Menéndez thought that he had found the City of the Caesars when he was told by natives in the Nahuel Huapi region that there was a city at the end of a great river full of Spaniards, houses, white shoes and fields sown with wheat to make bread. But he was simply being told of a real place: Carmen de Patagones.

That the natives were so impressed and given to exaggeration and, indeed, that Carmen should fuel myths and legends among white men, is hardly surprising. The memory of Gamboa's doomed colonies still lingered in the eighteenth century and, despite three centuries of colonial government in northern Argentina and Chile and maritime exploration on both coasts, no one really expected there to be a city in Patagonia.

Carmen came into being because of a change in attitude that took place when the viceroyalty of Peru was divided into smaller self-governing colonies, one of which was the viceroyalty of the Río de la Plata with its capital in Buenos Aires. The second viceroy, Juan José de Vertíz y Salcedo, received the following royal decree, dated 23 March 1778, from his superior, José de Gálvez, visitor-general of New Spain, explaining the need for a coastal bulwark far to the south:

> ...in order to prevent the English and their insurgent colonists from attempting to establish a base in Bahía San Julián or whaling along the same coast... His Majesty has resolved to issue exact orders to the viceregent... that, as soon as possible, a formal Settlement and population is made of the said Bahía San Julián with a view... to forming a whaling station equal to the one maintained by the Portuguese at Santa Catalina [Santa Catarina, in southern Brazil]... taking advantage of the abundant salt-lakes found in that location to supply Buenos Aires.

Gálvez decreed that four settlements be created, intending to people them with colonists from Galicia, Asturias, Castile and León. He, like many others in the Spanish court, was familiar with Falkner's reports, and envisioned a chain of fortresses capable of sending expeditions deep into the interior to explore the rivers as far as the Andes. Vertíz duly issued the orders and sent four ships south carrying 120 infantrymen and artillerymen, seventy black slaves, cooks, carpenters, surgeons, artisans, chaplains, and 94 sailors.

On 22 April 1779 the fort of Nuestra Señora del Carmen was established by royal commissioner Francisco de Viedma y Nárvaez on the south bank of the Río Negro, some 580 miles south of the city of Buenos Aires. In June or July a flood destroyed the makeshift settlement and it was decided to move to the north bank. Three months later, the first settlers began to arrive, mainly Spaniards from the town of Maragatería in León, who were forced to make their homes in caves around the bay.

Other settlements were found in southern Patagonia, and for a brief period there were colonies in a bay close to Península Valdés, at Puerto Deseado, and at a site named Floridablanca, not far from present-day Puerto San Julián. None of these was successful. The captains in charge of the projected towns were unable to find fresh water and natives were too close and too belligerent to allow the settlers to make progress. King Charles III of Spain, on finding his fleets fully occupied with the British navy and the insurrection of Tupac Amaru in Peru, could not spare vessels for such insignificant schemes as those in Patagonia and withdrew his support. In 1783 Vertíz ordered the abandonment of all the colonies of southern Patagonia. In 1790 a fresh attempt was made to establish a fort at Puerto Deseado, but in 1806 English forces destroyed the building and the colonists abandoned the region.

Carmen was all alone, but somehow, thanks to the proximity of the river, and, relatively speaking, of Buenos Aires, the town prospered. Houses were built, the gravelly soil was tilled, and the hardy colonists, from some of Spain's poorest regions, committed themselves to remaining on this far-off coast. Towards the end of 1810, following the May Revolution, the newly installed junta in Buenos Aires took control of Carmen and decided to make use of its remote location by building a prison for dissidents there. In April 1812 a group of royalists who had been condemned to ten years of exile led a rebellion against the fort's commander and stole a boat on which they sailed to Montevideo. For more than two years Carmen was, in effect, a royalist outpost in independent Argentina, but in June 1814, when forces led by County Mayoborn Admiral William Brown seized control of hitherto Spanish-controlled Montevideo, Carmen was fully incorporated into the newly baptized United Provinces of the River Plate

By 1816 Portuguese Brazil had become wary of its Spanish-speaking neighbours, all of which had seceded from Spain in a series of brief but sometimes bloody skirmishes. Having become embroiled in Uruguay's struggle for nationhood, the huge northern power routed the most important local power-broker, José Gervasio Artigas, and in 1821 annexed the country in a display of force designed to extend its empire and impress the nascent Argentinian nation. The following year, Brazil declared its independence from Portugal and in 1826, angered by ongoing Argentinian military support for insurgents in Montevideo and the Uruguayan interior, declared war on Argentina, sending out a blue-water navy to take on Argentina's smaller coastal fleet, which was supplemented by privateers. Both fleets were made up predominantly of British seamen.

Brazilian ships had successfully blockaded the River Plate, so most Argentinian and foreign vessels sailed south, first to Ensenada, near La Plata, and then to Carmen de Patagones. In February 1827 a fleet of ships carrying Brazilian, British and American troops, all under the command of Englishman James Shepherd, raided the settlement. Their mission was to destroy Carmen and, with the support of the local natives and the Pincheira family—infamous Chilean bandits who had fought for the royalist cause in Chile—establish a Brazilian stronghold from which to send troops to Buenos Aires overland via the pampas and from the southern seas.

But on 27 March 1827 the residents of Carmen, perhaps inspired by the defeat of English naval forces by the citizenry of Buenos Aires in 1806 and 1807, rose up against the Brazilians and successfully resisted the invasion. Peace followed and the people of Carmen returned to their domestic labours.

In 1844 Murrel R. Robinson published a report "On the Town of Carmen and the Río Negro" in the *Journal of the Royal Geographical Society of London*. He writes that there are some 1,230 inhabitants—"800 Spaniards, 280 Africans, 150 Indians (slaves)"—and gives a description of a sort of shanty town showing some signs of promise:

The town or village, which is irregularly and badly built, stands on the side of a steep sandstone bank, rising above the river to a height of fifty feet; its most prominent object is a ruinous mud fort, erected by Viedma at the formation of the settlement. There are seven pieces of ordnance mounted upon it which are occasionally discharged, to the great peril of fort and gunners. The houses are of one story, and of mud bricks; some few are lime-washed: only the most wealthy persons have glass in their window frames. The principal street, if it can be called by such a name, runs along a slight ridge on the bank before mentioned; it is about 500 yards in length and 19 in width...

The total number of houses and huts inn the town may amount to 100 on the north and 30 on the south bank of the river...

Robinson's paper, published ostensibly for reasons of general scientific interest, directs itself from time to time at merchants and farmers in the Falklands, for whom, he suggests, Carmen could be an important source of horse and sheep. Falkner's vision of the Falklands as a base for British incursions into the continent may not have come true, but it is clear that Britain was already maintaining quasi-colonial trading relations with Patagonia without the need for the raising of any flags.

These days, the only remains of the colonial town are the Nuestra Señora del Carmen church, the caves where the first settlers made their homes, a series of tunnels that once connected separate areas of the original fort, and seven Brazilian imperial flags seized during the 1827 war. (In the 1960s the Brazilian government attempted to recover the flags, offering to asphalt the streets in exchange, but Carmen's municipal authorities rejected the offer.) The south bank is now occupied by the city of Viedma. Unlike Carmen which, despite the "de Patagones" in its name, is officially in Buenos Aires province, Viedma is the capital of Río Negro province and, therefore, within Patagonia

In 1986 Raúl Alfonsin, the first president to assume power after the military dictatorship, decided that Argentina needed a new capital. Brazil had done this in the 1956 with the creation *ex nihilo* of Brasilia, in order to foster development in the Amazonian heartland and also to take politics out of the playground of Rio de Janeiro. Buenos Aires had—and still has—a similar reputation as a perfect city for corrupt, lazy, hedonistic politicians and bureaucrats. In 1986 the national executive proposed the establishment of a new federal capital in the conurbation comprising Viedma, Carmen de Patagones and Guardia Mitre.

Needless to say, the bill was not passed, and Carmen, like the City of the Caesars, remains an almost-place.

Chapter Six

SOUNDING THE SOUL: FITZROY, DARWIN AND JEMMY BUTTON

"FitzRoy: Yammerschooner!
Darwin: Captain FitzRoy, can you hear me?
FitzRoy: Shhhh! Me hiding.
Darwin: Hiding from what?
FitzRoy: Heredity."

Kirk Wood Bromley, *On the Origin of Darwin* (2004)

PUERTO SAN JULIÁN

An hour's walk along the coast south of Puerto San Julián is the tomb of Lieutenant Robert H. Sholl of HMS *Beagle*. On a cloudy day it is a bleak spot; the road is stony and few cars ever come by this way. Only walkers with an interest in maritime history and Patagonia's erstwhile role as an exporter of cheap lamb chops make the trek to see the tomb and, a mile or so further on, the abandoned, rusting skeleton of the Swift meatpacking plant. The bronze plaque above the overgrown grave, which is now protected by a low fence, says, in Spanish: "Here lies Robert Sholl, officer of the *Beagle*, who passed away on June 20, 1828." Volume I of the *Beagle* narrative records that he had been ill for ten days and as a midshipman "of high character" would be dearly missed by all his friends. A signpost announces that Paraje Tumba Scholl (*sic*) is now for *playa y pesca*—a beach (though only for those with a seal-like resistance to the cold) and a fishing spot. Numerous further plaques record dedications from the Argentinian navy to the seaman who died in this forlorn spot.

Apart from the grave, there is nothing to recall the epic voyage of the *Beagle* nor the presence of Robert FitzRoy and, later, Charles Darwin on Patagonian soil. Their separate, but fatefully linked, ambitions were not about hoisting flags, looting towns or massacring natives—they came only for knowledge. But what they perceived in Patagonia would profoundly affect both men. The logbooks of one would lead to the new science of meteorology, and the spidery scribblings of the other changed the history of thought. Less important to history perhaps, but more painful for those concerned, were the consequences of the *Beagle* voyages for Darwin and FitzRoy as friends and for four Fuegian natives who never asked to be involved in this very British adventure.

Captain Phillip Parker King, Captain Pringle Stokes, Captain FitzRoy and Charles Darwin are the authors of the massive four-volume *Narrative of the Surveying Voyages of His Majesty's Ships* Adventure *and* Beagle *Between the Years 1826 and 1836 Describing Their Examination of the Southern Shores of South America and the* Beagle's *Circumnavigation of the Globe*, first published in 1839. FitzRoy was the main author of this work, using logbook notes kept by Stokes and King while preparing Volume I (which is officially under the authorship of King) but more reliant on his own journals for Volume II (where he is named as author). Volume III is based on the journal of the young scientist, Charles Darwin, who joined the *Beagle* for its second voyage. The original notes have been published as the *Beagle Diary*, while Volume III itself has appeared countless times as *The Journal of Researches* and, more commonly, *The Voyage of the Beagle*—a definite article earned perhaps but not entirely fair on the endeavours of King and FitzRoy. Volume IV is an appendix to Volume II, consisting mainly of weather tables, compass readings, tidal records, notes on Fuegian vocabulary and measurements of native body parts and heads (partly to put an end to the legend of the Patagonian giants).

Printed in 1839, it is a magnificent record of two historic voyages and a unique compendium of observations on natural history, weather, life on board and the indigenous peoples of Tierra del Fuego. If the two voyages of the *Beagle* represented together a scientific landmark for their highly detailed accounts of the shoreline and intricate bays of southern South America, the *Narrative* also set a new standard as a work of scientific literature with its remarkable descriptions of both the coast and the interior of Patagonia.

First Voyage 1826-30

On 22 May 1826 HMS *Adventure* and HMS *Beagle* set out from England under the command of Phillip Parker King, son of the governor of New South Wales and an illustrious sailor, who was on board the former. The *Beagle* was captained by Pringle Stokes, a conscientious officer but rather too frail for the voyage he was undertaking.

King and Stokes were to establish accurate readings of the longitudes for Montevideo and Cape Santa Maria and then sail on to map the coast from the mouth of the River Plate on the Atlantic coast to the island of Chiloé in the Pacific. They also had specific instructions to explore the labyrinthine channels of Tierra del Fuego, the graveyard of so many Royal Navy ships. Britain had already established colonies in the Caribbean, Southeast Asia and Africa, but it was widely accepted that a sure hold on the empire's mercantile and territorial interests depended on finding viable sea passages through the Americas.

After crossing the Atlantic, the ships sailed into Montevideo, which along with Buenos Aires was the last convenient point of contact with civilization for those voyaging south. They left the Uruguayan port on 19 November 1826 and sighted the Patagonian coast about eight days later, harbouring at Puerto Santa Elena on the 28th. The first thing they saw there was less than propitious:

> We found the spot which the Spanish astronomers of Malaspina's Voyage
> (in 1798) used for their observatory, the most convenient for our

purpose. It is near a very steep shingle (stony) beach at the back of a conspicuous red-coloured, rocky projection which terminates a small bay, on the western side, at the head of the port. The remains of a wreck, which proved to be that of an American whaler, the *Decatur* of New York, were found upon the extremity of the same point; she had been driven on shore from her anchors during a gale.

The sight of the wreck, and the steepness of the shingle beach just described, evidently caused by the frequent action of a heavy sea, did not produce a favourable opinion of the safety of the port: but as it was not the season for easterly gales, to which only the anchorage is exposed, and as appearances indicated a westerly wind, we did not anticipate danger.

For the following sixteen months King, Stokes and their team of surveyors were occupied exploring the shores of Tierra del Fuego and stretches of the Atlantic coast of southern Patagonia. The Magellan Strait, the weather and the open sea presented their usual challenges, a sealer and a schooner purchased during a visit to Rio de Janeiro were lost, and there were bizarre highs ("hummingbirds in snow showers") as well as times of misery, shock and horror—but the work proceeded and the crews kept together.

In March 1828 Stokes was sent off to survey Patagonia's Pacific coastline from the western mouth of the Strait to the Gulf of Peñas. Covering 400 miles and five degrees of latitude, this stretch of coast was subject to meteorological mood swings at the best of times: sudden hurricane squalls—known as williwaws—and vicious black storms were often followed by long periods of paralyzing calm. The ship's deck was constantly awash and one of the ship's crew died from "inflammation of the bowels".

Stokes was overcome by the monotony of the environment they were faced with and succumbed to depression. By the time the *Beagle* had rendezvoused with the *Adventure* in the Strait, Stokes' deputy, Lieutenant Skyring, had become concerned at his superior's ill-health. King was summoned over to his cabin but was unable to raise his fellow seaman's spirits.

The *Beagle* was anchored off Port Famine in June 1828, when Stokes noted in his journal:

Nothing could be more dreary than the scene around us. The lofty, bleak, and barren heights that surround the inhospitable shores of this inlet, were covered, even low down their sides, with dense clouds, upon which the fierce squalls that assailed us beat, without causing any change... Around us, and some of them distant no more than two-thirds of a cable's length, were rocky inlets, lashed by a tremendous surf; and, as if to complete the dreariness and utter desolation of the scene, even the birds seemed to shun its neighbourhood. The weather was that in which... "the soul of man dies in him."

The last quotation, which Stokes had taken from the poet James Thomson (1700-48), might have been an allusion to the illness or burial of Lieutenant Sholl, who died around this time.

But perhaps it was utterly personal. On 1 August Pringle Stokes took a gun, placed it against his head and pulled the trigger. The shot was not fatal and a surgeon tried to save his life. For four days Stokes was delirious, then improved slightly and was able to converse with King, confessing that he had hopes of recovery. On 12 August, after a period of lingering pain, he died.

ROBERT FITZROY

On 15 December 1828 Robert FitzRoy assumed captaincy of the ninety-foot, 235-ton HMS *Beagle* in Montevideo.

FitzRoy was the second son of the second marriage of Lord Charles FitzRoy, son of Augustus Henry, third Duke of Grafton, to Lady Frances Anne Stewart, eldest daughter of the Marquis of Londonderry. He was born in 1805 in Suffolk and schooled at Rottingdean and Harrow. The Graftons were a favoured, if illegitimate, branch of royalty, resulting from a liaison between Barbara Villiers and King Charles II. (The family name FitzRoy is the traditional one for an acknowledged royal bastard, from the Norman French son (*fils*) and king (*roi*)). Young Robert inherited class, wealth, military connections and, on his mother's side, a degree of mental instability. In 1820, when FitzRoy was fifteen and already studying at the Royal Naval College, Portsmouth, his uncle, the third Marquis of Londonderry, Viscount Castlereagh, slashed his own throat with a letter-opener.

In his late teens and early twenties FitzRoy earned many academic and maritime distinctions and rose speedily from volunteer on the *Owen*

Glendower to midshipman on the South American station and flag-lieutenant to Sir Robert Waller Otway.

With 23-year-old FitzRoy—highly strung but a very able leader—in command, the *Beagle* resumed its duties. The new captain sailed his newly-loaded ship out of the Plate on 30 January 1828. His first challenge was to weather a vicious wind off the coast of Buenos Aires province called the *pampero*, which throttled the topsails and blew two seamen off the rigging.

Two months later, FitzRoy took the *Beagle* into a strait near Cabo Negro, Tierra del Fuego, and had his first glimpse of the natives of what he called the Yapoo Tekeenica tribe, his generic misnomer for the diverse tribes of indigenous Fuegians. (In a classic example of linguistic confusion, *Teke uneka* in the native language actually meant "I do not understand you.") These stocky, hirsute people, with rotten teeth and mere rags for clothes—most probably members of the Selknam tribe, given their location—would have shocked FitzRoy's gentlemanly sensibilities and perhaps offended his strictly hierarchical class instincts.

> Their features were… peculiar; and if physiognomy can be trusted, indicated cunning, indolence, passive fortitude, deficient intellect, and want of energy. I observed that the forehead was very small and ill-shaped, the nose was long, narrow between the eyes and wide at the point; and the upper lip, long and protruding. They had small, retreating chins; bad teeth; high cheekbones; small Chinese eyes at an oblique angle with the nose… The head was very small, especially at the top and back; there were very few bumps for a craniologist.

FitzRoy was a keen phrenologist, but his primary concerns were cartographic and, for the moment, the Fuegians were little more than exotic fauna.

In his official capacity as captain surveyor, FitzRoy's job was to take small boats into the bays and channels of Tierra del Fuego, often for weeks at a time, and to make charts along the way. He also named the places he saw, usually after those who had served in some way, hence Otway Water (after his patron) and Skyring Water (after the officer who had made way for him to become captain of the *Beagle*). FitzRoy delighted in these derring-do adventures, but the austral winter was closing in and in July the *Beagle* and a schooner called the *Adelaide* sailed north to the relative warmth and calm of Chiloé to rendezvous with Captain King and the *Adventure*. There the three crews remained until the spring, preparing their ships for another voyage south. Jonathan May, the ship's carpenter, also built a new whaleboat to be used on survey expeditions in the Fuegian channels.

After cruising past Desolation Island in December 1829, the *Beagle* rested off Landfall Island, a protected anchorage about forty miles from Cabo Pilar at the western entrance of the Magellan Strait. Here FitzRoy saw for the first time members of the Yahgan tribe, though none of the Europeans would have known they were any different from the Selknam they had met in the eastern channels.

The Yahgan wanted no trinkets and beads, but rather knives, tools, weapons—and boats. They pestered FitzRoy and his crew, constantly pointing to desirable objects and demanding them, but not enough to persuade the seamen to abandon their sheltered harbour.

The Yahgan soon became bolder. After they attacked two crewmen on Landfall Island on 27 December and stole their clothes, FitzRoy and a small contingent went ashore to look for the offenders. They were forced to retreat when the Fuegians stood their ground armed with clubs, spears and even cutlasses which, FitzRoy deduced, must have been obtained from sealing vessels that visited the area. Whether these weapons had been the result of barter or theft was not known, but the Englishmen sensed that they were in the presence of natives who were at best obstinate, and at worst hostile and bellicose.

When, in early February, the tribesmen stole the whaleboat May had constructed at Chiloé, a fateful turn of events was set in motion. FitzRoy, whether out of a sense of justice or aristocratic chagrin, decided to pursue the Fuegians in order to punish them. Taking two hostages to provide directions, FitzRoy and his men rowed and sailed up and down the jagged shores, peering into the shadowy woods in search of the thieves. On 12 February one of the crew climbed a hill from which he spied a group of people he guessed belonged to the thieving party. The English sailors decided to rush the camp:

> After a long search we discovered the Indians in a cove, at some distance
> from that in which they were on the previous day; and having ascer-
> tained this point, taken a good view of the ground, and formed our

plans, we returned to our companions, and prepared for surprising the natives and making them prisoners. My wish was to surround them unawares, and take as many as possible, to be kept as hostages for the return of our boat, or else to make them show us where she was; and, meanwhile, it was an object to prevent any from escaping to give the alarm.

13th. Whether the men belonging to the tribe had returned during our absence, was uncertain, as we could not without risk of discovery, get near enough to ascertain: but, in case we should find them, we went armed, each with a pistol or gun, a cutlass, and a piece of rope to secure a prisoner. We landed at some distance from the cove, and, leaving two men with our boat, crept quietly through the bushes for a long distance round, until we were quite at the back of the new wigwams; then closing gradually in a circle, we reached almost to the spot undiscovered; but their dogs winded us, and all at once ran towards us barking loudly. Further concealment was impossible, so we rushed on as fast as we could through the bushes. At first the Indians began to run away; but hearing us shout on both sides, some tried to hide themselves, by squatting under the banks of a stream of water. The foremost of our party, Elsmore by name, in jumping across this stream, slipped, and fell in just where two men and a woman were concealed: they instantly attacked him, trying to hold him down and beat out his brains with stones; and before any one could assist him, he had received several severe blows, and one eye was almost destroyed, by a dangerous stroke near the temple. Mr. Murray, seeing the man's danger, fired at one of the Fuegians, who staggered back and let Elsmore escape; but immediately recovering himself, picked up stones from the bed of the stream, or was supplied with them by those who stood close to him, and threw them from each hand with astonishing force and precision. His first stone struck the master with much force, broke a powder-horn hung round his neck, and nearly knocked him backwards: and two others were thrown so truly at the heads of those nearest him, that they barely saved themselves by dropping down.

All this passed in a few seconds, so quick was he with each hand: but, poor fellow, it was his last struggle; unfortunately he was mortally wounded, and, throwing one more stone, he fell against the bank and expired. After some struggling, and a few hard blows, those who tried to secrete themselves were taken, but several who ran away along the beach escaped: so strong and stout were the females, that I, for one, had no idea that it was a woman, whose arms I and my coxswain endeavoured to pinion, until I heard someone say so. The oldest woman of the tribe was so powerful, that two of the strongest men of our party could scarcely pull her out from under the bank of the stream. The man who was shot was one of those whom we had taken in the boat as a guide, and the other was among our prisoners. Mr. Murray's coats were found in the wigwams divided into wrappers to throw over the shoulders.

...That a life should have been lost in the struggle, I lament deeply; but if the Fuegian had not been shot at that moment, his next blow might have killed Elsmore, who was almost under water, and more than half stunned, for he had scarcely sense to struggle away, upon feeling the man's grasp relax. When fairly embarked, and before we asked any questions, the natives seemed very anxious to tell us where our boat was; but pointed in a direction quite opposite to that which they had previously shown us. We guarded them carefully through the night, and next morning (14th) set out upon our return to the *Beagle*, with twenty-two souls in the boat. My object was, to put them in security on board, run down the coast with the ship to some harbour more to the eastward, and then set out again upon another search; carrying some of my prisoners as guides, and leaving the rest on board to ensure the former remaining, and not deceiving us. We made tolerable progress, though the boat was so over-loaded, and on the 15th reached the *Beagle* with our living cargo. In our way we fell in with a family of natives, whose wigwams and canoes we searched; but finding none of our property, we left them not only unmolested, but gave them a few things, which in their eyes were valuable.

The theft of the boat had been a definite turning point. But now a Fuegian had died at British hands—the first instance of such an act on record—and FitzRoy was no doubt both distressed and frustrated. His authority as captain, and as gentleman, was being directly challenged by a gang of primitives and his surveying work was being sidelined because of a criminal act.

The prisoners were keen to show the Englishmen where the missing boat was, but with 22 people on board a 25-foot whaleboat FitzRoy was aware that another chase was impracticable. Instead, they returned to the

Beagle. The hostages were fed and clothed and the *Beagle* weighed anchor and sailed south-east to Cape Castlereagh. After several days of plying the shores in two boats with crew members and native guides, the men found the missing boat's leadline in a "lately deserted" wigwam. But after two further weeks of searching in vain, during which FitzRoy saw only fires and deserted camps, all the hostages except for three children escaped.

By now the surveying had been completely eclipsed by the futile chase. FitzRoy, suppressing his anger, decided to turn a personal disaster into a moral scheme:

> This cruise had also given me more insight into the real character of the Fuegians, than I had then acquired by other means, and gave us all a severe warning which might prove very useful at a future day, when among more numerous tribes who would not be contented with a boat alone. Considering the extent of coast we had already examined, we ought to be thankful for having experienced no other disaster of any kind, and for having had the means of replacing this loss.
>
> I became convinced that so long as we were ignorant of the Fuegian language, and the natives were equally ignorant of ours, we should never know much about them, or the interior of their country; nor would there be the slightest chance of their being raised one step above the low place which they then held in our estimation. Their words seemed to be short, but to have many meanings, and their pronunciation was harsh and guttural.

Unless this language gap could be bridged, FitzRoy deduced, there could be no useful knowledge gleaned on behalf of the crown. Nor could there be any improvement or moral education for the tribesmen. The captain made two important decisions. First, he resolved to have a new boat built in order to continue with his hydrographic work. Second, he decided to take permanent hostages.

The first Fuegian to be kidnapped, some time in March 1830, was Fuegia Basket, an eight-year-old Yahgan girl who, wrote FitzRoy, "seemed to be so happy and healthy, that I determined to detain her as a hostage for the stolen boat, and to try to teach her English." Her ludicrous nickname alluded to the wicker boat that FitzRoy's sailing master, Murray, had used to sail back to the *Beagle* when the whaleboat was stolen. She became, according to FitzRoy, a "pet on the lower deck", and the captain and crew found her a charming commodity to have on board.

The next captive was called York Minster after the castellated promontory named by Cook that loomed over the spot where he had been seized. FitzRoy records that the young man "was sullen at first, yet his appetite did not fail; and whatever he received more than he could eat, he stowed away in a corner; but as soon as he was well cleaned and clothed, and allowed to go about where he liked in the vessel, he became much more cheerful."

Surveying March Harbour, five days after taking York, FitzRoy saw smoke rising from a cove. Rocks and gunfire were exchanged as the crew chased the natives into the bush. They came across items of lost equipment on the shore, indicating that here were the culprits who had stolen the whaleboat. The next morning, a third Yahgan was arrested after a brief skirmish; he was christened, rather pathetically, Boat Memory, and was given some food and allowed to sleep once he was aboard the *Beagle*.

Ostensibly still bent on finding the whaleboat, FitzRoy's motives were changing. He noted in his journal: "Three natives of Tierra del Fuego, better suited for the purpose of instruction, and for giving, as well as receiving information, could not, I think, have been found." Evidently scientific aims and the practical aspects of seamanship—for these natives could presumably indicate the safest channels and aid the foreigners in reading the seas and weather systems—were beginning to merge with religious and moral intentions.

With the three natives on board, the *Beagle* continued with its surveys of the Fuegian coast. In his entry for 14 April, FitzRoy notes the following important piece of information:

> The master returned, and surprised me with the information that he had been through and far beyond Nassau Bay. He had gone very little to the northward, but a long distance to the east, having passed through a narrow passage, about one-third of a mile wide, which led him into a straight channel, averaging about two miles or more in width, and extending nearly east and west as far as the eye could reach.

The *Beagle's* master, Murray, had discovered a second east-west passage between the Atlantic and Pacific, which was duly christened the Beagle Channel.

On 11 May, near the Murray Narrows, between Isla Navarino and the Dumas peninsula of Isla Hoste, FitzRoy's ship met three canoes looking to trade with the Englishmen. He recounts the abduction and naming of the last hostage, who he noted belonged to a more malleable branch of the Yapoo tribe:

> We gave them a few beads and buttons, and some fish; and, without any previous intention, I told one of the boys in a canoe to come into our boat, and gave the man who was with him a large shining mother-of-pearl button. The boy got into my boat directly, and sat down… "Jemmy Button", as the boat's crew called him, on account of his price, seemed to be pleased at the change.

Jemmy Button was probably a Halakwalup, as he spoke an entirely different language to the other three captives.

The notion of kidnap occurred to FitzRoy spontaneously, or so he claims in the journal. But this apparent attempt to qualify his decision is an admission that taking a native in this manner was rather ordinary. Bruce Chatwin later imagined this scene in his travelogue, *In Patagonia*: "Heedless of danger, the boy persuaded the uncle to paddle up to the pink man's canoe. A tall person in costume beckoned him and he leapt aboard. The pink man handled the uncle a disc that shimmered like the moon and the canoe spread a white wing and flew down the channel towards the source of pearl buttons."

Chatwin appears to be making an attempt to get inside the mind of the victim, perhaps to counter the fact that all the voices we have about Patagonia come from the conquerors and discoverers, and never the native peoples. But, characteristically, he romanticizes the abduction, falling in with the pink men who barter for God and do whatever they please with the destinies of savages. David Taylor calls this "a paradigm of colonial narrative", claiming that "its dramatic touches block rather than illuminate the larger significance." In 2000 writer and human rights advocate Sylvia Iparraguirre wrote a prize-winning novel about the Jemmy Button saga, *Tierra del Fuego*, in an effort to tell the story as Jemmy might have experienced it and to redress FitzRoy's "colonial gaze" through fiction.

FUEGIA BASKET. 1833.   JEMMY'S WIFE. 1834.

JEMMY IN 1834.   JEMMY BUTTON IN 1833.

YORK MINSTER IN 1833.   YORK IN 1833.

FUEGIANS.

Published by Henry Colburn, Great Marlborough Street, 1839.

THE FUEGIANS IN ENGLAND

Volume I of the *Narrative* closes with FitzRoy justifying his purpose in taking the Fuegians home to England:

> I had… made up my mind to carry the Fuegians… to England; trusting that the ultimate benefits arising from their acquaintance with our habits and language would make up for the temporary separation from their own country. But this decision was not contemplated when I first took them on board; I then only thought of detaining them while we were on their coasts; yet afterwards finding that they were happy and in good health, I began to think of the various advantages which might result to them and their countrymen, as well as to us, by taking them to England, educating them there as far as might be practicable, and then bringing them back to Tierra del Fuego… In adopting the latter course I incurred a deep responsibility, but was fully aware of what I was undertaking.

In August 1830 the ships sailed out of Rio de Janeiro for England, and it is from this point that Volume II of the *Narrative* takes up the story. During the crossing over the equator FitzRoy noted: "Far, far indeed, were three of the number from deserving to be called savages—even at this early period of their residence among civilized people—though the other, named York Minster, was certainly a displeasing specimen of uncivilized human nature."

FitzRoy claims that the natives told him that their countrymen "occasionally committed" acts of cannibalism and that when food was very scarce, the eldest women in their tribes were slaughtered. He writes that a large ox thrilled the captives, but a passing steamship heading into Falmouth harbour at night perturbed them. FitzRoy estimates the natives' ages as:

York Minster...............26
Boat Memory...............20
Jemmy Button.............14
Fuegia Basket................9

But he makes no connection between York being older and his being more belligerent.

FitzRoy funded the whole scheme to educate and civilize the Fuegians, though in response to an open letter to the Admiralty, he received a reply stating that the Lords Commissioners would "afford him [FitzRoy] any facilities towards maintaining and educating them in England, and will give them a passage home again."

By mid-October 1830 the *Beagle* was back in England. In November Boat Memory fell ill with smallpox. All four natives were then sent to the Royal Hospital, Plymouth, but when FitzRoy arrived in London he was informed of Boat's death. The three others were unaffected. FitzRoy's plan was to keep them in England for two to three years, and he arranged to have them provided with rooms and schooling at Walthamstow, on the north-eastern outskirts of London. On the coach taking them out of town, York was especially impressed by the statue of the blue lion—the crest of the Percy family—on Northumberland House.

Between December 1830 and October 1831 York, Jemmy and Fuegia resided at an infant school in Walthamstow, only seven miles from London but at that time a suburb lying in open fields. FitzRoy had secured the three Fuegians board and education through Rev. William Wilson, rector at Walthamstow, and an assistant preacher, Rev. Joseph Wigram, who was also secretary of the National Society for Providing the Education of the Poor in the Principles of the Established Church.

The headmaster, William Jenkins, and his wife gave the Fuegians a warm welcome to their school and set about providing them with a knowledge—so FitzRoy notes—of English and Christianity, as well as some basic grounding in "husbandry, gardening and mechanism". Fuegia and Jemmy made good progress and soon charmed their hosts with their grasp of English and impeccable behaviour. Jemmy liked to pepper his speech with quaint, fashionable expressions and was something of a dandy in his choice of dress; FitzRoy writes that he was "fond of admiring himself in a looking glass." York, however, was a moody man and did not enjoy sitting among two- and three-year-olds singing, clapping and repeating the ABC. FitzRoy's journal makes no attempt to disguise his preference for the company of the two younger Fuegians, and it is likely that York was left behind when the captain took his exotic guests to visit aristocratic friends and members of his family.

In the summer of 1831 the Fuegians had an audience with King William IV and Queen Adelaide. The latter presented Fuegia with a bonnet, put one of her rings on the girl's finger and "gave her a sum of money to buy an outfit of clothes when she would leave England to return to her own country."

York, who would have been about 27 or 28 years of age by this time, sank into a state of permanent melancholy. In his prime, he must have felt oppressed by the strait-laced atmosphere at the church school and the constant supervision of Jenkins and Rev. Wilson. London was full of prostitutes, but York had neither the money nor the social means to access that particular escape route. Unable to go out and choose a life and a partner, he fixed his attentions on the only female he could see every day and share conversation with: Fuegia Basket.

When not occupied with the Fuegians and other social engagements, FitzRoy spent the winter of 1830-31 in the Hydrographic Office of the Admiralty. FitzRoy and King, aided by Stokes and Skyring, had achieved a good deal in terms of ensuring safe passage between the Atlantic and Pacific, and FitzRoy, a meticulous and assiduous sailor, was busy supervising the draughting of charts based on his surveys.

The emerging rapport between Fuegia Basket and York Minster prompted FitzRoy to make haste in arranging to take them away from England and back to their homeland. His plans for their Christian education had only been partially realized, but FitzRoy was aware that any scandal involving the two natives (Fuegia becoming pregnant being perhaps the most probable and also most catastrophic disaster) would mean personal disgrace and possibly the end of his hitherto almost flawless naval career.

He was therefore deeply aggrieved when he was given to understand that there would be no follow-up survey—and hence no way of his personally accompanying the Fuegians home. Anxious to act and feeling responsible for their fortunes, he agreed to hire a merchant vessel called the *John of London* to carry him and his protégés to Tierra del Fuego and take him on to Valparaiso. FitzRoy even purchased some goats to take to leave behind on the islands.

A sudden change of heart at the Admiralty meant that FitzRoy would, in fact, return as a surveyor and again as captain of the *Beagle*. This time his commission, issued by Francis Beaufort, Hydrographer of the Navy, proposed that FitzRoy return by sailing westward through Australasia and the Indian Ocean. Among his supernumeraries were a young missionary named

Richard Matthews, the three Fuegians, FitzRoy's steward, a draughtsman-cum-artist, an instrument maker—and a budding young naturalist.

SECOND VOYAGE 1832-36

Travel writers love Darwin; he is the author they turn to for a profound quotation. He is an icon but was iconoclastic, scholarly but excitable, and his writings combine hard science with intelligent introspection. The extract most often cited in writings about Patagonia is this:

> Among the scenes which are deeply impressed on my mind, none exceed in sublimity the primeval forests, undefaced by the hand of man, whether those in Brazil, where the powers of life are predominant, or those of Tierra del Fuego, where death & decay prevail. Both are temples filled with the varied productions of the God of Nature:—No one can stand unmoved in these solitudes, without feeling that there is more in man than the mere breath of his body.—In calling up images of the past, I find the plains of Patagonia most frequently cross before my eyes. Yet these plains are pronounced by all most wretched & useless. They are only characterized by negative possessions:—without habitations, without water, without trees, without mountains, they support merely a few dwarf plants. Why then, and the case is not peculiar to myself, do these arid wastes take so firm possession of the memory? Why have not the still more level, greener & fertile Pampas, which are serviceable to mankind, produced an equal impression? I can scarcely analyse these feelings:—But it must be partly owing to the free scope given to the imagination. They are boundless, for they are scarcely practicable & hence unknown: they bare the stamp of having thus lasted for ages, & there appears no limit to their duration through future time.

This famous passage, entered under the date of 25 September 1836, was clearly written while Darwin was editing at Down House, near Orpington in suburban London. The prose is not typical of *The Voyage of the Beagle* (a.k.a. Volume III of *The Narrative of the Surveying Voyages of His Majesty's Ships Adventure and Beagle*). Much of this magnificent book is filled with cool, scientific observations based on geological findings and precise descriptions of flora and fauna. Even when Darwin makes notes on human behaviour he does so with an eye for patterns and generalizations.

For *The Voyage* is based closely on the log that Darwin kept on board—published as the *Beagle Diary*—and it strains to be an objective account. That later writers, from W. H. Hudson and Bruce Chatwin to journalists sent on sponsored trips to Patagonia, have seized on this after-the-fact, daydreaming moment of topographical melancholy rather than the dry details that form the core of Darwin's contribution says much about the glamour of the gloomy and the need for travel writing to avoid too much fun—or indeed, too many facts.

When the *Beagle* sailed out of Plymouth on 27 December 1831 Darwin was aged just 22. He was a naïve naturalist and a confirmed land-lubber—he would suffer terribly from sea-sickness during the following four years—but in some ways his life had been moving purposefully towards the *Beagle* adventure.

Darwin was born in Shrewsbury on 12 February 1809 at his family home, The Mount. He was the grandson of Erasmus Darwin, an advocate of Jean-Baptiste Lamarck's theory of evolution, on his father's side, and of Josiah Wedgwood on his mother's. As a child he attended the local Unitarian chapel, and in 1817 he joined the day school run by its preacher. From September 1818 he attended the nearby Anglican Shrewsbury School as a boarder

During the summer of 1825 Darwin helped his father care for Shropshire's poor as an apprentice doctor before going off in the autumn to the University of Edinburgh to study medicine. He did not enjoy the surgery classes and began to neglect his studies, and in the second year dedicated his time to natural history and Lamarck's theories. One of Darwin's mentors, Robert Edmund Grant, took him out to the shores of the Firth of Forth to research the life cycle of marine animals. Darwin joined the Pinnian Society, a gathering of natural history enthusiasts, where he presented a paper on eggs found in oyster shells. He also took an interest in classification and began to help out at the University Museum, which housed important botanical and biological collections.

Darwin's father was not overly impressed. In 1827 he enrolled his son onto a BA course at Christ's College, Cambridge, to qualify as a clergyman. But Darwin preferred riding and shooting to theology, and continued his naturalist's pursuits by becoming an adherent of the then fashionable hobby of collecting beetles. A cousin introduced him to Cambridge's Professor of Botany, the Rev. John Stevens Henslow, who ran a natural history course. Darwin attended and took a keen interest in the writings of William Paley, especially his famous argument for divine design in nature. Inspired by Henslow's tutoring, Darwin postponed his clerical career and, after reading Alexander von Humboldt's *Personal Narrative of a Journey to the Equinoctial Regions of America*, made plans to visit the Madeira Islands with some classmates after graduation to study natural history. But following a trip to Wales, a letter arrived from Henslow recommending Darwin as a naturalist for the unpaid position of gentleman's companion to Robert FitzRoy, captain of HMS *Beagle*, which was to leave in four weeks on an expedition to chart the coastline of South America. His father initially objected but was persuaded by his brother-in-law, Josiah Wedgwood, to agree to his son's participation.

The other young supernumerary, Richard Matthews, had been recruited by Rev. Wilson of Walthamstow. His aim was to sail to Tierra del Fuego and help the natives resettle, while he established a mission there. Still a teenager, Matthews was a fervent evangelist, inspired partly by the role model of his brother, a missionary in New Zealand. He no doubt expected his own godly work in the wilderness to mirror that of his sibling, and probably regarded the Fuegians on board as distant relatives of the Maoris. Wilson had raised a subscription to provide Matthews with all he needed to erect an English home beside his church in Tierra del Fuego.

The sailors probably expressed mere bafflement while loading Darwin's measuring instruments and storage boxes; as they carried on Matthews' hoard of soup tureens, chamber pots and white linen they enjoyed some "very fair jokes".

PHILOS AND FITZROY

By the time the *Beagle* had "crossed the line"—the term for voyaging past the equator—Darwin and FitzRoy had become acquainted with each other's character. Darwin had been accepted by the crew and had acquired the nickname "Philosopher" or "Philos", and as well as his own work-related schedules he shared several routines with FitzRoy. The two men usually lunched together shortly after noon and then both retired to write their journals, Darwin following the seasoned captain's habits of keeping copious and meticulous records.

Darwin had also to get used to FitzRoy's "severe silences" and his excessive bad humour in the mornings. In Bahia, Brazil, the two men had a huge row over the issue of slavery, FitzRoy expressing contempt for Darwin's more sympathetic attitude and suggesting for a moment that Darwin might have to leave the ship. But it was also FitzRoy's habit to make amends quickly.

As the only educated men on the *Beagle*, the pair spent many hours enjoying each other's conversation and there was mutual admiration. FitzRoy shared many of Darwin's scientific interests, and as a welcoming gift he gave his new companion a copy of Charles Lyell's *Principles of Geology*, which had been published in 1830. The book was to serve Darwin well, and he applied its knowledge every time he was able to go ashore.

FIRST VISIT TO PATAGONIA

Darwin's first voyage to southern Argentina took place in September 1832. He reconnoitred the area between Bahía Blanca and the Río Negro, where FitzRoy's team was surveying the shallow coastal waters and inlets. Darwin seemed more impressed by the natives and gauchos than by the landscape or nature, though he spent a fair portion of time studying the local "Ostriches"—flightless rheas—and collecting their eggs.

In the *Beagle Diary* entry for 14 September, Darwin notes: "I am spending September in Patagonia, much in the same manner as I should in England, viz in shooting." He shot deer, agouti and cavy, while another member of his party showed off his skill with the *boleadoras* and bagged a rhea.

He was not merely occupied in hunting and going for horseback rides. On 22 September he describes a pleasant cruise around a bay to Punta Alta where he found some rocks. "These are the first I have seen, & are very interesting from containing shells & the bones of large animals." He then moves onto the weather, which was pleasant and, in his opinion, "wasted" on the surrounding country. FitzRoy records the same excursion in his narrative, adding that the "cargoes of apparent rubbish" that his avid young passenger had brought on board were the "large fossil bones" of extinct species. In his commentary on this episode Professor Richard Keynes states that "This was truly a red-letter day for biology, marking the initial discovery of the first of the lines of evidence that eventually led CD [Darwin] to question and ultimately to reject the doctrine of the fixity of species."

When we read *The Voyage of the Beagle*, the Punta Alta explorations are expanded into an essay of several thousand words detailing the saline nature of the soils and the mud banks, and repopulating the crumbling cliffs with a plethora of incredible beasts:

> First, parts of three heads and other bones of the Megatherium, the huge dimensions of which are expressed by its name. Secondly, the Megalonyx, a great allied animal. Thirdly, the Scelidotherium, also an allied animal, of which I obtained a nearly perfect skeleton. It must have been as large as a rhinoceros: in the structure of its head it comes, according to Mr. Owen, nearest to the Cape Ant-eater, but in some other respects it approaches to the armadilloes. Fourthly, the Mylodon Darwinii, a closely related genus of little inferior size. Fifthly, another gigantic edental quadruped. Sixthly, a large animal, with an osseous coat in compartments, very like that of an armadillo. Seventhly, an extinct kind of horse, to which I shall have again to refer. Eighthly, a tooth of a Pachydermatous animal, probably the same with the Macrauchenia, a huge beast with a long neck like a camel, which I shall also refer to again. Lastly, the Toxodon, perhaps one of the strangest animals ever discovered: in size it equalled an elephant or megatherium, but the structure of its teeth, as Mr. Owen states, proves indisputably that it was intimately related to the Gnawers, the order which, at the present day, includes most of the smallest quadrupeds: in many details it is allied to the Pachydermata: judging from the position of its eyes, ears, and nostrils, it was probably aquatic, like the Dugong and Manatee, to which it is also allied. How wonderfully are the different Orders, at the present time so well separated, blended together in different points of the structure of the Toxodon!
>
> The remains of these nine great quadrupeds and many detached bones were found embedded on the beach, within the space of about 200 yards square. It is a remarkable circumstance that so many different species should be found together; and it proves how numerous in kind the ancient inhabitants of this country must have been'.

This passage provides us with a clear idea of how far Darwin's mind had travelled by the time he sat down to write *The Voyage of the Beagle*. From scattered, mis-spelt notes often written in a hurry or in a seasickness-induced temper, a comprehensive, vivid picture of zoological history was imagined. The blank horizontal of Patagonia was given a vertical past.

Keynes concedes that Darwin was probably not struck by the implications of his find until his return to England, when he was able to classify the fossils with his mentor Richard Owen. But it is intriguing to think of Darwin ruminating on the possibilities of evolution as he wanders the northern fringes of Patagonia—where the pampas of the north become arid and burnished and merge into a land that seems so barren and bereft of trees and animals as to seem to be on its own road to extinction.

Ever the Victorian traveller, Darwin's diary is also occupied with the weather and the views. On the 26th he remarks that "The weather is most beautiful.—passing from the splendour of Brazil to the tame sterility of Patagonia has shown me how very much the pleasure of exercise depends on the surrounding scenery."

Jemmy Goes Home

In October the *Beagle* returned to the River Plate to re-supply and Darwin went gallivanting in Buenos Aires and Montevideo. On 26 November they set sail for the south again, this time bound for Tierra del Fuego, where FitzRoy planned to return the "civilized" natives to their homeland, and also for the Falkland Islands. (They made landfall on the latter on 1 March 1833, just two months after the United Kingdom had seized possession of the islands from the Americans, who had ousted the Argentinians.)

Darwin's diary for December and March 1833 gives us plenty of insight into how an open-minded, educated young Victorian viewed less developed societies. The narrative is exclamatory from the outset. Apart from the three Fuegian passengers, Darwin had had at this stage no encounter with the tribespeople, yet he draws quick, certain conclusions.

> When we landed the party [of four Fuegian males] looked rather alarmed, but continued talking & making gestures with great rapidity.—It was without exception the most curious and interesting spectacle I ever beheld. I would not have believed how entire the difference between savage & civilized man is.—It is far greater than between a wild & domesticated animal, in as much as in man there is greater power of improvement.

There is a kind of grotesque comedy to the encounter. Darwin is particularly enthralled by their facial expressions—"distrustful, surprised &

startled"—and is particularly taken with an old man who does a kind of chicken dance before him while clucking and patting Darwin on the chest and back. As far as Darwin is concerned, the Fuegians' "language does not deserve to be called articulate," consisting of little more than gargling, guttural clicks and the sound a man makes when he is "encouraging a horse."

"I believe if the world was searched, no lower grade of man could be found," he remarks while watching a group of Fuegians scrub about for shellfish on a stony beach. When even small groups of natives gather to challenge the presence of the *Beagle* party, he has little respect for their territorial pride and regards their courage as "like that of a wild beast". He describes them as "Cannabals" and "thieves". He, like FitzRoy before him, completely misreads the Fuegians' propensity to "steal": "Jemmy's own relations were absolutely so foolish & vain, as to show strangers what they had stolen & method of doing it," he notes.

Once again, the Englishmen are perturbed by the Fuegians' persistent importuning. Darwin notes the native word, as he understands it, for "give me":

> While in the boats I got to hate the very sound of their voices, so much trouble did they give us. The first and last word was "yammerschooner". When, entering some quiet little cove, we have looked round and thought to pass a quiet night, the odious word "yammerschooner" has shrilly sounded from some gloomy nook, and then the little signal smoke has curled upwards to spread the news. On leaving some place we have said to each other, "Thank Heaven, we have at last fairly left these wretches!" when one more faint halloo from an all-powerful voice, heard at a prodigious distance, would reach our ears, and clearly could we distinguish—"yammerschooner".

Darwin's impressions are also coloured—and sometimes drained of colour—by the natural environment. "The gloomy depth of the ravine well accorded with the universal signs of violence," he writes, and again: "The whole landscape has a monotonous sombre appearance." He seems to swing between contempt for monotony on the one hand and an obscure fear of cataclysm on the other. This seeming paradox should not surprise us. The influence of the Romantics notwithstanding, the early Victorians had not yet risen to the challenges of the Alps and other mountain wildernesses. Beauty was still only accorded to nature which was either amenable to a gentle stroll or, ideally, modified and manicured by man with the purpose of improving it.

Darwin explored the forests of Good Success Bay, named by Cook during his first voyage in the *Endeavour*. Out on his rambles, the curved, twisting trees, the masses of root buried in moss and lichens, and the dense canopy that blocks out the weak rays of the sun all impressed Darwin as a kind of icy version of the Tropics. His senses assailed, he draws a stark conclusion: "In this still solitude, death instead of life is the predominant spirit," a phrase immediately followed by an admission of "delight... that this part of the forest had never before been traversed by man."

On 23 January the four boats proceeded down Ponsonby Sound, escorted by many canoes, and moved into Wulaia (a.k.a. Woollya) Cove, on Isla Navarino, where the mission was to be started. Jemmy's mother, two sisters and four brothers came to visit. The crew and settlers were engaged in setting up some primitive dwellings while the Fuegians looked on, bemused.

Three small huts were built and the provisions were unloaded from the boats and stored in them in order to discourage thievery. If his general impressions gave rise to anthropological assertions typical of his times, in other respects Darwin was enlightened. His view on the establishment of a mission reveals a sceptical and, as it turned out, prescient assessment of the Bible-bearing colonists: "The choice of articles showed the most culpable folly & negligence. Wine glasses, butter-bolts, tea-trays, soup turins, mahogany dressing case, fine white linen, beavor hats & an endless variety of similar things shows how little was thought about the country they were going to."

Nonetheless, gardens were planted with potatoes, carrots, turnips, beans, peas, lettuce, onions, leeks and cabbages. By 27 January the preparations were complete and Rev. Richard Matthews and the three partially anglicized Fuegians settled down to run the mission. Yet as soon as Matthews and his party were left behind, they were surrounded by noisy natives. Groups advanced with stones and stakes. They plundered all the belongings and prevented Matthews from obtaining food and wood.

Darwin and FitzRoy returned with some sailors on two boats to Wulaia Cove on 6 February to check up on the mission but en route noticed that many of the natives walking along the shore were wearing strips of English cloth. Arriving at the settlement, they found that the mission had been looted and the gardens trampled. Rev. Matthews, despairing, returned with the boats.

The three Fuegians were left to fend for themselves, and promised to carry on with the mission. Darwin, however, expresses pity for Jemmy Button's predicament, caught between two cultures without the education to manage his dilemma. "I do not suppose, any person exists with such a small stock of language as poor Jemmy, his own language forgotten, & his English ornamented with a few Spanish words, almost unintelligible." He has a sense of foreboding as they bid the Fuegians goodbye: "I am afraid whatever other ends their excursion to England produces, it will not be conducive to their happiness.—They have far too much sense not to see the vast superiority of civilized over uncivilized habits; & yet I am afraid to the latter they must return."

When FitzRoy returned to Wulaia on 12 February, the Fuegians had repaired the mission huts and the gardens were replanted. After staying at the mission for a few days the crew headed back to the *Beagle*. Matthews was subsequently taken in the *Beagle* to New Zealand, where he joined his brother and continued his missionary work.

After leaving the mission, the *Beagle* sailed for the Falkland Islands. Though the colony seemed at times far busier than Patagonia, with many ships arriving, Darwin noted that its days as the "Botany Bay for Buenos Aires" were long gone and that it was yet another eerily quiet spot on the globe He protested at having so little to write in his journal. On 4 April the *Beagle* and a newly acquired schooner, the *Universe*, voyaged back to the Patagonian mainland, briefly pausing in the San Matías Gulf, which Darwin describes as an "El Dorado to a Geologist" in view of its miles of exposed strata, rich in organic remains.

PATAGONIA AGAIN

Darwin's next departure for the south was in August 1833 to the seas off Carmen de Patagones, where the *Beagle* was occupied with surveys. He spent more than a month riding back from the mouth of the Río Negro to Buenos Aires. But summer was fast approaching and FitzRoy's expedition in the southern islands had to be recommenced.

After sending a small boat up the River Plate to obtain fresh water, the *Beagle* and *Adventure* left Montevideo on 6 December and continued south. The ships arrived at Puerto Deseado on 23 December. During the next few weeks the *Adventure* stayed in port while its masts were repaired. The *Beagle* anchored a few miles within the entrance, in front of the ruins of an old Spanish settlement.

Darwin's *Voyage of the Beagle* describes this as a "new country... the whole aspect bears the stamp of a marked and individual character. At the height of between two and three hundred feet above some masses of porphyry a wide plain extends, which is truly characteristic of Patagonia. The surface is quite level, and is composed of well-rounded shingle mixed with a whitish earth. Here and there scattered tufts of brown wiry grass are supported, and still more rarely, some low thorny bushes. The weather is dry and pleasant, and the fine blue sky is but seldom obscured. When standing in the middle of one of these desert plains and looking towards the interior, the view is generally bounded by the escarpment of another plain, rather higher, but equally level and desolate; and in every other direction the horizon is indistinct from the trembling mirage which seems to rise from the heated surface."

Darwin sees little prospect for settlement of such a terrain: "The result of all the attempts to colonize this side of America south of 41 degs., has been miserable. Port Famine expresses by its name the lingering and extreme sufferings of several hundred wretched people, of whom one alone survived to relate their misfortunes. At St. Joseph's Bay, on the coast of Patagonia, a small settlement was made; but during one Sunday the Indians made an attack and massacred the whole party, excepting two men, who remained captives during many years. At the Rio Negro I conversed with one of these men, now in extreme old age."

The zoology seems to be on a par with the dryness. Yet Darwin discovers black beetles, three carrion hawks, a few finches and insect-feeders. In the guts of an ibis he finds grasshoppers, cicadae, small lizards and scorpions. He is drawn to the guanaco, "an elegant animal in a state of nature, with a long slender neck and fine legs". He watches the herds closely, and long passages of the *Voyage of the Beagle* are littered with rhetorical questions, small experiments, inventories of behaviour driving towards generalizations and, where evidence is lacking, speculation and suggestion. Books by other naturalists are incorporated into the text and species are studied alongside other members of the same genus to further consolidate observations. While the *Diary* presents his explorations in chronological order, Darwin compresses time in the *Voyage of the Beagle* and allows his data to mingle to produce a wholly scientific document.

The second major Patagonian expedition took Darwin and FitzRoy to Puerto San Julián, into the Magellan Strait, to Puerto del Hambre, to the Río Santa Cruz, back to the Falklands, and once again to Tierra del Fuego. In March 1834, just over a year after they had last seen Button and his companions, the *Beagle* dropped anchor at Wulaia. The settlement was in ruins and apart from a few turnips and potatoes, the vegetable patch was trampled. FitzRoy records that there was no sign of any natives, and:

> An anxious hour or two passed, before three canoes were seen in the offing, paddling hastily towards us, from the place now called Button Island. Looking through a glass I saw that two of the natives in them were washing their faces, while the rest were paddling with might and main: I was then sure that some of our acquaintances were there, and in a few minutes recognized Tommy Button, Jemmy's brother. In the other canoe was a face which I knew yet could not name. "It must be some one I have seen before," said I,—when his sharp eye detected me, and a sudden movement of his hand to his head (as a sailor touches his hat) at once told me it was indeed Jemmy Button—but how altered!

Jemmy, like his companions, was stark naked and "wretchedly thin". But he could still speak English and he dressed to sit down with FitzRoy for dinner, at which he used his knife and fork like an English gentleman. He told FitzRoy that York, supported by some of his brothers, had stolen all his possessions and paddled off with them in a large canoe, taking Fuegia with them.

Jemmy was not, it seems, especially distressed. He was living with his family, and a young wife, at a safer spot than Wulaia. He had "plenty birdies", "plenty fruits" and "ten guanaco in snow time" and he was wealthy enough to give FitzRoy a gift of a bow and a quiver full of arrows, and to present him with two fine otter skins—one for FitzRoy, one for Bennett, the bosun—as well as two spear heads for Darwin.

FitzRoy reflected that Jemmy, as a solitary representative of the civilized world, was powerless to change the habits of his people. He decided against leaving Matthews for another attempt at establishing a mission and as they said goodbye once again, the captain's only hope was that "perhaps a shipwrecked seaman may hereafter receive help and kind treatment from Jemmy Button's children."

Darwin's remarks on the Fuegians go beyond the sentimental and the particular. He ponders the distance in mental ability between a Fuegian and Isaac Newton and wonders: "Whence have these people come? Have they remained in the state since the creation of the world? What could have tempted a tribe of men leaving the fine regions of the North to travel down the Cordilleras the backbone of America, to invent & build canoes, & then to enter upon one of the most inhospitable countries in the world?"

We should read these questions both as the musings of a proto-anthropologist and as the interrogations of a mind attuned to geological history. For Darwin was asking the same questions about the sea shells he found on the plains of Patagonia, and in both the *Diary* and especially in the *Voyage of the Beagle* we can hear a mind edging towards a theory of natural selection:

> In the cases where we can trace the extinction of a species through man, either wholly or in one limited district, we know that it becomes rarer and rarer, and is then lost: it would be difficult to point out any just distinction between a species destroyed by man or by the increase of its natural enemies. The evidence of rarity preceding extinction, is more striking in the successive tertiary strata, as remarked by several able observers; it has often been found that a shell very common in a tertiary stratum is now most rare, and has even long been thought extinct. If then, as appears probable, species first become rare and then extinct— if the too rapid increase of every species, even the most favoured, is steadily checked, as we must admit, though how and when it is hard to say—and if we see, without the smallest surprise, though unable to assign the precise reason, one species abundant and another closely allied species rare in the same district—why should we feel such great astonishment at the rarity being carried one step further to extinction? An action going on, on every side of us, and yet barely appreciable, might surely be carried a little further, without exciting our observation. Who would feel any great surprise at hearing that the Magalonyx was formerly rare compared with the Megatherium, or that one of the fossil monkeys was few in number compared with one of the now living

343.—Un Yapoo Tekeenica (Fueguino) frente a su choza. Dibujo del natural, por C. Martens, del buque "Beagle".

monkeys? and yet in this comparative rarity, we should have the plainest evidence of less favourable conditions for their existence. To admit that species generally become rare before they become extinct—to feel no surprise at the comparative rarity of one species with another, and yet to call in some extraordinary agent and to marvel greatly when a species ceases to exist, appears to me much the same as to admit that sickness in the individual is the prelude to death—to feel no surprise at sickness—but when the sick man dies to wonder, and to believe that he died through violence.

The potential of the land—its potential for science—is played off against its deathliness and dereliction. In his entry in *Voyage of the Beagle* for 22 April 1834, Darwin writes: "The country remained the same, and was extremely uninteresting. The complete similarity of the productions throughout Patagonia is one of its most striking characters. The level plains of arid shingle support the same stunted and dwarf plants; and in the valleys the same thorn-bearing bushes grow. Everywhere we see the same birds and insects. Even the very banks of the river and of the clear streamlets which entered it, were scarcely enlivened by a brighter tint of green. The curse of sterility is on the land, and the water flowing over a bed of pebbles partakes of the same curse. Hence the number of waterfowl is very scanty; for there is nothing to support life in the stream of this barren river."

Two days later he reflects that "like the navigators of old when approaching an unknown land, we examined and watched for the most trivial sign of a change. The drifted trunk of a tree, or a boulder of primitive rock, was hailed with joy, as if we had seen a forest growing on the flanks of the Cordillera."

The Origin of Species, which dealt the fatal blow to revealed religion, is shot through with a quasi-missionary zeal and a fierce will to believe in the evidence of nature; the *Voyage of the Beagle*, which might have been the romantic record of a young man's rite of passage, is primarily a precise, often pedantic, account of empirical observations. In Patagonia especially, Darwin worked hard to describe, to give life, colour and meaning to the most godforsaken landscapes he had ever seen. When the soil offered only a repellent blank, he dug beneath the surface to give the land history and depth.

THE LONG WAKE

The second *Beagle* voyage was a daring, dramatic undertaking, and though the discovery of variation in finches on Galapagos Islands was later popularized as a scientific watershed, Patagonia represented a highly significant stage of the trip. Its chief legacy was a scientific insight that would change man's perception of the world and his place in it. Even during Darwin's lifetime, his volume of the *Narrative* outsold the volumes collated and written by FitzRoy many times over. The publication of *The Origin of Species* on 24 November 1859 revolutionized the history of thought across all disciplines. It propelled Darwin into the tiny group of truly world-famous thinkers and made Darwinism the orthodoxy among scientists and, eventually, western society as a whole.

Darwin later reflected on the importance of the *Beagle* voyage: "As far as I can judge of myself I worked to the utmost during the voyage from the mere pleasure of investigation, and from my strong desire to add a few facts to the great mass of facts in natural science." Where Paley had found an intricately designed watch on his imaginary beach, Darwin had found a seeming chaos of geological data. But Darwin also confessed that the voyage had affected his soul:

> Whilst on board the Beagle I was quite orthodox, and I remember being heartily laughed at by several of the officers (though themselves orthodox) for quoting the Bible as an unanswerable authority on some point... But I had gradually come... to see that the Old Testament from its manifestly false history of the world... from its attributing to God the feelings of a revengeful tyrant, was no more to be trusted than the sacred books of the Hindoos, or the beliefs of any barbarian.

Some four decades after the *Beagle* experience Darwin continued to reflect on his time with the Fuegian natives. Jemmy Button makes an appearance in *The Descent of Man* (1871), where he is portrayed as a remarkably enlightened "intermediate" primitive who "with justifiable pride, stoutly maintained that there was no devil in his land."

FitzRoy's legacy is a complex affair. He produced maps of lasting importance, and his navigational acuity and weather observation techniques were peerless. The creation of the British Meteorological Office in 1854 was a direct consequence of FitzRoy's conscientious, courageous work on the high seas of the South Atlantic and in the shallow, rock-strewn bays of Patagonia and Tierra del Fuego.

There were other, more personal consequences to emerge from the voyage, and from his meeting with Darwin. In 1837 FitzRoy was awarded a gold medal by the Royal Geographical Society. In the same year he noted in his diary, "Is it not extraordinary, that sea-worn, rolled, shingle-stones and alluvial accumulations, compose the greater portion of these plains? How vast, and of what immense duration, must have been the actions of these waters which smoothed the shingle-stones now buried in the deserts of Patagonia!"

Yet during the next two years, while working on the *Narrative*, something changed in his mind. FitzRoy admits to having read books "by geologists who contradict, by implication, if not in plain terms, the authenticity of the scriptures" and that "while led away by skeptical ideas and knowing extremely little of the Bible, one of my remarks to a friend was 'this could never have been effected by a forty days' flood'." Fearing that such ideas might infect the minds of young sailors, he asserts his commitment to a literal reading of the Bible, using two main arguments: one, that the rock layers containing sea shells aree proof of Noah's Flood; two, that if the six days of creation were in fact aeons, the grasses and trees would have died out during the long nights.

The man who had given Lyell's geologizing handbook to Darwin had become a Christian fundamentalist. He may have spent long hours during the voyage reading the Bible, with the awesome tempests outside adding their own force to the doom-laden prophecies of the Old Testament. His manic-depressive tendencies surely also played a part. In 1836 he married Mary Henrietta O'Brien, who may have been an influence, though there is almost nothing in the way of letters to indicate that she was a religious fanatic.

FitzRoy's career moved on. He became a Member of Parliament and then governor of New Zealand and after worked in a steam shipping firm, but never mastered any of these occupations in the way he had the office of ship's captain. In December 1859 he entered into correspondence in the columns of *The Times*, under the pen-name "Senex" ("old man") refuting claims by paleontologists that flint axes found on the banks of the River Somme were 14,000 years old. FitzRoy argued that the Bible's own dates were the literal truth, following the genealogies of the Bible in the manner of Archbishop James Ussher, which date the world as a mere 6,000 years old.

In his engaging biography *Evolution's Captain*, Peter Nichols describes FitzRoy's reaction to the sensation generated by *The Origin of Species*:

> Darwin sent a copy to FitzRoy, in recognition of their connection and the fact that, but for FitzRoy, there would have been no book—no Darwin as history was just beginning to perceive him. This was clear to both men, horribly so to FitzRoy. He had provided Darwin with the vehicle for his conclusions… FitzRoy hated the book. "My dear old friend," he wrote to Darwin, "I, at least, *cannot* find anything 'ennobling' in the thought of being a descendant of even the *most* ancient Ape."

During the next five years, FitzRoy, the man who had been appointed captain because of a suicide, struggled with awful depression. On Sunday morning, 30 April 1865, he went into his dressing room just before eight o' clock. He picked up a razor and cut his throat.

It is grimly fitting that a final, long-term consequence of FitzRoy's voyages would be the establishment of a Christian mission in Tierra del Fuego, and that the name of Jemmy Button would surface one more time in circumstances that dashed FitzRoy's earlier hopes that he might one day help a shipwrecked sailor.

Despite the tragic-comic farce of Matthews' first assault on the Fuegian soul, the mere fact that there was a corner of the planet where Stone-Age Fuegians existed was sufficient temptation to all puritans who believed naked tribes were a crude caricature of sin as well as to those well-meaning Christians who believed that nakedness was evidence that here was an antediluvian society.

In 1841 Christian convert Allen Gardiner visited the Falkland Islands in order to explore the idea of establishing missions in nearby Patagonia and Tierra del Fuego. He returned to England to garner support and to establish, in 1844, the Patagonian Missionary Society. Gardiner and a group of amateur missionaries sailed out to Tierra del Fuego in 1850 with the aim of creating a floating mission that would roam the coasts, preaching to the native tribes and employing Jemmy as their translator and co-preacher. The men died of scurvy and starvation at Spanish Harbour (now Bahía Aguirre) in 1851.

The Secretary of the Patagonian Missionary Society, Canon G. Pakenham Despard, determined to persevere with the work of the mission and had a schooner built and named the *Allen Gardiner*. In 1854 a mission station was built on Keppel Island in the West Falklands, and over the next five years it made contact with the Fuegians, distributing food and clothes, and guiding them in Bible and agricultural instruction. Several of the missionaries learned the Yahgan language.

Amazingly, they were able to locate Jemmy—now in his forties—and they persuaded him to spend several months on the Falklands, along with his wife and children. Several other natives joined the Buttons on the voyage.

Everything seemed to be going well. The first party of Fuegians duly returned to their homeland, and a second group of nine natives—one of Jemmy's grown-up sons among them—was taken to the Falklands. But when this second party returned to Wulaia in October 1859 the whole scheme fell apart. It seems that, in an effort to clamp down on theft, the natives had been searched before being allowed to disembark, and that a number of stolen items were recovered. Then, when the captain and crew of the *Allen Gardiner* went ashore unarmed, they were massacred by the natives. The cook escaped in a dinghy and was eventually rescued alive to tell the tale. Jemmy was transferred to the Falklands to give evidence at an inquiry, but no punitive action was taken and he was allowed to return to Wulaia. The official conclusion of the Falklands authorities was that the missionaries had been naïve and had brought down disaster upon themselves. Jemmy died in 1864 in an epidemic of a measles-like disease brought in by sailors.

News of the slaughter reached England in May 1860 but received scant attention in the press. John and Mary Gribbin, in their biography *FitzRoy*, believe that "news of the killings and of Jemmy Button's part in them must have reached FitzRoy… just at the time when he was already upset by the publication of the *Origin* and feeling guilt about his part in providing Darwin with the material on which the theory of natural selection was based."

In 1863 the Rev. Waite Stirling joined the team on Keppel Island, and subsequent attempts at establishing stations, at Leuaia and Ushuaia, were more successful. In 1864 the Patagonian Missionary Society became the South American Missionary Society. By the 1870s many of the local

Fuegians had converted to Christianity; however, the native population dwindled to such an extent over the next couple of decades that the Fuegian mission was closed down in the opening years of the twentieth century.

For his efforts, Stirling, who liked to refer to himself as "God's Lonely Sentinel", was summoned to London to be consecrated as Bishop of the Falkland Islands. Until well into the twentieth century the Bishop of the Falkland Islands had Episcopal authority over the whole of South America.

Despard brought with him his thirteen-year-old adopted son, Thomas Bridges, who was to learn the Yahgan language and take Christian-Fuegian relations to a new level, even while observing the by then inevitable disintegration of the native culture.

There have been a number of retellings of the Jemmy Button drama—most of them along the lines of fictionalized histories. In Spanish the best known are Chilean author Benjamin Subercaseaux's *Jemmy Button* (1954), Eduardo Belgrano Rawson's *Fuegia* (1991) and Sylvia Iparraguirre's *Tierra del Fuego* (1998). English-language versions include Nick Hazlewood's *Savage* (2000), Richard Lee Marks' *Three Men of the Beagle* (1991) and Harry Thomson's 625-page *This Thing of Darkness* (2005), which takes its title from *The Tempest* (Act V, Scene I: "This thing of darkness I acknowledge mine."

The proliferation of re-workings should come as no surprise. The FitzRoy-Darwin-Button story incorporates heroic discovery, scientific revolution, exotic visitors and romance. Did FitzRoy fall in love with Fuegia? What did he and Philos talk about in the captain's cabin as the storms blasted outside? Did York ever manage to escape the glare of the vicar's wife and visit a whore in Hackney? It is remarkable that there has never been a blockbuster film of the tale. Perhaps Hollywood will focus on the Darwin-FitzRoy drama instead, though one can only imagine how Bible-wielding atavists would protest at the screening of *Creation: the Movie* or *The Scientist and the Sailor*.

OTHER TOMBS

Darwin's tomb is in Westminster Abbey. FitzRoy's grave can be visited in the churchyard of All Saints, Upper Norwood, in south London; a Grade II listed monument, it was restored in 1997. Down by the Magellan Strait on a forsaken strip of land above Port Famine is the lonely grave of Captain

Pringle Stokes who, as the inscription on the beech wood cross tells us, "died from the effects of the anxieties and hardships incurred whilst surveying the western shores of Tierra del Fuego."

Chapter Seven

Y WLADFA:
THE WELSH IN PATAGONIA

"Ni gawsom wlad sydd well   "We've found a better land
Yn y Deheudir pell,   In the far South.
Patagonia yw: It is Patagonia.
Cawn yno fyw mewn hedd,   We will live there in peace
Heb ofni brad na chledd,   Without fear of treachery or war,
A Chymro ar y sedd: With a Welshman on the throne.
Boed mawl i Dduw."   Praise be to God."

Verse sung on board the *Mimosa*, quoted in R. Bryn Williams,
Gwladfa Patagonia

The province of Chubut is named after the river that flows through it, the Tehuelche word for which was *chupat*, meaning "transparent". Perhaps the natives were struck by the gleaming vitality of the river in this dry, dusty land, and by the thin, meandering line of green that accompanies it on its

500-mile journey from Carreras in the Andes to Playa Unión near Rawson, where it meets the Atlantic. Or perhaps in their tireless wanderings they had been to the upper reaches of the river where the water is cool and crystalline.

During the seventeenth and eighteenth centuries some of the early settlers used the word *Chupat*. Among them were Spanish missionaries, including Jesuit father Nicolás Mascardi who discovered the Nahuel Huapi lake in 1670. Since *Chupat* sounds like *chupar*, the Spanish verb "to drink"—as in alcohol—the name was at some stage modified to Chubut.

In the mid-eighteenth century the San José fort was established at Península Valdés—at around the same time Carmen de Patagones was founded—but repeated raids by tribesmen led to the project being soon abandoned. A hundred years later the desert above the Chubut valley was still without any kind of fixed settlement. Only the Tehuelche knew how to survive on its meagre resources—berries, guanacos, rheas, foxes—and how to eke out an existence on its wind-blasted wastes.

The "Gwladfa" Project

The nineteenth-century booms in metal, slate and coal mining had a devastating effect on agricultural communities in Wales and led to social conflict between workers and their English bosses. In the 1830s and 1840s riots broke out in both rural and urban areas. A government inquiry into the state of education in Wales, carried out by three English commissioners who spoke no Welsh, concluded that the Welsh were ignorant, idle and immoral, and that the main causes of their turpitude were the Welsh language and nonconformity. The 1536 Act of Union had banned Welsh monoglot speakers from public office; the language was increasingly under pressure in the workplaces and in academic spheres, and by 1870 children were forbidden to speak Welsh in schools.

There were very few Welsh national institutions. Although the Calvinistic Methodists were organized along all-Wales lines, the established Church consisted of four westerly bishoprics of the archdiocese of Canterbury, with the Congregationalists and Baptists having virtually no central organization. The Welsh legal system—the Courts of Great Session—was abolished in 1830, making the legal and administrative structure of Wales identical to that of England.

The idea of establishing a specifically "Welsh" community in another part of the world emerged at the beginning of the seventeenth century. Several attempts were made—remote and scarcely populated Newfoundland proved a popular choice for aspiring colonists—but none was entirely successful. By the 1840s, the notion of an isolated settlement was more widely discussed as emigration from Wales reached unprecedented levels and long-established Welsh communities in the United States became aware of the gradual disappearance of their national characteristics. The 1849 Gold Rush tempted many to the promising new states of California and Wisconsin, but Australia, New Zealand, Brazil and Uruguay were also viable options for Welsh migrants. In 1850, 200 Welsh settlers were enticed to the fertile pampas of Rio Grande do Sul in southern Brazil. But since Argentina was also opening its borders to mass immigration, it became an attractive possibility too.

The origins of the Patagonian venture can be traced to 1856, when a society was formed in Camptonville, California, with the aim of promoting the creation of a Welsh settlement. At the society's inaugural meeting, Patagonia was suggested for the first time as a possible location. A circular letter was sent to Welsh newspapers to appeal for support in Wales, and nonconformist minister Michael D. Jones responded by organising a public meeting in Bala.

After travelling widely in the US in the late 1840s, Jones had seen how Welsh people, by reason of their language, were always at a disadvantage. Over time the cultural identity of all emigrants was diluted and, he believed, the result would be a loss of religion. The answer he proposed was an entirely Welsh settlement (*Wladfa*) free of external control. Jones thus provided the New Wales project with an ideological foundation. As Glyn Williams writes in *The Welsh in Patagonia*: "The propaganda campaign which aimed to encourage potential emigrants to choose Patagonia as their destination was not only couched in terms of the conventional relationship between emigration and opportunity but was also a concerted political campaign against the existing social, political and economic situation in Wales itself."

In 1861 an Emigration Society was established, and after perusing FitzRoy's journal, the members decided that the lower Chubut valley would be a suitable location for a settlement. They had the backing of the Argentinian consul in Liverpool and also of Argentina's influential interior minister Guillermo Rawson. Funds were raised, a proposal to the Argentinian government was drafted and two delegates were elected: Liverpool typographer Lewis Jones and Rugby- and Oxford-educated Welsh landowner Sir Thomas Duncombe Love Jones Parry, who put up at least £750 of his own money to sponsor the colony. Michael D. Jones' wife Anne had a private fortune and contributed the bulk of the funds for this first trip.

In late 1862 they sailed—on separate ships—for the Chubut valley, stopping over in Buenos Aires en route. It is probable they were only authorized by the Argentinian government to travel as far as the lower reaches of the Río Negro, then the limit of government-controlled territory, but sailed on past Carmen, to an inlet FitzRoy had claimed was calm and serviceable for anchoring ships. This they referred to as New Bay (Golfo Nuevo).

According to Abraham Matthews, one of the chief chroniclers of the early stages of the Welsh colony, Lewis Jones and Love Jones Parry "went up a river a little and had a glance at the valley." Then they sailed to Buenos Aires and signed a draft agreement that would enable the Welsh to send some two to three thousand families to Patagonia during the following decade, with the assurance that all would obtain titles to land. The agreement they signed with the Argentine authorities was rejected by Congress by 21 votes to five, but they could fall back on another land law passed in 1862 that granted 124 acres to all settler families. There was no promise of autonomy and no explicit material support from the Argentinian government.

Undeterred, Lewis Jones and Love Jones Parry, now back in Wales, regrouped with the Emigration Society and began to look for settlers. It is not clear whether prospective emigrants were told of the Congress' decision not to give any special recognition to the Welsh colony, as this was hardly likely to generate enthusiasm. But Lewis Jones had great faith in Rawson, and travelled around Wales giving lectures while Michael D. Jones published a leaflet promoting emigration. Their focus was on industrial areas, and the greatest number of emigrants came from Mountain Ash, Aberdare, Rhosllanerchrugog and Ffestiniog in Wales, and from Liverpool and Birkenhead on the Mersey. Anne Jones' money was made available as credit for the purchase of a vessel. Soon there were about 200 emigrants on the list, ready to disembark in April 1865. But then negative reports on Patagonia appeared in two newspapers, one in the US, the other in North Wales. Most likely the notices were a counter-campaign intended to induce prospective emigrants to opt for North America, but some people were also familiar with Darwin and other writers who had written of an arid, inhospitable land; in any case, names began to drop off the list.

Still, after forceful pro-colony campaigns led by Michael D. Jones, a 447-ton tea clipper, the *Mimosa*, was chartered and a May 1865 departure was scheduled. The ship was not suitable for passengers, so Anne Jones was once again asked to provide funds (Matthews estimates £2,500, a fortune at the time) to cover the reconditioning costs, as well as a lifeboat.

Three months before the emigrants set out from Liverpool, Lewis Jones and Edwyn Roberts were sent to prepare for their arrival. When they reached Carmen de Patagones, Jones was able to persuade some merchants to let him have provisions and animals on credit. They also arranged for 500 sheep to be driven down from the pampas—but raids by natives meant that many of these were lost.

On 10 June, the two men sailed south on the schooner *Juno* and landed at a wide bay just south of Argentina's Península Valdés, which they baptized officially New Bay. When the depleted flocks arrived, Jones decided to head north and collect a second load, leaving Roberts on the desolate shore with four of his men. While they waited, the men decided to dig a well for fresh water, for which one of them was stationed at the bottom to fill the bucket with earth. One day, when it was Roberts' turn to man the bucket, the men went on strike and left him down there while they got drunk. The alcohol fortunately stirred compassion in one of the men and Roberts was finally allowed up.

On the evening of 28 May the *Mimosa* sailed out of Liverpool for the coast of northern Patagonia. On board the vessel were 153 Welsh men, women and children, all carrying all their possessions and a dream of creating a New Wales.

GLANIAD: THE LANDING

On 28 July 1865 the *Mimosa* made landfall at New Bay. A number of children had died during the voyage and others had been born. When they set foot on dry land most of the passengers were in good spirits.

Yet what they saw on disembarking was rather less than a paradise found. In the words of one settler, "The region is poor, very poor for trees; a lot less than Caleb [probably Lewis Jones] said." Another colonist wrote to his wife: "You may be of the opinion that it's not possible to be happy here." Shortly afterwards, Lewis Jones returned aboard another vessel, a schooner called the *Mary Ellen*, with a new supply of horses, cattle and sheep. This was to be the settlers' last contact with the outside world for many months.

No one had considered that the Welsh were arriving in the middle of winter and that there would therefore be no prospect of a harvest for a whole year. The land was dry, cold and hard, and there was literally nothing to be done. The beach was featureless and desolate. There were no houses or people, no roads or tracks, and hardly any landmarks. On the day of the landing one young man, David Williams, went up a hill to take in the view and never came back—he was probably tired and disoriented and so perished wandering off across the plains in the wrong direction.

Things got worse. There was no clear plan for travelling overland to the river valley—a journey of about forty miles. During the enforced delay some people decided to try to sow wheat fields, but these were doomed as it hardly ever rained on the bay and the land was unsuitable. Even milking the Argentinian cows was a challenge as they were used to roaming wild on the pampas, where they were reared by the gauchos only for their hides and tallow.

William Jones of Bala sent a letter about the first few days to his "dear uncle and friends" dated 7 November 1865. It was published in the Welsh press in 1867 and this version reads:

> I have never been so disappointed by anything. The region is nothing like we read and heard about it before and I must say that [name omitted] has told tremendous lies about the region.
>
> Well, I'll tell you myself about the area, as I see it, after travelling hundreds of miles in several directions, by day and by night. When we disembarked in New Bay all we could see were dunes covered in some kind of short, spiky grass, like the ones you see in Wales, with an old, sterile appearance. Then we saw two or three people with buckets on their shoulders who were going to dig in search of water, but the water was very salty, almost as salty as the sea...
>
> It's an almost infinite plain, without trees or rocks, only different types of grasses and bushes, some reaching above head-height, so it is

very difficult to move around and only the luckiest comes out of it with their skin intact…

There are neither cattle nor the wild horses that we heard about, not even one, nor wild animals of any kind… There are lots of wild sheep [guanacos] but no one to catch them.

…But the worst thing here are the men, the clumsiest and most useless bunch that ever could have come together. Most of them are coal miners and salesmen with no experience of working the land…

…Money has no more value than the stones as regards progress, as there is nothing to buy.

No sooner had the new settlers christened their new home on the beach Porth Madryn—after Love Jones Parry's estate at Nefyn on the northwest coast of Wales—than they decided to move on. Most of the men made their way overland through the arid plains. Stunted bushes of thorn and tufts of dark-coloured grasses made crossing difficult, and there were no trails. Their thirst was intolerable and many were compelled to wet their lips using their own urine. The women and children, meanwhile, were taken to the river aboard the *Mary Ellen* and nearly starved in the process.

The new settlement at the mouth of the river, named Rawson (now the provincial capital of Chubut) was founded on 15 September 1865 when it was visited by Colonel Julián Murga, who arrived a few weeks after the first settlers to raise the Argentinian flag. But it was October before many families reached the river and most had to wait weeks or even months before they were allocated their holdings. These were traced out close to each other for fear of raids bythe indigenous Tehuelche.

NATIVE KNOW-HOW
Summer passed and all the sheep had either escaped or perished. The charity of the Argentinian government permitted the Welsh to buy a small boat, essential supplies and seeds. Yet the settlers were not farmers, and sowed wheat according to where the vegetation looked greenest. Nor had they the skills to hunt animals such as the guanaco, rhea or Patagonian cavies. They occasionally shot a bird or rodent, but probably more through luck than judgment since only a handful of the men could use a rifle. They began to build shelter from the elements, but they were living on borrowed time, and without urgent help the colony was doomed.

In July 1866 they were visited by tribesmen. In exchange for three bottles of gin and a mere whiff of cognac (being Presbyterians they had not brought a profusion of liquor) the natives gave the settlers meat. The nomads also taught the newcomers to turn to hunting for their subsistence and to raise funds by exporting feathers and skins to Buenos Aires. The Welsh never needed to build a single defensive bulwark around their settlement—and this at a time when bands of native warriors were carrying our raids and murdering and looting a few hundred miles to the north.

This was a remarkable state of affairs. As Geraint D. Owen writes in *Crisis in Chubut* (1977):

> Nowhere did the colonists display greater shrewdness and humanity than in their relations with the Indians of Patagonia. At the outbreak of the Indian troubles in 1868, the Government had seen fit to provide the Welsh with rifles and ammunition, and to instruct them in the organization of militia. The weapons were never used except for hunting. Strong ties of friendship developed between the Patagonian Indians and the Welsh, which were not wholly commendable in the eyes of the Argentinian Government, but which materially benefited the colonists when their position seemed untenable.

It is also surprising how open the nomads were to the idea of a permanent colony in the valley, especially when one considers that only a few years before around 1,500 Araucanian and pampas natives had attacked Bahía Blanca. The situation may have been helped by the fact that the Argentinian government paid compensation to the Tehuelche, but it seems that they also valued the opportunity to trade with a fixed post in this region rather than having to travel as far as Carmen de Patagones.

Not all was peace and harmony, however. In 1871 a group of natives entered the camp during the night and made away with sixty or so horses, many of which were used for tilling the land as well as serving as a means of transport.

Nothing caused the Welsh more trouble than the shortage of water. In general, the early years were extremely tough as crops failed due to a lack of rain. To make matters worse, periods of drought were followed by flooding. Heavy rains meant that most—and occasionally all—of the valley would, every four to six years, be inundated. But the bursting of the banks suggested a possible solution to the aridity of the farmlands. The settlers, led by Aaron Jenkins—whose wife Rachel proposed the systematic use of canals—soon established Argentina's first ever irrigation system, digging deep troughs that extended three or four miles to each side of a fifty-mile stretch of river.

However trying the material circumstances, much of the anguish felt by the settlers was spiritual. Welsh folktales and mythologies, many of them derived from Celtic literature, abound in images of a barren wilderness. For the Celtic saints, the deserts were a place of trial and toil, endured by the faithful in order to facilitate direct communication with God. One settler is said to have described his new homeland thus: "If God made the earth, the devil made Patagonia and he made it as like his own special home as two pies." Some of the colonists decided to return to their homeland or move to other countries.

Enormous difficulties had to be overcome in order to move produce, or indeed to travel at all. It took six to eight hours to ride from the riverbank to Puerto Madryn. Unshod, the horses became lame after around 150 miles. Nonetheless, while the Tehuelche educated the Welsh in hunting and fishing techniques and exchanged game, horses or ostrich feathers for bread and sugar, a rudimentary local economy evolved. Over the first decade significant progress was made in the lower Chubut valley and the colony achieved a degree of self-sufficiency in the production of cheese, barley, wool and alfalfa. According to Geraint Owen, "In 1876 the colony was able to boast that its exports of wheat, butter, seal-skins... and other commodities had reached the respectable total of £7000. The colony could relax enough to hold annual Eisteddfodau, and regard its initial miseries and privations as things of the past by celebrating its 'Gwyl y Glaniad' (The Festival of the First Landing) with concerts, races and other pleasant distractions."

Expansion and Exploration

Between 1874 and 1876, 500 newcomers arrived from Wales and a further 27 migrants from New York. There was an almost continuous trickle of immigrants over the coming years, with peaks in 1880-81, 1885 and, to a lesser extent, in 1907-10. Flour mills and other agricultural machinery were imported from the US. By 1885 wheat production had reached 6,000 tons, with grain samples produced by the colony winning gold medals at international expositions in Paris and Chicago.

During the 1870s and 1880s chapels were built, companies were created and a co-operative society was established in 1885 to handle exports to Buenos Aires and beyond. Towards the second half of 1886 a steamer called the *Vesta* docked, bringing 465 further immigrants who had been contracted to work on a railway line from the Chubut valley to New Bay. The project was envisioned as a means of exploiting the increased yields in the valley, but in reality the tonnages of grain involved, the infrequency of harvests and the fact that there was unlikely to be any demand from passengers made the line something of a white elephant. As Lewis Jones once again played a central role, the new railhead was named Trelew (or Lewis Town) after him (the official foundation date of the town is considered to be 20 October 1884, when the National Congress passed the law to build the railway).

Newspapers were published. The first were *Y Brut*, which appeared in manuscript form in early 1868, *Seren Patagonia*, in August of the same year, and *Ein Breiniad*, which followed in 1878. All of these were short-lived and unable to build up local support. In 1891, however, Lewis Jones founded *Y Drafod* as a Welsh weekly which survived as such until 1961. (Today it is published as a quarterly, mostly in Spanish.)

The settlers christened the Chubut valley Afon Camwy (or Vale of the Twisting River). New settlements were established at Gaiman and Dolavon (Welsh for "meadow" and "river" respectively).

As early as the 1870s some of the Welsh had travelled north and west in search of new pastures and, on at least one occasion, on a quest for gold. The exploratory escapade of one group, which had returned not via the valley but by heading north-north-east across sixty miles of desolate plain, was mythologized locally as *Hirdaith Edwyn* (Edwyn's long journey).

From the 1880s onward parties of Welsh men—sometimes accompanied by Argentinian officials and Tehuelche guides—regularly travelled up the valley of the Chubut river. These expeditionary teams had regular contact with bands of natives led by some of the leading *caciques*—Galats, Sac-Mata, Chiquichan, Foyel and Saihueque—and most of the encounters were peaceful.

In 1885, following a spate of poor harvests, a public meeting was organized in Gaiman. The Welsh settlers sent an official letter to Luis J. Fontana, Chubut's first governor, requesting his support for a scheme to find suitable land for a new settlement in the foothills of the Andes. An ex-

pedition into that region was also seen as an opportunity to search for valuable minerals and metals.

The expedition was to be led by John Daniel Evans, an accomplished rider and trail-finder. In 1884 he had had what was regarded as a miraculous escape when he and three of his friends were attacked by indigenous tribesmen. The other three men were mutilated and killed, but Evans escaped on his horse Malacara, who made a courageous leap down a steep slope and into a deep canyon. The place where they were attacked is known as the Valley of the Martyrs.

Evans' group began its long journey across the plains on 16 October 1885. At Cwm Hyfryd ("Pleasant Valley") they arrived in a landscape that actually looked like Wales. This became the site of another Welsh settlement, named in Spanish Colonia 16 de Octubre. The towns of Trevelin (1875) and Esquel (1906) were founded. Both Trevelin and Cwm Hyfryd became so successful agriculturally that the Chileans began to take an interest. Rainfall on the western slopes of the Andes feeds the rivers that flow through the valley. If strict watershed rules were followed, the Chileans argued, Cwm Hyfryd would be a part of Chile. In 1902 a plebiscite was organized by the settlers and by a vast majority they decided that they would prefer to be a part of Argentina rather than Chile.

Evens settled in Trevelin. Outside his house a gravestone reads, in Spanish:

HERE LIE THE REMAINS OF
MY HORSE, MALACARA, WHO
SAVED MY LIFE DURING THE
ATTACK OF THE INDIANS IN
THE VALLEY OF THE MARTYRS
ON THE 4-3-1884 AS I WAS
RETURNING FROM THE
CORDILLERA
R.I.P.
JOHN D. EVANS

As the Welsh began to roam and explore, their sons' attitudes to settlement changed. Around 1900 one poet penned a verse about what he called the "Welsh Argentinian", and it is clear that the native gaucho was a role model:

He is a Welshman of blood and kindred,
But he speaks a rough Spanish;
He boasts that he has no taste
For his mother tongue on his lip.

The Welsh gaucho in the poem carries a whip and boasts a belly full of strong drink and empty pockets. The author praises his bravery and horsemanship, contrasting it with the drudgery of farm work:

He was not author nor bard
Or musician, gentleman or tramp
And yet he is talented, and handsome
In the growth of the plains tradition
At an eisteddfod or chapel he never shows.
About religion he cares but little.
His all is the "Asaw"
And a mare that can run like the wind.

BECOMING A MINORITY

In 1890 there were 2,500 Welshmen living in Gaiman and Rawson and their environs, and about 100 Argentinian officials. Four years later the population had grown to 3,000, but the new arrivals were mainly other foreigners, mostly Italians. At the same time, the British government campaigned to stimulate migration to Canada, Australia and South Africa, as opposed to Argentina.

In addition, Argentina's immigration policy was being modified and it was believed that the predominance of one community in a specific area could threaten national unity. This belief was not prompted by any incident in the Chubut valley but rather by rumours of a projected insurrection by Italians in Buenos Aires.

Today, the town which has best preserved its Welsh connections is Gaiman, where an annual Eisteddfod is held and where "Welsh teas" are served every afternoon in a dozen quaint tea shops. Part of the Argentinian tourist trail, the Welsh colony is also regarded as a major element in Patagonia's myth-riddled history; it seems not quite to belong here, its survival confounds ordinary historians, and it offers a peculiar link to the Mersey, to Liverpool and to the Welsh heartland.

By 1920 Welsh immigration had ceased and the Chubut valley, now green and pleasant, was home to a new wave of immigrants, mainly from southern Europe. The Welsh clung to the Bible (their children were baptized with names from the Old and New Testaments) and their cultural past; one observer described the Welsh group as Argentinian by birth but Welsh by sentiment. These were the "Us", still living on farms dotted along the riverbank, while the "Them" were Catholics settled in the built-up areas and adapting rapidly to the Argentinian way of life. This division is still felt in the Chubut valley.

MYTHOLOGIES AND MISCREANTS

Between 1814 and 1914 about 100,000 Welsh people left their country and headed for pastures new, mainly to the US, Australia or New Zealand. Yet, as a source of popular myth and nationalist idealism, the Patagonian settlement has been more significant than any of these. Certainly the dedicated cultural output, from books and pamphlets to websites and Welsh-language television documentaries, has been hugely disproportionate to both the numbers of Welsh people involved in the Argentinian *Gwladfa* and its relevance to Latin American history and culture.

Several books have rendered the Welsh narrative in purely heroic terms. The two "Bibles" of Welsh Patagonian history are Abraham Matthews' *Hanes y Wladfa Gymreig yn Patagonia* (1894) and *Y Wladva Gymreig yn Ne Amerig* (1898) by Lewis Jones. These chronicles are gritty and largely free of nationalistic zeal or religiosity, and yet manage to imbue the Welsh adventure with an almost mythic heroism. One of the ploys used by Matthews is to introduce Biblical colour when writing about the Tehuelche: "We read in the Bible that Elisha wore a hairy cape of leather and a leather loincloth. Isn't it also true that John the Baptist wore a similar garment?... They live in tents, as they are called in the Bible, as the Israelites lived in the wilderness."

Matthews was a preacher—for a spell the colony's only preacher—and scriptural references are to be expected. But he skips quickly over obstacles and mistakes, excusing the early blunders by invoking Lewis Jones' youthful passion for a new land. Above all, he, like many Welsh-language commentators, seeks to depict the colony as something unprecedented in history. The book—and the story *per se*—is a celebration of existence on the periphery. Exile is the route to the greater glory of the Chosen People. The Tehuelche, soon to be extinct, are the doomed doppelgangers of the Welsh. They can relate to one another because both communities have been persecuted, but only one will be elected to survive.

A modern version of this approach was adopted by R. Bryn Williams in 1965 when he provided the text for a short volume intended to look back on a century of Welsh culture in Patagonia:

> I have mentioned the thousands who had already emigrated from Wales, but this event was quite different. It is doubtful if there has ever been anything like it in the history of any country. Here we have a number of ordinary people venturing to an unexplored part of the world, without certain means of livelihood, and into the midst of primitive Indians, with only their dreams to lead them on and their faith to sustain them. And the little committee in Liverpool was attempting to establish a new country in the furthermost reaches of the earth with no practical experience of pioneering, having little or no knowledge of business, without support in Wales, and completely lacking in financial resources.

The very layout of Williams' book has a mythic structure, with chapter headings such as "The Landing" proceeding through "Quarrels" to a chapter called simply "The Flood". (With a few slight changes, it could easily be adapted to echo the Pentateuch.) But the "Indians" were not, in fact, as "primitive" as the planners and key players in the Welsh colony. At least they possessed the skills and know-how to make use of the land and centuries of contact with the climate and topography on which to make informed decisions about settlement and movement. The Welsh, for their part, were sometimes foolhardy and ignorant, and they were arguably misled by the men they most respected.

There is little doubt that the story of the Welsh in Patagonia has a symbolic value for nationalists. As Glyn Williams, in his *The Welsh in Patagonia*, says: "It is significant that Welsh speakers are far more familiar with this part of the nation's history than are those Welsh people who do not speak the language." Perhaps the real significance of the Patagonian Welsh colony resides in its uniqueness—or to phrase it less generously, in the simple fact that the Welsh in Britain have no other settlement they can look to when they wish to spin romantic, heroic narratives about overcoming hardship and keeping the faith with the divine Welsh tongue.

Eluned Morgan, the daughter of Lewis Jones, was born in 1870 on the ship *Myfanwy* en route to Patagonia (Morgan means "sea-born"). Between 1903 and 1908 she was educated in Wales and worked for a spell at the Cardiff Free Library. She started writing in order to enter the eisteddfod competitions in the Chubut valley, and is best known in Wales as the author of *Dringo'r Andes* (1904), about Patagonia, and *Plant yr Haul* (1915), about the Incas. She also wrote an account of a sea voyage from London to Patagonia, *Gwymon y Môr* (1909).

To date, *Dringo'r Andes* has not appeared in English but there is a Spanish translation by Irma Hughes de Jones, who edited *Y Drafod* for fifty years, published in Rawson as *Hacia los Andes* (1982). While Morgan is alert to the complexities of the Welsh presence in a region where all colonizers bear some responsibility for the oppression of the natives, she idealizes the relationship between the Welsh settlers and the Tehuelche as symbiotic and based on shared values.

DEMYTHOLOGIZERS AND DETRACTORS

In *Crisis in Chubut*, Geraint D. Owen portrays the Welsh settlement of the Chubut valley as a drawn-out tragedy of errors and disasters which ultimately led to such misery and disorder "that the desire of many of [the colonists] to resettle under British administration was strong enough to initiate a number of projects for their removal at the beginning of the present century." In a long chapter titled "Struggle and Disillusionment" Owen details the sequence of disasters: the lack of communication with the outside world; general economic instability and frequent catastrophe wreaked by the perennial floods; the absence of economic or even moral support from Buenos Aires; and colonization from other countries encouraged by the government of Julio A. Roca, which would, ultimately, erode the all-important homogeneity of the Welsh settlement.

Following severe floods in 1899, 1900 and 1901 the local economy went into a sustained slump and the community began to consider emigration from Chubut, first to Canada and later to South Africa. There was support—and pressure—for such a move not only from both of these countries (and from Britain) but also from the Welsh Patagonian Committee in Wales which viewed the settlement in Chubut as a potentially dreadful (not to mention embarrassing) humanitarian crisis as well as a futile waste of energy and industry.

In 1965, on the occasion of the centenary of the landing of the *Mimosa*, Welsh academic Bobi Jones (a.k.a. Professor Robert Maynard Jones) wrote an article in the Welsh-language current affairs monthly *Barn* under the title "Patagonian Farce":

> The Patagonian celebrations in Wales this year have been rather unreal. Many deceived themselves that the emigration has been a success, that it is wonderful to think that there is an exotic land beyond the Southern hemisphere where people preach in Welsh, that there is some future to Welshness in the shadow of the Andes. That is, we deceive ourselves that the emigration was worthy of note, that it has some historical value, and we inflate the whole thing to seem a significant element in our national life.

By 1965 the Welshness of the Chubut community was at the lowest point in a long curve of decline. Few spoke the language, chapel congregations had dwindled and economic gloom across Argentina had affected the Welsh too. Their co-operative company had gone bust, and there was no money for anything but a low-key annual eisteddfod and a barbecue.

The centenary did, however, prompt media coverage and some reflection among Welsh nationalists and cultural leaders. Since then there has been an increase in traffic between Wales and Patagonia: teachers are sent from the motherland to Afon Camwy to teach Welsh, Young Patagonian students are sent to Lampeter University and Trinity College, Camarthen, on cultural exchanges, and VIPs come and go between Trelew and Cardiff. In 1995 Princess Diana visited Gaiman's Ty Te Caerdydd teashop and, after a few songs by the local choir, ate a raspberry tart. On 31 August the town honours her memory. Sporting contests are held between the two nations and tourism has steadily increased since Bruce Chatwin profiled some of the local Welsh Argentinians in his *In Patagonia* (1977).

If there were dozens of Welsh colonies in South America no one would pay any attention to the communities strung along the Chubut river. But, at least from a distance, the *Wladfa* can be imagined as a huddle of hardy survivors spread out along a single green valley in the desert. Their presence is an affront to nature; they bring colour to a dun and dusty landscape. Speaking their exotic tongue beneath the Red Dragon and meeting in the cold Patagonian evenings to sing in choirs, the descendants of those who sailed on the *Mimosa*, the *Myfanwy*, the *Vesta* and all those early ships also challenge the Argentineness and the Englishness of Patagonia. They are, in fact, only the best known of many isolated immigrant colonies that settled and prospered across Patagonia: the Germans of Río Pico, the Boers of Sarmiento, the Yugoslavs of Punta Arenas. But the Welsh forged what amounts to a national epic from an enterprise that was, in the words of Alun Davies, "at once bold, bungling and rather magnificent". It is the bungling, somehow, that makes the story worth telling.

Chapter Eight

KING OF PATAGONIA:
ORLLIE ANTOINE AND THE
ARAUCANOS

"Les Indiens d'Araucanie et de Patagonie m'ont librement proclaimé
leur roi et ont adopté mon drapeau bleu, blanc et vert... Le Chili n'a
jamais eu aucun droit sur ces deux pays, ni par conquête, ni par submission volontaire."

Manifeste d'Orllie Antonie 1er (1863)

Pedro de Valdivia, sent by Pizarro to conquer and colonize Chile, led his
troops south of the Maule river in the early 1550s. He was able to establish a chain of fortified towns in the heavily forested region and at the
outset managed to subdue pockets of Mapuche settlement, rewarding his
soldiers by giving them use of the enslaved natives in finding and exploiting gold deposits. A few of the younger Mapuche, known to white men
as *araucanos* or Araucanians, were employed as grooms, and they quickly
learned to ride. Some stole horses and galloped to freedom, and a handful
formed their own cavalry units.

One of Valdivia's former pages, Lautaro, led his people in a general uprising in December 1553. They destroyed the fort at Tucapel and, when
Valdivia sent in troops, the Mapuche responded with renewed ferocity.
Valdivia was captured, and all the Spaniards were slain. The fact that no
one on the losing side survived to narrate the debacle has given Lautaro a
unique prominence in Chilean folklore. Neruda wrote that he "wore a suit
of lightning", and was the invincible, impossible father of the nation. There
are many versions of the final scene, when Lautaro captured and killed the
conquistador—the best known tells that, on the day of his execution,
molten gold was poured down Valdivia's throat.

From this period on, the Mapuche, of trans-Andean origin, began to
colonize areas of Argentinian Patagonia, transmitting their culture to other

native groups. This process, known as Araucanization, effectively swallowed up the scattered peoples of the pampas as well as groups of northern Tehuelche nomads and created a vast, loosely organized confederation with a common language and a basic canon of beliefs and customs. At the same time, many Mapuche had regular dealings with Spanish colonists, with whom they traded cattle and hand-woven textiles for ironware, cloth and trinkets. There were, however, numerous attempts by the colonial armies to penetrate further south and for 200 years there was mutual mistrust, and any peace deals that were struck between the two sides were fragile and limited.

By the middle of the eighteenth century Spain had grown weary of the tensions. Grudgingly, the authorities in Santiago de Chile were forced to accept that the natives of the southern lake region and beyond were *inencomendable*—a Castilian term to admit that their foes were too militant to be enslaved. The necessary paperwork was issued, and in 1777 Araucania was officially recognized as a separate kingdom, outside the rule of the Spanish monarchy.

Armies led by Bernardo O'Higgins and José de San Martín won independence for Chile in 1818. During the first two decades, the newly installed creole leaders were fully occupied resolving immediate political and economic crises, and addressing mining-related matters that were mainly linked to the northern region. Yet, as border issues with Peru, Bolivia and Argentina began to surface, the government realized that the long, thin country would not be fully recognized and esteemed as a nation until it embraced the lake district and beyond.

The far south had always been "closer" to Santiago in logistical terms. Ships visiting Punta Arenas often docked at Valparaiso and the Fuegian native population never presented any significant obstacles to establishing settlements. In 1843 Fuerte Bulnes (Fort Bulnes) had been built at Puerto del Hambre (Port Famine), followed in 1849 by a penal colony. Port facilities had also been established at Punta Arenas. The new town thrived, thanks to the traffic generated by the California Gold Rush, and became an export hub for seal skins, coal, firewood, and lumber. Thus Mapuche territory—most of the land between the Biobío river and Palena, including Chiloé Island—was viewed as a humiliating anomaly. How could armies that had shaken off the Spanish yoke fail to overwhelm a force composed mainly of poorly armed militia?

By the 1850s Argentina was beginning to contemplate pushing south beyond the Río Colorado to colonize the plains of Río Negro and Chubut. Wary of her huge neighbour's undeclared territorial ambitions, Chile looked again to Araucania and Congress decided to send Colonel Cornelio Saavedra to the region with orders to build forts and advance the government's control southward, gradually encircling the Mapuche lands.

KINGDOM COME

The fiercely independent spirit of the Mapuche was no obstacle to a flamboyant, ambitious and single-minded Frenchman's goal of becoming their ruler. It is far more likely that the man in question, Orllie-Antoine de Tounens—better known as the King of Patagonia—was only encouraged in his venture by finding that his soon-to-be subjects were of a kindred spirit.

Orllie (sometimes spelt Orélie) left little in the way of primary sources. His memoirs are chaotic and incomplete, and regally one-sided in their account of his life and work. But we do have some of his edicts and a manifesto, as well as a now classic historical résumé, *El reino de la Araucanía y Patagonia* (1936), written by Chilean author Armando Braun-Menéndez.

He was born on 12 May 1825 in La Chèze in the Dordogne, the second child of an impoverished family of nobles. In his autobiography he skims over his upbringing and early adulthood, but while working as a low-ranking lawyer in the local court, he began, in the words of Braun-Menéndez, to "fall ill with geography." He devoured accounts of the voyages of La Pérouse, Cook, Dumont d'Urville, d'Orbigny and other maritime adventurers, which gave him dreams of becoming an explorer and fed an incipient ambition to become a leader of men and a hero of France. To satisfy both of these urges, he needed a land his compatriots had not yet conquered. It would have to be *l'Amérique*. In his memoirs Orllie claims he left France with the grandest of visions: his aim was "to unite the Hispano-American republics under the name of a single constitutionally monarchic federation divided in seventeen states."

In 1858 Orllie packed a couple of suitcases and sailed for South America, visiting the Atlantic ports and making his way to Coquimbo in northern Chile. These first experiences of the New World, and later visits to Santiago and Valparaiso, where he made his home for two years, did not allow him scope to put into action his master plan. In the settled towns of northern and central Chile it was plainly obvious that the local authorities would fiercely resist any attempt to change the form of government.

When he heard about the resistance encountered by Chilean armies in the south, Orllie saw a glimmer of hope. What the new-born nation saw as an obstacle—the *frontera,* the line beyond which the Mapuche maintained their rule—was for him a threshold demarcating a region in need of civilized government and guidance. After making contact with some Mapuche *caciques* and a group of French colonists in Valdivia, Orllie continued south in October 1860 and managed to gain an audience with Quilapan, the son of a ferocious warrior, Manil, and a chieftain whose power-base encompassed the eastern slopes of the cordillera.

A sworn enemy of Chile, Quilipan gave Orllie a *mestizo* guide, whose advice and mere presence allowed the Frenchman—now joined by two countrymen, Lachaise and Desfontaines—to penetrate further into Mapuche lands. To impress his future minions, Orllie modified his appearance, allowing his curly locks to flow as far as his waist and wearing a prophet's beard. He also sported a handsome pothook cavalry sabre and, as a token of respect, wore a Mapuche poncho.

With Quilapan's support, doors began to open. Many of the Mapuche agreed that they wanted independence. They believed that it was their land, and they would indeed support a separate and sovereign kingdom.

Braun-Menéndez claims that the Mapuche, like the Incas, had a legend often spoken of by the *machis* or wizards in which a white man came to put an end to war and enslavement. But the *caciques* may have expressed support for Orllie merely in the belief that their cause might be better served with a European acting on their behalf.

Orllie soon found himself in a position to issue his first edict. We do not know who was there to understand (or not) the prince regent's announcement to his future subjects in French-hued Spanish, but the passage, dated 1 November 1860, was later published in Paris:

> Considering that Araucania does not depend on any other state; that it is found to be divided into tribes and that there is need of a central government... we decree the following:
>
> Article one
>
> A constitutional hereditary monarchy is founded in Araucania; Prince Orllie Antoine de Tounens is designated King.

Article two

In the case that the King should leave no descendants, his heirs will be taken from other branches of his family, following an order previously established by royal edict.

Article three

Once State bodies are constituted, royal edicts will have the force of Law.

Orllie made Desfontaines his minister of justice and together they drafted a constitution and wrote letters of presentation to the Chilean president, Manuel Montt, and to the minister for foreign affairs. Numerous decrees were promulgated throughout November: the king reserved the right to create "nobles at will"; christenings, weddings and funerals would be free to all his loyal subjects; legislative sessions were to be announced in the daily newspapers. An egalitarian note runs through these foundation texts; funerals for royals were to be the same as those for minions. Though the kingdom would observe the Catholic service, God was notably absent from the constitutional paperwork, perhaps reflecting Orllie's Masonic leanings.

According to Orllie's account, three days after his edict was announced in the Mapuche regions south of Valdivia, chieftains from other areas of Patagonia made contact with him. They, too, wanted to serve in the new kingdom. The king dictated his bounteous response to all his subjects "present and absent".

Considering that the indigenous peoples of Patagonia have the same rights and interests as the Araucanians, and that they solemnly declare their wish to be united with these, in order to form but one single nation under a Government of Constitutional Monarchy. We have ordered and we order as follows: Patagonia is reunited today with our Araucanian Kingdom.

As far as the Frenchman was concerned, he was now sole and supreme head of state for all the southern lands of Chile at least as far as the Magellan Strait—and all Argentinian territory south of the Río Negro. All the tribes in his dominion were now equal, from the tent-building Tehuelche of Chubut to the mussel-gathering Yahgan of Tierra del Fuego.

Once back in Valparaiso, he spread the news of his peaceful—indeed passive—conquest in the local newspapers and sought support from compatriots, seducing them with the promise of a *Nueva Francia* or "New France". He created a blue, white and green flag (one was given to each of the key *caciques*) and had coins minted for the nation bearing the inscription *Nouvelle France*. But when he tried to attract other French settlers to join his court, they responded with a polite, somewhat condescending refusal. Orllie was left feeling embittered and lonely. Even worse was the utter indifference of the Chilean authorities; the royal pronouncements and press releases stirred up little reaction and news of the monarchy was not picked up by the newspapers in Santiago.

Orllie travelled south again. He gave his guide an IOU which, he said, would be paid out in full by the Araucanian exchequer as soon as the finance minister was elected and a treasury created. Having failed to persuade the Chileans about the momentous fact of his coronation, he dedicated his energies to informing the indigenous tribes that he was their king and that he would lead them in their defence of the *frontera* at the Río Biobío. After a brief but sober ceremony, witnessed by spear-wielding *caciques*, Orllie withdrew to his hut and busied himself with the day-to-day business of government.

Following a series of meetings with groups of leading chieftains, Orllie began to gather support to take a small army north in order to negotiate a peace deal with the Chilean authorities that would, he believed, be favourable to the kingdom. Not all the natives, however, supported the proposed royal alliance of tribes, not least because there was not a peso in the crown coffers, and many were begin to weary of Orllie's ostentatiously generous IOUs.

At about this time news of his movements began to circulate among the authorities who controlled the frontier between Araucania and Chile proper. For information leading to his capture, a reward of fifty pesos was offered, sufficient to tempt his servant, Rosales, to betray him. On 5 January 1862, while riding on ahead mounted on the king's steed, Rosales advised the Chilean police and army, based at Nacimiento on the banks of the Biobío, that the king had made a camp just south, beside the Río Malleco.

As he was bathing and resting beneath an apple tree on the riverbank, the king was detained and taken away like a common criminal. Even so, a multitude of indigenous royal subjects were never far behind, boosting Orllie's confidence and no doubt perturbing the arresting officers. The following day he was transferred to Nacimiento to be interrogated by Colonel Cornelio Saavedra, now governor of the recently founded province of Arauco. From a historical perspective, this can be seen as a meeting between a Latin American military hero (Saavedra would go on to be Chile's minister of war) and a deluded madman, but at the time Saavedra was merely a senior officer in charge of a vital, if undesirable, outpost and Orllie was a king, of sorts. It was nonetheless surprising to Saavedra when the king haughtily enquired: *Parlez-vous français?* With the aid of a translator, he listened carefully to the king's demands to be "returned directly to the bosom of my family" before placing him in a dungeon on a charge of disturbing the peace and illegally entering territories controlled by indigenous groups.

Aware of the expeditious character of military justice, Orllie began drafting his will and testament, and put in writing the law of succession in his kingdom. He named his brother Juan de Tounens as his immediate heir and his nephew, Adriano Juan, as next in line. During the trial he argued that his intentions were philanthropic, and that he proposed to civilize the natives by "establishing primary schools… and with the influence of agricultural and artistic industry." When challenged over the title and meaning of "king", Orllie was forthright: "that territory [of Araucanian Patagonia] does not recognize Chilean laws and does not obey them and has always seen itself as independent and equipped to appoint its own rulers."

He was intractable throughout the trial, signing his confession "Orllie Antoine 1er". Rosales came forward and declared that Orllie had stirred up revolution among many of the *caciques*—naming Levin, Guantecol, Leucon, Levio and Villamis—which the king denied, stating forcefully that he had always intended to seek a peaceful accord with the Chilean government. He went on to explain his plan for a confederation of South American states and, to further ingratiate himself with his judges, he recommended Santiago as the "provisional capital".

His offers were in vain. He was imprisoned in the town of Los Angeles and declared to be a *loco*. The stress of such intense scrutiny caused Orllie to come down with a diarrhoeal fever—possibly typhoid or dysentery—a side-effect of which was that his regal mane fell out in clumps. On doctor's orders he was transferred to a hospital, despite the reservations of Colonel Pantoja, the officer who was charged with keeping him locked up. In his memoirs, Orllie recalls the fever as "a breather... but at what price" and recalls the extent of his tribulations:

> I was shrunken if not to the state of a cadaver then at least to that of a skeleton. During the past month and half I had not been able to write in a little book I used as a diary, having lost any sense of life's meaning, and I was impatient to get back to writing in it. Barely with the strength to get out of what served as my bed, I approached the jailer to ask him what day of the week it was, as I had no calendar. I also asked them to move me to a more comfortable room.

After nine months, Orllie was transferred to Santiago and, following an appeal from the French consul, allowed to board the warship *Duguay-Trouin* and sail for Brest. There he published his memoirs as well as memoranda attacking his Chilean jailers. Bizarrely, the Chilean consul in Paris launched a magazine called *La Couronne d'Acier* (taking its title from the "Order of the Steel Crown", one of the bogus honours the Patagonian king had created) and printed copies of Orllie's manifesto, which encouraged nationals to join him in the creation of a New France, "a crusade worthy of the nineteenth century". He also crossed the Channel to spend six weeks in England, seeking to foment international interest in his cause.

These various petitions, and attempts to win the support of the French government, inspired apathy in all, despite the forceful, and defendable case that Araucania was not a province of Chile at all but an independent state. Tiring of the indifference and ignominy, Orllie made plans to return, alone, to South America.

He sailed for Montevideo in 1869. After a botched attempt to reach Mapuche lands by crossing the pampas, Orllie sailed down to Carmen de Patagones and proceeded up the Río Negro. At Choele Choel he was apprehended by natives and, much to the king's chagrin, treated as an unwelcome intruder. Orllie's outraged protests fell on deaf ears, but in a rare moment of good fortune one of his captors was reminded of a certain Frenchman who had indeed befriended *cacique* Quilapan, son of Manil. Orllie was spared and his small entourage was permitted to travel westwards.

Meanwhile, back at the *frontera*, Saavedra was still in charge, by this stage a seasoned commander and diplomat pursuing his territorial ambitions behind a veneer of *détente* with the natives. The line of forts, protected by a moat, had shifted south, penetrating deep into Mapuche territory along the coastline and, by degrees, forcing the tribes into a controlled zone; only Quilapan and his indomitable mountain warriors were beyond the pale. In December 1869 Saavedra recorded in his official journal that he heard news of the arrival from the direction of the Argentinian pampas of "the adventurer Antonio Orllie, accompanied by a certain number of gauchos". Saavedra despatched faithful native messengers to investigate and called a parliament of *caciques* in the plaza at Toltén in order to create a combined fighting force of Mapuche and *criollos*. Some 800 foot-soldiers were armed for combat, with further reinforcements held on alert at the forts. To win over the *caciques* who expressed allegiance to Orllie, he made the following announcement: "I offer to whoever brings me the adventurer Orllie's head two *almudes* [an ancient measure equal to 0.8 bushels] or saddlebags of legal tender, and I authorize you to spread news of this offer to the outer reaches of the [Mapuche] land."

We have no details as to if or how Orllie learned of the military manoeuvres or the reward, but we know he fled, once again travelling through the Andes and crossing the steppes. The next reports were of his re-grown mane flowing as he rode down the streets of Montevideo. At the end of 1872 he was back in Paris, drinking Pernod at the Café Musard and holding meetings with journalist and entrepreneur M. Mahon de Monhagan and London-based banker Jacob Michael. They began to spin fresh rumours, giving a Francophobe slant to protests from the Chilean mission in Paris, and were able to encourage patriotic sentiment among a handful of noblemen and well-heeled merchants. These were issued with bonds and divested of funds to sponsor a colony. Orllie then returned to his kingdom under the pseudonym Juan Prat. He and his small entourage debarked at Buenos Aires, where they boarded the Pampita, a *pailebot* (a kind of schooner) heading for Bahía Blanca.

When interrogated at the southern port, Prat and his supporters protested that they were representatives of a banking firm that wanted to invest in farms at Bahía de la Unión, near Carmen de Patagones. But entry visas were refused.

Back in Paris yet again, Orllie convinced four of his political allies in the Dordogne to write a letter to the French Foreign Affairs Ministry, protesting against "the arrest of Orllie that took place on July 17, 1874, near to Patagones." In October 1876 Orllie took another ship to Buenos Aires, but got no further than the local French community hospital, where he had an intestinal blockage removed.

On 13 January 1877 Orllie embarked on the *Paraná* and sailed away from the shores of Latin America for the last time. The rest of his days were spent manufacturing the paraphernalia of royalty. The most prestigious medal the king could confer was the Royal Order of the Southern State, and he also bestowed hereditary peerages on worthy associates in France and overseas. Edward Michael of North Shields, son of banker Jacob, was made the Baron of Belgrano in perpetuity. Along with the flag there was now a national anthem, heraldic symbols and arms and countless coinages of illegal tender.

At last the Chileans began to miss him. A report was filed by the Spain correspondent of Valparaiso's *El Mercurio* newspaper. The writer had seen Orllie in the streets in France and reported that he was

> of good bearing, tall of stature, always sad and give to meditating, with his brow inclined no doubt owing to the burden of the crown that he has worn upon his head; he is seen wandering through the green hillsides, his demeanour gallant, his face expressive, his eyes searching. Yet he lacked, in his physiognomy and in his person, the distinction and majesty one would have expected of someone whose time has been spent on a Throne. Wearing a great hat, he walked down the boulevards, always smoking a huge cigarette, never showing that he knows that he is being observed.

On 17 September 1878 the king died.

THE ROYAL LINE

Writers and fantasists have embraced the figure of Orllie, partly because he is colourful, partly because he may have been insane, and partly because the citizens of republics seem to enjoy flirting with the notion of royalty. For all the irony that clings so easily to his persona, Orllie excites narrators too. Braun-Menéndez' book is pure romance, and later re-workings of the limited material—including Adolfo José Galatoire's *Quien fue el Rey de la Patagonia* (1972) and Claudio Morales Gorleri's *El Rey de la Patagonia* (1999)—balance farce and tragic-comedy with nostalgia and genuine respect.

To his descendants, Orllie is known as "The Founder". He was succeeded by King Achilles I, "The Diplomat", who remained in Paris, married to Queen Mary. As they left no heir, the mantle of monarchy was passed to the "seal keeper" and secretary of state Antonio II, "The Philosopher", who took up residence in Rio de Janeiro. In 1903 Laura Teresa I ascended to the throne, and was succeeded by Antonio III (1916-52). In 1952 Prince Philippe took his place on the virtual throne. To keep the scribes interested, he sent Braun-Menéndez a photograph of Orllie's tombstone in Tourtoirac, Dordogne, bearing the royal seal.

In 1959 Philippe published a 23-page *Bibliographie* under the aegis of the newly established Academy of Advanced Araucanian Studies to permit researchers and historians access to political, historical, botanical and folkloric resources pertaining to the kingdom of Araucania and Patagonia and so enable them to take a view on the "passionate and complex problem" of regal rights. He lives in France and does not use the regal title, preferring the common surname Boiry.

Yet he has kept alive the memory of Orllie-Antoine, and has shown his support for the ongoing struggle for Mapuche self-determination by authorizing the minting of coins in cupronickel, silver, gold, and palladium. He does not speak Spanish and first stepped on Patagonian soil in 1989.

When in 1996 Enrique Oliva, the Paris-based Europe correspondent for the Argentinian tabloid *Clarín*, claimed that the King of Patagonia was an impostor and his titles "as false as his presumed majesty", Philippe Boiry tried to sue him for 16,000 francs. The case was thrown out of court by the judge. He also presented titles showing he was a descendant of other royal dynasties, including those of Byzantium, the Kings of Israel, France, Hungary, England, Scotland, Sweden and Bavaria, among others. Philippe and his second wife, Princess Elizabeth of Araucania, live in Orllie Antoine's house at La Chèze. They have no children—but that fact should not be a significant hindrance to the survival of the kingdom.

THE "PACIFICATION"

With the French pretender out of sight, Saavedra's forces encircled Araucania with forts. In 1866 a huge swathe of land was declared state-owned, removing all native land rights and creating a monopoly system of the kind employed by the Americans in the Far West. The Mapuche struck back briefly in 1868, but were eventually coerced into accepting a truce. Saavedra had wanted to go further and finish the job, but he had neither political support nor sufficient military forces to realize his plan.

Then, in 1879, when Chilean forces were occupied with the War of the Pacific—during which Chile extended its territory northwards, cutting off Bolivia's access to the coast—the Mapuche rebelled again. This time Saavedra was given more soldiers and told to take his landgrab scheme to its natural conclusion: to crush the Mapuche rebels and colonize all their territory. Again following the model of the American frontier, a railway was laid, easing the movement of troops and supplies onto former Mapuche territory.

In 1881 and 1882 forts were established at Imperial and Villarrica. By 1893 the railway had reached Temuco, and telegraph lines were installed. Surveyors and land speculators were not far behind. Industry arrived and

forests were cut down. The area of the *frontera* was overrun with brothels and bars. The Mapuche shamans were forbidden from performing their healing and clairvoyance rituals. After 1882 a period of intensive immigration began, and the lake district was overrun with outsiders, including around 10,000 English, Swiss, German and French settlers.

Some time between 1912 and 1913 the American engineer and geographer Bailey Willis took the train into the lands that used to lie behind the *frontera* (the track now ran all the way to Puerto Montt on the Reloncaví Sound). Willis explored the region, admiring the Osorno and Calbuco volcanoes, and noting certain symmetries with North America:

> Compared with our Pacific Coast the change of scene may be likened to that from the orchards of California to the hill country of Oregon and the lake region of Puget Sound. From a city three centuries old [Santiago] one lands in virgin forests, where conditions of settlement are those of our pioneer West in the last decades of the nineteenth century. A rich volcanic soil and abundant rainfall support a dense growth of shrubs and fine trees, the like of which is not often seen outside the tropics. Overhead all is green, even the tree trunks; underfoot among strong, twisting roots all is morass and boghole. But cleared and drained it is a marvelously fertile land. Those who are bringing it into cultivation are Germans, colonists of the second generation. In Osorno sturdy boys and red-cheeked girls with long blond braids gathered round the bandstand to sing fine old songs of the *Vaterland*.

The slopes are still densely wooded in those parts of the lake district that were declared national parks in the 1920s, and Osorno, Puerto Montt and the smaller towns between them still have a makeshift feel. With the right evening light, the cool mists, the smoking chimneys atop wooden houses and the German signs for *Kuchen* all suggest a region where pioneers are still waiting for news from the frontier.

Many Chilean historians and just about all the school textbooks call the 1870s and 1880s the period of the "Pacification of Araucania". Mapuches call it *La Ultima Matanza* or "the Last Massacre".

Leonardo León, professor of history and geography at the University of Chile, has argued that the conflict was more akin to a mass riot, with all-out fighting between different Mapuche factions, between Chilean forces and the *mestizo* (part-Mapuche mixed race) populations, and also between *mestizos* and Mapuches:

> It was not a general "pacification" of anonymous citizens, but rather the eruption of inter-ethnic violence. The new bandits were the illegitimate children of the interracial, social and cultural mixing born of frontier society, whose past had been spent wandering the plains and crossing the mountains in search of subsistence or booty. When the Chilean occupation took place and Mapuche lands were appropriated, these [*mestizo*] people were persecuted, rounded up and uprooted, as part of a general process of social conditioning designed to transform them into the peons and day-labourers of the region's flourishing estancias and industries... the vast majority of them joined the ranks of peons working on wheat ranches, in forestry or on roadworks. Others, whose number we will probably never know, joined the ranks of renegades who have for years defined our geography through acts of rebellion and insubordination. These last were the protagonists of an anonymous history that renders fragile and inconsistent the myth of the Pacification of Araucania.

Chapter Nine

MYSTICAL TWITCHER:
W. H. HUDSON

"Days windless and serene to their very end, bright with a cloudless sky
and sunshine sweet and pleasant to behold, making the grey solitudes
smile as if conscious of the heavenly influence. It is a common saying in
this country that 'once in a hundred years a man dies in Patagonia.'"

W. H. Hudson, *Idle Days in Patagonia* (1893)

After a "storm-vexed" voyage down the Atlantic coast in December 1870,
the sea became a degree calmer. William Henry Hudson, the 29-year-old
ornithologist on board, had just closed his eyes when the old steamer that
was carrying him suddenly began to shudder in the most unnatural way.
The fragile hull had struck some rocks.

Hudson, as alarmed as he was worn out, dashed out of his cabin and
caught the mate and three sailors about to mutiny. Their captain was mortally sick and in no state to issue orders. The ship, it seemed, was doomed.

Out of nowhere the first engineer appeared, wielding a gun and
threatening to shoot the first man who made any attempt to escape. All the
passengers began to stream onto the deck, followed by the dying captain.
A sudden gust of wind blew the ship off the rocks and sent her bobbing
over the seething surf to come to a halt on the shore, where she stuck fast.

Little wonder that Hudson felt intense relief on arriving on dry land.
The first chapter of his famous travelogue-cum-memoir, *Idle Days in Patagonia*, is titled simply "At last! Patagonia." But that relief was mixed with
keen anticipation as Hudson, who had grown up in a rural neighbourhood near Buenos Aires, was realizing one of his dreams. All his life he
had watched flocks of migratory birds on their long flight south—and
now he was arriving at the magical place where they nested for the austral
summer. Hudson had read his Darwin and knew something about geology
and dinosaurs. He also knew all about Magellan and Trapalanda, and no
doubt a host of other legends. But, in his own words, his simple plan was

CALODROMAS ELEGANS

DOLICHOTIS PATAGONICA

to spend "twelve months on the Río Negro... watching and listening to birds."

As Hudson recounts in the second chapter, the plan became more complicated after he accidentally shot himself in the knee with a revolver. This took place while riding and staying at a ranch near the mouth of the Río Negro only a few days into his holiday. We can only imagine his sense of disappointment, and of the cruel irony of being so close to his beloved birds but unable to go off into the wilds and enjoy them.

Compelled to convalesce, Hudson says he "became an idler." Lying on his back through a long, sultry summer, his mind swatted away at the thoughts that buzzed in his head, "flitting, sylph-like things". Meanwhile, a new self evolved:

> I caught nothing, and found out nothing; nevertheless, these days of enforced idleness were not unhappy. And after leaving my room, hobbling around with the aid of a stout stick, and sitting in houses, I consorted with men and women, and listened day by day to the story of their small un-avian affairs, until it began to interest me. But not too keenly. I could always quit them without regret to lie on the green sward, to gaze up into the trees or the blue sky, and speculate on all imaginable things. The result was that when no longer any excuse for inaction existed use had bred a habit in me—the habit of indolence, which was quite common among the people of Patagonia, and appeared to suit the genial climate.

THE BOY AND THE BIRDS

In some ways Hudson is the poor man's Darwin. He is an expatriate, removed from the great centres of learning and the libraries; he is a naturalist, but too passionate about birdwatching to be a top-flight scientist; and, in any case, his eagle-eyed observations are interwoven with mystical flourishes that were admired by late Victorian Romantics a century ago but for most people now read rather like a lonely new ager's dizzy ramblings.

Yet Hudson was far more than a Victorian birdwatcher. Born in 1841 in Quilmes, in the province of Buenos Aires, he was the child of Anglo-American parents who had moved to Argentina from New England. Their first home, an *estancia* called Los Veinticinco Ombúes (after its garden of

25 *ombú* trees) was Hudson's playground and a sort of paradise for any inquisitive child. His father, however, struggled to adapt to working and living on the ranch.

Hudson's vistas were always vast and unbroken. The pampas—at least in some regions of Buenos Aires and La Pampa provinces—can seem more desolate than Patagonia because they are truly flat. The grasses, once lofty and feathery enough to hide lanky rheas, were by the mid-nineteenth century cropped low by cattle and sheep. If you see any trees at all, it is generally as a hazy mirage. On a clear day you can sense the curvature of the earth, of the horizon rolling away beneath huge skies.

But the grass here is far greener and richer than in Patagonia and the birdlife is teeming, especially where rivers, flood plains or lagoons are found. Giant *maguari* storks, roseate spoonbills, flamingos and egrets are common sights, and the marshes are a hiding place for scores of small tyrants and flycatchers whose vermillion and gold feathers can be spied flicking between the tall reeds. For birdwatchers, *Argentine Ornithology* (1888) and *Birds of La Plata* (1920), Hudson's portraits of the species found on the pampas, are seminal works. For others he is best known for his exotic romance novels, especially *The Purple Land* (1885), set in Uruguay, and *Green Mansions* (1904), about a revolutionary who takes refuge in the primeval forests of south-western Venezuela. In all his writings, nature is a vital force.

Hudson spent his childhood—lovingly recalled in *Far Away and Long Ago* (1918)—roaming the pampas, studying the plant, bird and animal life, and observing both natural and human dramas close to what was still a relatively lawless frontier. The Argentinian government, established in 1816, divided its limited military resources between fighting in civil wars and establishing rule over the semi-nomadic natives of the pampas. The ever-present threat of a native incursion no doubt added to the boy's excitement and sense of danger.

When a bout of typhus struck at the age of 15, he became introspective and sought company and comfort in literature. He read poetry, the classics, contemporary non-fiction, and also the *Origin of Species*, whose theories supported his own empirical observations of nature. After his mother died in 1959, Hudson was badly affected. Then his father died in 1868 and he felt his life was no longer firmly fixed in Quilmes. Raised as a country boy, he began to lead the life of a wanderer and to dedicate all his time to observing and writing about birds, plants, animals and the processes and patterns of the natural world.

Hudson's bird portraits always begin as detailed, factual accounts of plumage, nesting habits, song and behaviour in groups, and contain all the measurements and gender commentaries required to aid observation. But he is prone to closing his narratives with a subjective and unscientific flourish. Here is his opening for the Patagonian mocking-bird:

> The Patagonian Mocking-bird, which I met with during my sojourn on the Rio Negro of Patagonia, closely resembles the species just described [the common *calandria*], but is smaller, the plumage is a darker grey, and the irides are also of a darker green. It is a common bird, resident, lives alone with its mate, feeds on insects and berries...

So far, so dry. Here is the final section, remarking on the Patagonian mocking-bird's discovery of "new" notes and the ensuing audience reaction:

> After the new wonderful note has been sounded they all become silent and attentive, reminding one in their manner of a caged Parrot listening to a sound it is trying to learn. Presently they learn it, and are pleased with its acquisition as if they had discovered it themselves, repeating it incessantly. I noticed this curious habit of the bird many times, and on one occasion I found that for three entire days all the birds in a small thicket I used to visit every day did nothing but repeat incessantly two or three single notes they had borrowed from one of their number. The constant repetition of this one sound had an irritating effect on me...
>
> This bird usually sits upon the summit of a bush when singing, and its music is heard all seasons and in all weather from dawn till after dark: as a rule it sings in a leisurely, unexcited manner, remaining silent for some time after every five or six or a dozen notes, and apparently listening to his brother-performers. These snatches of melody often seem like a prelude or promise of something better coming; there is often in them such exquisite sweetness and so much variety that the hearer is ever wishing for a full measure, and still the bird opens his bill to delight and disappoint him, as if not yet ready to display his power.

The way the prose concedes but pulls back, yearns but is never satisfied, tells us more about Hudson than it does about the mocking-bird—which is no longer merely a sonorous mimic of other birds but a sensual flirt who toys with the desires of men. In such passages, there is as at least as much of Keats and Wordsworth in Hudson as there is of Lamarck and Darwin.

IDLE IDEAS

Hudson's Patagonia trip took place between December 1870 and August 1871. His expeditions in fact extended no further south than the banks of the Río Negro, but at the time it was right on the border of native country and Carmen was still the only sizeable settlement in the region

A factual report of the trip was published in March 1872 in London as an essay entitled "On the Birds of the Rio Negro of Patagonia". But the book was written from the mid-1880s onwards while Hudson was living in England. It began as a series of essays, some of which were published in Longman's and in the *Gentleman's Magazine*, and was only published in full in 1893. When reading *Idle Days in Patagonia* we have to take into account the twenty years of life that had passed between the trip and the narrative—perhaps the account of his choice to become an idler was not originally a philosophical one. We should also note that Hudson had only published four other books by 1893 and would go on to publish more than twenty prose works before his death in 1922. A further dozen or so were issued posthumously. In this sense *Idle Days in Patagonia* is an early, landmark work. As Ruth Tomalin says in her biography of Hudson: "Rich in experience of many kinds as that year had been, these Patagonia essays are often in deeper and quieter vein, dealing with adventures of mind and spirit. Recollecting in tranquillity, Hudson develops patterns of thought on a wide range of themes, many of which would recur in his later work."

During the trip Hudson travelled some 100 miles and encountered 126 species, 33 of them endemic to Patagonia. Among the latter was a new species, *knipolegus hudsoni*, or Hudson's black tyrant-bird. Yet the narrative of *Idle Days in Patagonia*, once the *Tempest*-like scene is over and the bullet lodged in the knee, does not busy itself solely with birdlife. Rather, the ornithological vignettes are punctuation marks in the story of a man who breathed deeply the fragrances on the air and who studied carefully the forms of foliage, the spikes and flowers of every tiny plant and dwarf tree struggling to survive on the dunes. Hudson relishes the "feeling of relief, of escape, and absolute freedom which one experiences in a vast solitude, where man has never been."

His mood becomes despondent when he dwells on the decline of the native peoples. He makes solitary peregrinations to the piles of stones that mark the graves of natives, almost certainly Tehuelche, which he describes as "Golgothas". Around the burial piles he finds exposed bones and skulls. He says he went not as collector, nor archaeologist, but solely to "indulge in mournful thoughts." He then connects the skull to the land and to his own private vision of the world; he imagines wearing the skull as a helmet, to serve as a kind of lens through which the arid wastes will reveal their true essence: "If by looking into the empty cavity of one of those broken un-buried skulls I had been able to see, as in a magic glass, an image of the world as it once existed in the living brain, what should I have seen?"

Hudson makes the case that Patagonia makes visitors ponder such questions, as the skull seems to belong there, to be part of the land. He focuses on the character of the landscape in the way that an abstract painter might. The empty eye sockets prompt Hudson to contemplate what forms and hues might have filled the field of vision of a native when he was alive and roaming the plains:

> There would have appeared a band of colour; its margins gray, growing fainter and bluer outwardly, and finally fading into nothing; between the gray edges the band would be green; and along this green middle band, not always keeping to centre, there would appear a sinuous shiny line, like a serpent with glittering skin lying at rest on the grass. For the river must have been to the aboriginal inhabitants of the valley the one great central unforgettable fact in nature and man's life.

LIFE IN DEATH

Hudson develops a philosophy of mental and physical health through communing with nature. He praises the winter climate of Patagonia, and says the winds of the summer are mitigated by the dry, pure air. He describes an encounter with a wealthy Spanish tradesman who suffered from grievous asthma and who, on visiting Patagonia, was in a short time restored to perfect health. He went back to his home in Buenos Aires, but fell ill again. Finally, despairing, he returned to Spain, back to a familiar milieu, assuming he would be well there. But this man was a pursuer of false goals, says Hudson, and as a "child of civilization, a man of the pavement" he could not live without the luxuries of banter in the café and a game of dominoes with friends of an evening. Hudson is disdainful of the sad man's trials:

> As these things which he valued were merely dust and ashes to me, I did not sympathize deeply with his discontent, nor consider that it mattered much which portion of the globe he made choice of for a residence. But the facts of his case interested me; and if I should have a reader who has other ideals, who has felt the mystery and glory of life overcoming his soul with wonder and desire, and who bears in his system the canker of consumption which threatens to darken the vision prematurely—to such a one I would say, TRY PATAGONIA. It is far to travel, and in place of the smoothness of Madeira there would be roughness; but how far men go, into what rough places, in search of rubies and ingots of gold; and life is more than these.

Idle Days in Patagonia ranges far and wide in its themes and arguments. Hudson interweaves culture into the narrative, alluding along the way to the works of Bacon, Melville, Kingsley and Lewis Carroll. He writes about the bird-music of South America; about differences between the eyesight of "savages" and that of civilized man; and about eye colouring in birds, man and animals. His final chapter is called "The Perfume of an Evening Primrose", about scents and their power over memory. These are the themes he revived again and again in later works, especially in his fiction, where he could test and explore his theories.

In August—which Hudson calls the "April of the Argentine poets" to aid his northern hemisphere readers—the weather turned bitter and snow fell. When discussing this carpet of snow, he focuses on "the quality of whiteness" in nature and its effect on the mind.

> Snow is... most intimately associated in the mind with the yearly suspension of nature's beneficent activity, and all that this means to the human family—the failure of food and consequent want, and the suffering and danger from intense cold. This traditional knowledge of an

inclement period in nature only serves to intensify the animism that finds a purpose in all natural phenomena, and sees in the whiteness of earth the sign of a great unwelcome change. Change not death, since nature's life is eternal; but its sweet friendly warmth and softness have died out of it; there is no longer any recognition, any bond; and if we were to fall down and perish by the wayside, there would be no compassion; it is sitting apart and solitary, cold and repelling, its breath suspended, in a trance of grief and passion; and although it sees us it is as though it saw us not, even as we see pebbles and withered leaves on the ground, when some great sorrow has dazed us, or when some deadly purpose is in our heart.

Hudson's seemingly scientific prose gives way to a personification of winter, and for the first time he writes specifically of "animism". It is tempting to trace from this meditation on whiteness a link to Darwin's reflections on the negativity and emptiness of the plains. Perhaps whiteness was, for Hudson, the final form of Patagonian blankness, permitting a purity that gives rise to a quiet, attentive state of mind, a trance-like oneness with the environment, and a watchfulness that is almost animal.

In Chapter Thirteen, "The Plains of Patagonia", Hudson takes as his starting point Darwin's rhetorical question: "Why, then—and the case is not peculiar to myself—have these arid wastes taken so firm possession of my mind?" Hudson proceeds to turn the latter's bafflement into an affirmation:

Judging from my own case, I believe that here we have the secret of the persistence of the Patagonian images, and their frequent recurrence in the minds of many who have visited that grey, monotonous, and, in one sense, eminently uninteresting region. It is not the effect of the unknown, it is not imagination; it is that nature in these desolate scenes... moves us more deeply than in others.

It is as if the blank canvas facilitates mental—or mystical—access to nature, to whatever lies beneath or inside nature. In this context, one can only speculate on what birdlife might signify for Hudson: atoms of buzzing life and energy swirling across the dead zone, concentrations of beauty thrown into relief by the blurred, bland ugliness of the setting.

Hudson writes that he learned to listen to the silence, contemplating the effect of his shouting aloud in such a lonely place. All travellers have, of course, done this in deserts, dunes and caves—to express glee, power or simply to affirm their presence and the fact of being alive—but Hudson wonders if to shout would not, in fact, be wrong, the consequence of a "lawless and uncertain thought". Instead, he allows himself to fold inwards, to stop talking, to barely listen and—let us not forget he was a birdwatcher—even cease from observing. The result of this: the end of thought.

> I had become incapable of reflection; my mind had suddenly trans-formed itself from a thinking machine into a machine for some unknown purpose. To think was like setting in motion a noisy engine in my brain; and there was something there which bade me still, and I was forced to obey. My state was one of *suspense* and *watchfulness*: yet I had no expectation of meeting with an adventure, and felt as free from apprehension as I feel now when sitting in a room in London... I was powerless to wonder at or speculate about it; the state seemed familiar rather than strange, and although accompanied by a strong feeling of elation, I did not know it—did not know that something had come between me and my intellect—until I lost it and returned to my former self—to thinking, and the old insipid existence.

This suspension of intellect, which Hudson had not experienced in the humid pampas—with their raucous southern screamer birds and buzz-saw cicadas, and where the sweat prickles so intensely you can almost hear it—was borne of desolation. Like Thoreau, whom he admired, Hudson had sensed something uncanny, deeply moving and, in its way, delightful in being alone in nature.

Going Home?

In 1874 Hudson left Argentina for England, never to return. He told his brother he wanted to live in the land of his father's father and to set down on paper the results of all his scientific pursuits. But he was outraged at the way industry and its processes had usurped nature in his ancestral home-land, and would later describe his adopted England as "a glorified poultry farm".

Nor did Hudson's private life bring happiness. Poverty and ill-health may have occasioned his marriage in 1876 to a woman much older than himself. Together, they lived precariously on the proceeds of two boarding houses until she inherited a house in the Bayswater district of London, where Hudson spent the rest of his life.

Somehow, while swatting away troublesome thoughts, the idler had reached a firm conclusion: that the biblically sanctioned notion of a natural world created for man to conquer and dispose of at will was simply unsustainable. To Hudson, the natural world, the environment, was sacred and not there solely to be exploited. He contrasted nature's richness with the artificial pleasures that most men valued—newspapers, finance, current affairs, city life—and which he despised. He viewed nature as a way out of the tiresome, very English town-and-country dichotomy, and as a means to finding health as well as moral well-being.

His writings and civic efforts focused on two areas: first, in-depth descriptions of the flora and fauna of Argentina and other South American countries; secondly, appeals for laws to protect birds and other animals in Britain. The former was the vital evidence to support the latter. But Patagonia and the pampas were still exotic for London's readers and Hudson finally achieved fame with his books on the English countryside—*Afoot in England* (1909), *A Shepherd's Life* (1910), *Dead Man's Plack* (1920), *A Traveller in Little Things* (1921) and *A Hind in Richmond Park* (1922).

The romances gained Hudson the attention of some leading authors in Britain, among them Joseph Conrad, Ford Madox Ford, Edward Garnett and George Gissing. As a "voice in the wilderness" he was compared by critics to Henry David Thoreau. When the so-called "back to nature" movement emerged in Britain after the First World War, it was these and not Hudson's ornithological writings or memoirs that were regarded as authoritative texts. But even in *Green Mansions*, a romantic fantasy, the principal character in the novel is arguably the forest. In *The Purple Land*, Hudson wrote, "Ah, yes, we are all vainly seeking after happiness in the wrong way.... We are still marching bravely on, conquering Nature, but how weary and sad we are getting."

Hudson died on 18 August 1922 in London. His birthplace at Quilmes, converted into a small, pleasant little house museum in his memory, is at the southern edge of greater Buenos Aires, the ugly suburban sprawl that extends for miles around the capital. There is still some greenery, but it is hard to imagine what it might have been like for an English family—and their bird-loving little boy—to live so far away from their origins in an empty place ruled by *caudillos* and military men. In contrast, the stretch of the Río Negro that Hudson explored has hardly changed at all.

HUDSON'S INFLUENCE

Were Hudson writing today, he would no doubt find an audience in the green movement. Yet, as Tomalin notes, few refer to him: "Today his constant readers number perhaps, world-wide, a few hundreds. In Britain alone his followers, in name at least, total hundreds of thousands, still increasing yearly. Few of these have ever heard of him."

Perhaps this is the price paid for any leader of a quiet revolution. John Galsworthy, who provided introductions to several of Hudson's works, wrote in 1915:

> Hudson, whether he knows it or not, is now the chief standard-bearer of another faith... All Hudson's books breathe this spirit of revolt against our new enslavement by towns and machinery... His work is a vision of natural beauty and of human life as it might be, quickened and sweetened by the sun and the wind and the rain, and by fellowship with all the other forms of life—the truest vision now being given to us, who are more in want of it than any generation has ever been. A very great writer; and—to my thinking—the most valuable our age possesses.

But perhaps Hudson leaves behind a sharp existential warning, too. In Ernest Hemingway's *The Sun Also Rises*, Jake notes his rival's reading matter:

> Then there was another thing. He had been reading W. H. Hudson. That sounds like an innocent occupation, but Cohn had read and reread *The Purple Land*. *The Purple Land* is a very sinister book if read too late in life. It recounts splendid imaginary amorous adventures of a perfect English gentleman in an intensely romantic land, the scenery of which is very well described. For a man to take it at thirty-four as a guide-book to what life holds is about as safe as it would be for a man of the same age to enter Wall Street direct from a French convent...

Sinister? Intensely romantic? Hudson's works, taken together, portray a life fully lived, if only for a brief period. The intensity and the introspective fire that burn through all the fiction and memoirs may be partly a consequence of melancholy, of Hudson's longing for Argentina and for a return to a state he felt he had almost achieved in his twenties. But some of the energy also derives purely and simply from the land and the strange, silent motions of birds, foxes, guanacos and *gauchos* in northern Patagonia. "Slow down" is the message, unnerving, unwavering and—perhaps fatally—unheeded.

Hudson put it in the starkest terms:

> The man who finishes his course by a fall from his horse, or is swept away and drowned when fording a swollen stream, has spent a happier life than he who dies of apoplexy in a counting-house or dining-room; or who, finding that end which seemed so infinitely beautiful to Leigh Hunt (which to me seems so unutterably hateful), drops his face on the open book before him.

Sadly, that is how he died, far from the pampas, and far from Patagonia.

Chapter Ten
PATAGONIA CONQUERED, 1870-1922

"Our President lately recalled the fact that vast areas existed in South America still unknown to geography, which were not only interesting on account of the rich products they may be presumed to contain, but also for the variety, beauty, and charm of their landscapes."

Dr. Francisco P. Moreno, *Explorations in Patagonia* (1899)

"*Ma yshorsks ysher*: I like your wife."

From the appendix to George C. Musters, *At Home with the Patagonians* (1871), showing useful Tehuelche phrases

After centuries of relative insignificance, Patagonia became strategically important to Argentina and Chile in the last quarter of the nineteenth century. Within a relatively short period both countries colonized the remaining wildernesses of their respective territories and wiped out the

native tribes who had ties to the land dating back some 13,000 years. For both nations, conquering Patagonia was important as a symbolic act; it demonstrated power and authority; it embodied the triumph of the white, urban ruling classes; and it also signified closure, tying hitherto separated regions to the capital cities and to each other.

Some factors merely prompted the nations to look south; others spurred them on with urgency. Orllie Antoine de Tounens was hardly a serious threat to Chilean statehood and was arrested and exiled without a military challenge from his Mapuche supporters. The Welsh settlement, though growing steadily, was small and isolated, and had accepted Argentinian sovereignty without protest.

The Mapuche, however, did represent a serious problem. In Chile they had been encircled and subdued by Saavedra's armies, but in Argentina the Mapuche and other natives of the southern pampas—many of whom had been "araucanized" (absorbed into the Mapuche culture)—were responsible for *malones*, or raids, on cattle ranches during which they made off with herds of cows together with horses and sheep. As well as the obvious economic cost of these incursions, the presence of native warriors frightened many landowners. At the political level they were an affront, and the fact that Mapuche rustlers were trading their stolen animals with Chilean ranchers enraged Argentina's military and political elite.

There were three further, equally pressing issues that spurred both governments to look south. The first and most sensitive problem was that the relationship between the governments in Santiago and Buenos Aires was soured by mutual distrust and the belief that each was a threat to the other. As late as 1875, Chile, notwithstanding the now century-old colony at Carmen de Patagones and the Welsh settlements along the Chubut valley, had expressed an intention of creating three colonies between the Magellan Strait and the Río Negro.

The second, ever-present, obstacle to both nations' perceived dominion over their lands was the British. Since 1833 the Falkland Islands had been under British control and there was regular maritime traffic between the islands and the coasts of Patagonia and Tierra del Fuego. Even if the days of Drake and Cavendish were long gone, there was a lasting suspicion (stretching into the present day) that the nation of *piratas* was fully capable of regarding Patagonia as a colony or quasi-colony even if she had never raised a flag on the mainland.

Historian Colin Lewis argues that a further key motive for Argentina's colonizing the whole of its vast interior was to quell "diplomatic disputes between Argentina and several European countries arising from the fate of immigrants... For several years after 1869, the British Emigration Commissioners regularly published warnings advising against emigration to Argentina, stressing the dangers of lawlessness and insecurity in the frontier. Similar concerns were voiced in Germany and Italy."

THE INVENTION OF ARGENTINA

By the middle of the nineteenth century Argentina wanted, more than anything else, immigrants. The 1853 constitution reads: "The federal government will foment European immigration and cannot restrict, limit nor tax the entry into Argentinian territory of any foreigner whose aim is to work the soil, improve industry or teach arts and science."

Many of the principles contained in the new constitution had reflected the vision of the diplomat and political theorist Juan Bautista Alberdi, who became famous for his slogan *gobernar es poblar*, "to govern is to populate." In his *Bases y puntos de partida para la organización nacional de la República Argentina* (1852), Alberdi explained the purpose of encouraging colonization of the interior:

> Do we wish to plant and nurture here in America the liberty of the English, the culture of the French, the work ethic of the man of Europe and of the United States of America? Let us bring here living examples of all these in the customs of the men of these countries and root them here... This is the only means by which America, today a desert, will become an opulent world in a short time.

To this seemingly pragmatic attitude was coupled widespread support for Domingo F. Sarmiento's argument that Argentina needed to quash all forms of rural barbarism, which for him meant not only the native and *mestizo* populations, but also the gauchos and Afro-Argentinians who had been serving in the private armies of the dictator Juan Manuel de Rosas since 1829. In his political treatise-cum-novel *Facundo* (1845), Sarmiento looked ahead to a whiter, brighter time: "In ten years a million industrious Europeans, spread throughout the Republic, teaching us how to work, will exploit new wealth and enrich the country with their qualities; with a million civilized men civil war would be impossible."

Many maps of the period described the land south of the Río Negro as *tierra de nadie* or no man's land—which prompted the government to offer generous land grants to settlers willing to begin a new, hard life in the empty spaces. European colonies had been created in the 1850s and 1860s in several northern provinces and now it was time to look south.

Although the 1853 Argentine constitution putatively recognized indigenous peoples as citizens of the Republic, the reality was discriminatory. The ruling class in Buenos Aires and the central provinces knew that to open up new lands in the south meant dislocating and dispossessing the Tehuelche and Mapuche.

REMINGTON ROCA
Sometimes he is "General", sometimes "Presidente", but everyone knows him as Roca. Julio A. Roca's middle name was Argentino. His nickname was *Zorrito* or "Little Fox".

Since independence Argentinian armies had been involved in frequent territorial campaigns in the north, east, west and centre of the country, and as early as the 1830s forts had been established on the fringes of northern Patagonia. The *conquista del desierto* (desert campaign or conquest) led by Roca in 1878-79 was to change the landscape of Patagonia dramatically and irreversibly. Whereas settlement in the previous 350 years had been sporadic and concentrated on the coast, Roca planned to send armies sweeping across the pampas and up the river valleys into the foothills of the Andes. In 1874 he sent a letter to the minister of war and navy, Adolfo Alsina:

> Static forts in the middle of the desert kill discipline, weaken the line and only protect a very limited radius. In my opinion the best fort and the best wall, in order to make war against the Indians and overwhelm them in a single shock-movement, consists in sending out mounted units which invade the [native] encampments incessantly, surprising them when they least expect it... I commit myself to executing this plan in two years: one to prepare it, another to execute it.

Roca was given his two years. Using Gatling guns and the brand-new Remington machine-guns his armies stuck firmly to the simple plan of

shock tactics and merciless treatment of the natives. Many of the latter, riding bareback across the plains and often escaping in families or large groups, were unarmed. Only about 2,000 plains Indians survived the extermination, and many of these were rounded up and shipped to the Isla Martín García in the River Plate delta, where they died of disease. It is said that Roca paid his junior soldiers according to how many pairs of human testicles they brought back.

Much of the *conquista* involved finding and pursuing small groups of natives. A report dated 13 July 1879, intended for Colonel D. Eduardo Racedo and signed by an officer named Juan A. Alvarez, is typical. Alvarez describes how a search for a group of Ranquel tribesmen near a stream called Arroyo Lacha in the vicinity of the Río Colorado dragged on and on without any success. "There were 26 Indians in the formation, of whom 10 or 12 had spears, the others were unarmed," he reports, and then wonders why the natives would not take on his troops. "As we explored the stream, we continued our pursuit, but seeing that they always fled, I separated Captain Albornoz with four soldiers to see if in this way we could, using a smaller unit, give them the courage they were not demonstrating. The Captain was in pursuit for a long time, until, persuaded of the absolute cowardice of the Indians, he returned and regrouped with my units."

The weather was atrocious throughout the winter campaigns, and there were outbreaks of smallpox among both soldiers and captured natives. But much of the "action" was dull and uneventful. Alvarez says, "I should have liked to seize Cacique Baigorrita and offer him to Your Excellency as a trophy of my campaign, but all hopes of achieving that were dashed by the fatality of destiny."

The *conquista* was, then, a melancholy and desultory slow grind over the cold deserts, punctuated by spasmodic acts of ultra-violence against unprepared, unequal foes. Yet it was, on Roca's terms, a huge success. In October 1878 the Argentinian government baptized Patagonia as an official territory and named its capital as Mercedes de Patagones. In 1880 the Argentine citizenry rewarded Roca for his pains by electing him president. He served six years then and a further six years between 1898 and 1904, the longest period in office of any Argentinian president. During his first watch the *conquista* was advanced to the far south. In 1881 Argentina and Chile signed a treaty recognizing Argentinian sovereignty over virtually all of Argentina and defining the east-west border as the line following the high peaks of the Andes. (In Patagonia this line is not always the watershed and the accord has been a source of many disputes as well as an object of derision for many nationalistic Chilean historians.) Chilean president Aníbal Pinto had little choice but to agree to the treaty to prevent Argentina from siding with Peru and Bolivia in the War of the Pacific.

Though Roca's principal ambition was to reach as far as the Río Negro, there was always a more complete vision behind the *conquista* programme. In 1884, after a final push by military forces, the territories of Chubut and Santa Cruz were established. The penal colony of Ushuaia, in Tierra del Fuego, was founded in the same year. Roca had it all.

The speed and comprehensiveness of the military campaign, tied to the plain fact that in just two years Argentina had evolved into a truly vast and potentially great nation (it is the eighth largest on the planet), turned Roca into a symbol of national pride and brute power. Historian David Rock claims that with the *conquista*, the idea of Argentina as "a nation graced by Nature and by God, predestined for power and greatness" was born, and goes on to say that this would in turn give rise to the intimate and lasting association between nationalism and the armed forces.

Yet conquest did not lead to the peopling of Patagonia. The campaign was financed by prior land sales, and some twenty million acres of land snatched from the tribes was shared out between 381 speculators and military bigwigs. As a consequence, Argentina became not so much nation as an untilled, unpopulated wilderness; the ideals of Sarmiento, Alberdi and Roca were so much dust blowing over the steppes.

Many of the forts established by Roca and his successors are now the main towns and cities of Patagonia. Even resorts such as San Martín de los Andes and Junín de los Andes were created as military posts. As the first tourists began to arrive in northern Patagonia in the early twentieth century (the visit of super-rich Aarón de Anchorena and his friends to San Carlos de Bariloche in 1902 is often cited as the first package tour) these towns, in their shift from frontier posts to fleshpots, offered little in the way of "culture" and no one settled there to actively develop the land or other resources. To this day, the Mapuche of San Martín protest at the exploitation of their limited water supplies for tourism.

If the agreement with Chile had settled any issues relating to the main frontier, an advance into Tierra del Fuego was also part of the overall plan of the *conquista del desierto*. Mixing cynical fatalism with *faux* paternalism, Senator Miguel Cané pronounced in 1899:

> I do not have confidence in the destiny of the Fuegian race. I believe that the implacable law that condemns inferior organisms will apply to them, as it is applying itself elsewhere around the globe; but it is the… obligation of civilized societies to do whatever they can to prolong the existence, to better the well-being of these defenceless, destitute races, as the physician who takes care of the hopeless patient does.

Cané wanted to apply social Darwinism in the land where the theory had—perhaps—first been intuited. Others believed indigenous blood might be acceptable if diluted. A year after Cané's remarks, a senior legislator made the following appeal: "I do not want that a parallel be established: on the one hand the Indians, on the other the Argentinians, as the North Americans did and still do with the blacks. I want the immediate mixture, with the conviction that, in a generation, the savage will disappear, for it is an undeniable fact that the superior civilization destroys, prevails over, overpowers, the inferior one."

They need not have worried; between 1900 and 1922, Fuegian blood would be spilt too fast to be diluted.

BUENOS AIRES HERALD

As part of the general inward flow of migrants, British traders and workers arrived in Buenos Aires and other major cities. In 1876 the English-language *Buenos Aires Herald* newspaper was founded, and only three years later it had gained enough credibility and recognition within Roca's circle to be invited to send a correspondent to follow the *conquista*. The *Herald* was fully behind the campaign, its editorial of 1 January 1879 exhorting rapid and decisive action: "Now is the time to move in this direction. Let this be done, and push settlements close up to the Río Negro frontier, the strains to which public finance is driven will be relieved, and we do here what the United States have done at the north."

But other sections of the paper show us how expatriates in the capital, which was, at that time, very far indeed from the action, viewed the relocation and rounding-up of natives. Here are the short notices for Friday, 3 January 1879:

- The 1,200 Remingtons with which government intends arming the Rural Police will be sent to the camp districts in ensuing weeks
- 123 more Indians have been sent in from Trenquelauquen [in the far west of Buenos Aires province]
- We have been asked by various persons for information as to how to set about obtaining a little Indian of those lately sent in as prisoners… We may also be allowed to say that it is very foolish to take Indians as they are dirty and mischievous; they will lay hands on anything they see…
- The masked balls on the 31st were a decided success
- General Roca, the Minister of War, is again very sick, we must trust only of a light temporary ailment

LADY AT LEISURE

Even as Roca's soldiers were galloping in formation from the north and east and the plains tribes were fleeing on foot or on mounts in a westerly direction, a member of the English gentry was advancing from the south. On 14 December 1878 the daughter of the seventh Marquis of Queensberry, Florence Dixie, visited Patagonia with her husband, her two brothers, and family friend Julius Beerbohm, who had already visited Patagonia a few years earlier.

Conversations with Beerbohm and a reading of George Chatworth Musters' 1871 *At Home with the Patagonians* had fired her imagination. At the beginning of the book that came out of the trip, *Across Patagonia* (1880), Dixie also claims psychological reasons:

> Precisely because it was an outlandish place and so far away, I chose it. Palled for the moment with civilization and its surroundings, I wanted to escape somewhere, where I might be as far removed from them as possible.
>
> Many of my readers have doubtless felt the dissatisfaction with oneself, and everybody else, that comes over one at times in the midst of the pleasures of life; when one wearies of the shallow artificiality of modern existence; when what was once excitement has become so no longer, and a longing grows up within one to taste a more vigorous emotion than that afforded by the monotonous round of society's so-called "pleasures".

Like Hudson before her, Dixie sought solace. But her text falls short of his mystical minimalism and is, rather, tiresomely whimsical, repetitive and full of ostrich hunting, campfire chit-chat and sleeping al fresco. It is not that the prose is interestingly monotonous, as some kind of formal response to the long, tedious rides and dreary dun-coloured landscape, but—like so many accounts of self-indulgent equestrian escapades—the narrative suffers from the uniquely tiresome monotony of glee. The literature of constant action can be curiously static for the reader.

Dixie is often to be found admiring the scenery—in the Victorian sense of an edifying element. Fernanda Peñaloza, in her essay "A Sublime Journey to the Barren Plains" (2004) argues that Dixie, the first British woman to travel across Patagonia, "uses the landscape as a testing ground for exploring herself." This, she believes, is evident in the way that Dixie expresses her "enjoyment of the sublime", citing Burke's belief that "greatness of dimension is a powerful cause of the sublime" and understanding the sublime to be an encounter "with excess" and the impact of that excess "on the subject's sense of self". In short, the sublime is that area of experience that stretches our ability to describe what we are going through.

A typical urge to record the sublime is this short passage:

> Scenes of infinite beauty and grandeur might be lying hidden in the
> Silent solitude of the mountains which bound the barren plains of the
> Pampas, into whose mysterious recesses no one as yet had ever ventured.
> And I was to be the first to behold them—an egotistical pleasure, it is
> true; but the idea had a great charm for me, as it has had for many
> others.

Dixie is evidently impressed by the vastness of the Patagonian landscape—
though she also sees "infinite beauty" in its recesses.

And what of the massacre unfolding to the north? Nowhere, between
the secrets, the wonder and the alien thrill, is there any space for history
or current affairs. As Peñaloza writes, "Dixie turns Patagonia into an empty
space, devoid of 'civilisation', resulting in a narrative without historical reference to the political or economic content of her journey."

If Dixie brought anything new to the discourse of Patagonian travel
writing, it is simply that her expressions of the sublime are focused on
herself, as a woman. But in failing to see beyond her horse's ears, she was
not challenging or subverting the masculine gaze at all, merely ignoring it.
Peñaloza points out that almost all of the narratives we have are written by
men and many of them are typically masculine "conquest" narratives.
Almost as an aside, she adds: "The barren plains, the desert and the
Cordillera all seem so easily to convey masculine metaphors of power."
This sleight of hand allows her to move coolly from the prior observation
that most writers on Patagonia are male to a description of the scenery
itself as "hyper-masculine".

Surely it is not the land that *conveys* such metaphors ("barren" is only
used of women) but how men perceive both the land and their actions
upon it. If we regard the land, rather, as a woman, it adds metaphoric
potency to Roca's heroic ride down to the Río Negro. Was he, in his macho
imagination, fertilizing the sterile plains as he fired round after round into
the bare chests of the cowardly *indios* and had his horse prance, gaucho-
style, in pools of blood?

BORDERS: EL "PERITO" MORENO

From the mid-nineteenth century scientists and explorers were sent out
from Buenos Aires and Santiago de Chile to bring back information about
natural resources, native populations and mining prospects, and to gather

data that could be used to prepare detailed maps of hitherto unknown regions. Chief among them was Francisco Pascasio Moreno, the first explorer and scientist from the Argentinian academy to achieve anything like fame beyond his own shores.

He was born in 1852 in Buenos Aires. His mother, Juana Thwaites, was of British descent and he was taught to speak English. Moreno and his brothers and sister were encouraged by their father to be nature-lovers and collectors and in 1866 he gave them an attic in which to create a small museum. On trips to Palermo park and the banks of the River Plate they collected bugs, soil and mud samples, bones and flowers. When he was 19 Moreno began to explore the pampas, and travelled to the lake at Chascomus in Buenos Aires province to collect fossils.

After a short spell as an employee in his father's insurance company, Moreno decided to dedicate his energies to his growing collection. At the age of 21 he set out on his first journey to southern Argentina, which took him to Carmen de Patagones. His second trip in 1874 brought him to the mouth of the Santa Cruz river. These encounters with the coast stirred up a desire to penetrate the interior, despite the inherent dangers.

Initially there was limited government support for Moreno's explorations. In 1875 he became the first Argentinian ever to reach Lago Nahuel Huapi in north-western Patagonia. On 22 January 1876 he hoisted the national flag on its shores. At the end of the same year Moreno and another Argentinian explorer, naval officer Carlos Moyano, sailed up the Santa Cruz from the Isla Pavón. On this trip they discovered Lago San Martín, explored numerous rivers in Patagonia, and on 4 March 1877 encountered the towering pinnacle known to the Tehuelche as El Chaltén ("smoking mountain", because of the wisps of cloud that make it appear like a volcano). They renamed it Monte Fitz Roy. The next day they christened the lake at the western end of the Santa Cruz river Lago Argentino, and raised a flag at the site now known as Punta Bandera (Flag Point).

By naming and claiming the land for the nation Moreno was only being a good patriot. He wanted to draw attention to the potential for development in Patagonia. But members of the urban ruling class in Argentina were too comfortable sipping cognac at the Jockey Club in Buenos Aires to visit their vast estates and, in any case, the nearby pampas provided easy wealth for a minimum of investment.

There was no perceived tension between science and industry. Knowledge was achieved by observing and measuring, but also by killing (fauna) or removing (flora, indigenous tools and skeletons) and collecting. As the quotation at the opening of this chapter makes explicit, Moreno saw no conflict between the "rich products" of the earth and the "variety, beauty, and charm" of a landscape.

With regard to the natives, Moreno was ambivalent. He firmly believed that they had knowledge to share and rejected the more extreme creole position that development meant annihilating them. Yet he was unable to embrace their "otherness" and believed that the only solution was to employ and educate them in the manners and modes of Europeans and creoles. In his *Viaje a la Patagonia Austral* (1879), an account of the 1876-77 expedition which first appeared as a column in the *La Nación* newspaper, he writes:

> It is commonly believed that for Patagonia to be successfully settled, the extermination of the Indians is necessary. If the latter, with their savage pride, do not ask of the soil what it does not voluntarily give them, it is because they despise sedentary life and prefer to succumb to the fasci-

nation that they feel for the endless horizons of the desert... The day that the Tehuelche, and all the other pampas tribes for that matter, come to appreciate our civilization instead of being taught our vices, and are treated by us as fellow human beings, we will have them working on our [Río] Gallegos farms, performing the same services as our gauchos.

Back in Buenos Aires later that year, Moreno decided to donate his now sizeable collection of fossils, archaeological artefacts, rocks and flora and fauna samples, as well as his library, to the province of Buenos Aires. This formed the basis for the La Plata Museum of Natural Sciences, directed by Moreno as of its founding in 1886.

In 1880 Moreno went on a second expedition to northern Patagonia. He was taken prisoner by a band of Tehuelche led by the *cacique* Saihueque (sometimes spelt Sayhueque), one of the most powerful tribal leaders of the western plains. Moreno was condemned to death, but escaped on 11 March, the day before he was due to be executed. In 1884-85 he carried out new explorations of the territory south of the Río Negro.

Moreno was a tireless traveller, and spent much of his life on stagecoaches, ships, walking, on horseback and, as railways fanned out west and south, on trains. His unique knowledge of the interior gave him the confidence to become a self-appointed spokesman for the future of Patagonia. He wanted the oligarchy to go out into the wilderness and exploit, and in 1897 he wrote the following call to action:

It is necessary that we, Argentines, reverse as soon as possible our abandonment of the exploitation of the Republic and of the natural riches it offers. To think of that abandonment is painful; and if from time to time there appears an isolated effort toward a more favourable reaction, it breaks down before the difficulties that arise from our ignorance of the land... We lack a sure foundation, that is a complete knowledge of the geography, geology, and meteorology, of the fauna and flora; and we who strive to assemble this knowledge as rapidly as may be and who combat the indifference of the public and the selfish interests of those who exploit the ignorance of the majority for their own gain, we may not falter in our task, for we are convinced that the Argentine Republic will never occupy the position to which she is entitled in the concert of nations unless the national welfare be founded on bases of firmer character than those that now exist.

In Patagonia Moreno had observed how the watershed did not lie on the high peaks in areas where very ancient rivers had worn deep clefts into the Andes and caused lakes on the eastern slopes to flow west into the Pacific, and occasionally in both westerly and easterly directions. In the late 1890s he was tasked to address the disputes with Chile over boundaries, and moved to London with his family to present his case to a board of neutral arbitrators; he also lectured on Patagonian themes at the Royal Geographical Society. The final accord, which recognized Argentina's borders, was signed by King Edward VII at the end of 1902.

For his endeavours, Moreno was recognized as a *perito* or expert. To this day, Argentinians use the nickname *El Perito Moreno* as a term of endearment, something like "Cleverclogs Moreno", but the title relates to his expert knowledge of geology and his involvement in frontier disputes that almost drove Argentina and Chile into all-out war.

In August 1903 the Argentinian government awarded Moreno 25 square leagues (175 square miles) of state-owned land beside Lago Nahuel Huapi. Three months later Moreno presented three square leagues of the wilderness to the nation in order to create Argentina's first national park, which was established in 1934. There are now eleven national parks in Argentinian Patagonia.

Argentina has been described by author Jimmy Burns as "the land that lost its heroes." During the past century many iconic figures have been exiled or denigrated. Thus Eva Perón went from being a stateswoman to a slut. Tango legend Carlos Gardel's life-long bachelorhood has led some authors to suggest that he was gay—and they intend it as a smear. Diego Maradona is a national icon for some, a drug-abusing national shame for others. But Francisco Moreno is generally viewed with the same kind of admiration as that expressed by his fellow scientist and friend Bailey Willis in *A Yanqui in Patagonia* (1947):

> Dr. Francisco P. Moreno... was a rare personality... Among men of Moreno's nationality personal ambition is more often than not the ruling motive. But he was selfless where knowledge of the truth was his objective... He grasped the latent possibilities of Patagonia for settlement and

development as a national asset and his vision was that of a practical scientist; he realized the necessity for exact information on resources...
...Moreno's was the voice of a prophet in the wilderness. He was not heard.

For Argentinian cultural critic David Viñas, Moreno, for all his aspirations to be scientific and sympathetic to the native cause, was a man of his time and inextricably a part of the *conquista* scheme:

> Though... one supposes that [Moreno] aims to be objective—especially if one considers the obsessively neutral tone of his books—the connotations that define the power-seeking programme of Roca's generation surface in every sentence. The men of the '80s were absolutists and if they grasped the whole of humanity it was through a doing away with diversity... as a consequence Moreno is used to seeing the Indians not as individuals but as fragments of a whole... if the Victorians regarded their own body as a contretemps, the Indian's body was a scandal. The only thing they could do was cover the former with a hoop skirt, bows and laces, and eliminate the latter by manhunts, head measurements and museums.

In any case, the hero was only ever honoured in name. When Moreno died in 1919, a notebook in his desk recorded his last wishes:

> ...I am 66 years old and haven't a cent! I have given eighteen hundred leagues to my country and a National Park for the benefit of future citizens, so that they may find solace and renewed strength to serve this country. Yet I have not so much as a square meter of land to give my children to bury my ashes! It was I who staked the claim over eighteen hundred leagues of disputed territory for Argentina, when no one else would defend those lands and secure Argentinian sovereignty over them. Still there is no place for my ashes, not even a 20cm by 20cm box. My ashes would take up so little space. Yet if they were spread out they might stretch across all the land I acquired for my country. It would no doubt be a very thin layer but it would be visible to the eyes of those who are, in fact, grateful.

NATIONAL PARKS

Moreno's name is now commemorated by both the little-known Parque Nacional Perito Moreno, in central Patagonia, and the Glaciar Perito Moreno, the key attraction of Argentina's Parque Nacional Los Glaciares in southern Patagonia.

Yet he was by no means the only Latin American to champion the preservation and protection of the Patagonian wilderness. Turin-born Salesian missionary Alberto de Agostini was a keen explorer, a mountaineer and also an accomplished photographer, and his images of southern Patagonia helped to disseminate knowledge of the Andean peaks. A Chilean national park eighty miles west of Punta Arenas is named after him.

In the same country's lake district, German zoologist Bernardo Philippi, originally commissioned to gather flora and fauna by the University of Berlin, was employed in the 1840s by the Chilean government to survey the inland lakes in the Osorno and Llanquihue areas. His reports led to a law turning all vacant lands into state property that facilitated immigration—especially from Philippi's homeland—but also allowed the creation of parklands in the 1920s. In this respect he was very much the Chilean Moreno, raising an awareness of the environment while simultaneously opening it up for deforestation and development.

One of Latin America's best-loved reserves, the Parque Nacional Torres del Paine in Chile's XI Region, has become a talisman for Patagonia. The jagged granite ridges of the Paine massif rise majestically above the surrounding plains, and the park's 935 square miles—located in a transition zone between the subpolar forests of the Magellanic region and the steppes—contain an impressive variety of ecosystems and habitats that shelter the Andean condor, puma, Patagonian grey fox, lesser rhea and guanaco as well as many threatened species. Like most protected areas in Patagonia, Torres del Paine started as ranchland and was only later adopted as a national park; homesteads and grazing animals can still be seen around its periphery.

ANARCHY ON THE SHEEP FARMS

Introducing his 456-page memoir *A Story of Patagonia* (2003), John Locke Blake prepares his readers for what will be the common thread to his narrative:

Most of the people we are going to hear about had one thing in common: their lives revolved around, and depended upon, the *sheep* [his bold and italics]. This humble animal, in all its shapes, sizes, colours and breeds, has provided food, clothing and wealth for man for thousands of years. It has provided the basis for whole cultures and ways of life, and Patagonia—which is the real subject of these musings—would not have been settled if not for the sheep.

The conquest of the desert opened up the pampas and steppes beyond for farming. The first settlers in southern Patagonia—what is now the province of Santa Cruz—were English and Scottish sheep farmers, some of whom had fought alongside Roca and his *criollo* armies. Some Scots had migrated from the Falklands. Uprooted violently and exiled from their own homelands in the Highland clearances of the 1840s, they were willing to forcibly remove another civilization for the chance to become local lairds themselves.

In 1874 Henry Reynard, an English trader, arrived in Punta Arenas. Ignoring the local predators (puma and *carancho* hawks) and the fact that the place already had its own woolly livestock in the form of the guanaco, Reynard decided to import sheep to the region. He brought them over from the Falkland Islands and ran them on Elizabeth Island, a small island in the Magellan Strait, where they multiplied and soon spread to the mainland.

Reynard leased and settled Estancia "Oazy Harbour" but did not purchase it, later moving to a new site in Argentina where he founded an *estancia* called "Cañadón de las Vacas". The news travelled fast and Englishmen poured in. Moreno's sidekick, Carlos María Moyano, had been appointed governor of Santa Cruz and was given specific orders to encourage settlement, including inviting people from the Falkland Islands. For a period questions of sovereignty were put to one side; Moyano even went so far as to travel to the Falklands, where he met and married a local girl, Ethel Turner.

The first Romney sheep arrived from England around 1885, sent by wool barons from the Falklands. Some settlers drove pedigree Merinos from Buenos Aires province during a two-year, 1,700-mile journey. None of these hardships deterred the pioneers.

Settling in the south, however, was no holiday, as the harsh wind in

summer and the bitter cold in winter make even the towns ghostly. Tough Scots who had suffered several seasons in the Falklands had to face massive challenges in the new country—one settler, William Halliday, lost all his belongings on the very first night when the fast tide came up the Río Gallegos and took away his cargo.

The city of Río Gallegos was founded in 1885. A visitor to the town noted: "The normal language seems to be English, one has the feeling of being in Old England or at least in the Falklands. Except for the government officials, everything else is in English: the money, the sheep, the drinks, the ladies and the gentlemen." Pubs such as the White Elephant were a home from home.

In 1911 the British Club of Río Gallegos was opened. A portrait of its founder, George MacGeorge, looks down on the gloomy wood-panelled interior. The owners boast that the club has the only snooker table in Patagonia (though no one uses it) and *estancieros* still come to play cards and have a glass of Scotch.

Englishness has survived in people's faces and in surnames, but sheep have not prospered in Patagonia. In the late 1930s, Patagonia was, behind Australia, the world's second largest wool-producing region. The wool market collapsed in 1966, however, and never recovered. Patagonian lamb's meat—*cordero patagónico*—is revered throughout Argentina, but is hardly exported. In 1991 a million and a half sheep were killed when Chile's Mount Hudson volcano erupted. But the most serious problem for Patagonia has been the sheep themselves; they eat everything and their hooves, unlike those of the guanacos, destroy the thin, fragile layer of grasses that grows there. The far south was never as green as the humid pampa, but man-made desertification has turned huge swathes of the region into barren wasteland.

Lonely Outposts

Look at a detailed map of Patagonia, especially the southern tip, and the only sign of life along many of the lonely gravel roads is an arrow pointing off to an *estancia*, often far away from the junction and hidden behind rolling hills. Just as towns such as Bariloche memorialize the tribes that were massacred to make way for them, so *estancias* often carry indigenous names. Estancia Tapi Aike, Estancia Pali Aike and Estancia Camasú Aike all incorporate the Tehuelche word for "place". In northern Patagonia the names are more likely to be influenced by the Mapuche tongue. There is Estancia Tipiliuke, from the Mapuche for "inverted heart", an allusion to the shape of the mountains; and Estancia Huechahue, where the name means "battleground".

Others reach out to distant homelands—Estancia Glencross, Estancia Helsingfors, Estancia La Siberiana—to heroes (Estancia Skyring), to local linguistic tics (Estancia Quien Sabe—as in "Who Knows Ranch"), or simply to nature: Hill Station, Punta del Lago, Stag River. These last may suggest a lack of imagination, but in the arid steppe, there is no doubt that those who spend their lives in remote *estancias* have an intimate relationship with the one river or hill or rock formation that gives character to their homestead.

Imagined from a distance as romantic, poetically isolated havens of human warmth and honest labour, *estancias* are also desperate places of boredom, loneliness, economic insecurity and miserable routine, especially during the terrible winters that punish the far south. In his 1961 memoir *A Patagonian Panorama*, expatriate author Tom Jones writes: "Whether it is the dreary and crude climate of Patagonia or the lonely life in the camp after the day's work or remorse after a bout of hard drinking, I cannot say, but I have known, some very intimately, well over 20 people who have committed suicide."

TIERRA DEL FUEGO: THE WINNERS

While the land-grabbing in north and central Patagonia had been taken forward by military forces working on behalf of Buenos Aires, Tierra del Fuego—far more remote, and not physically connected to the continent or the *patria*—was colonized by landowners.

In 1873 Spanish-born bookkeeper José Menéndez travelled south from Buenos Aires and was struck by the opportunities for trading; ships sailing around the Horn stopped to replenish, and natives exchanged pelts, ambergris and even grazing rights for trinkets and tobacco. Menéndez set up a trading post at Punta Arenas and became friendly with a Russian immigrant, Elias Braun, who farmed nearby. In 1895 Braun's eldest son, Mauricio, married Menéndez's eldest daughter, Josefina. It was the perfect alliance. In 1896 Menéndez founded the Estancia Primera Argentina (later Estancia José Menéndez) on the south bank of the Río Grande, in Tierra del Fuego. Its 550 square miles stretched from the Atlantic coast to the Chilean border, and comprised rolling plains, high hills and forests, with rivers and numerous lakes in its western part. In 1908 Mauricio Braun and José Menéndez created the Sociedad Anónima Importadora y Exportadora de la Patagonia, usually referred to as La Anónima.

Jose María Borrero's *La Patagonia trágica* (1928) is a book about the ambitions of José Menéndez and those who followed his lead in Tierra del Fuego and Santa Cruz. He sets the scene by taking us to Punta Arenas, where a statue of Magellan bears a bronze plaque: *A Hernando de Magallanes* (to Ferdinand Magellan). Below it is the name of the man who dedicated the inscription—José Menéndez—and the date in Roman numerals: MCMXX. Borrero imagines a dialogue between a young tourist and a local old man who bump into each other while reading the plaque:

"Who is this José Menéndez, who is so familiar with Hernando de Magallanes?"

"Don't you know him?" he enquired.

"Not at all," replied the young man. "And I read all about the history of the discovery of the Strait as I travelled here, and all the related stories, but this personage is never mentioned."

"Well you see," the venerable old man explained, with terrible, bloody irony, "he is nothing less than the avenger of Magallanes."

"How is he the avenger?"

"Yes, sir, yes, the avenger. Don't doubt it. Doesn't history tell us how savages murdered Hernando de Magallanes on a Pacific island? Well, José Menéndez, with other men of the same stamp and standing, killed almost all the Indians on this other island in the Atlantic... the dead is avenged."

Borrero's book is not a rigorous attempt to document the history of the removal of the Fuegian natives from their homeland but a polemical denunciation of the *estancia* class. He claims the Menéndez and Braun families, as well as the Montes, Suárez, Petterson, Stubenrauch and Hobbs, were able to exercise absolute control over commerce and governance in Punta Arenas, "a place totally isolated from the educated, scientific world."

Initially European settlers had used "bullets, poison and alcohol", writes Borrero. In exchange they received exotic skins, ostrich feathers, gold and just about anything else the natives produced. This, he argues, was the foundation of Patagonia's "ridiculous 'aristocracy'". But, he argues, these bar-owners-made-good began to be concerned about the Tehuelche, Selknam, Yahgan and other tribes. On the one hand, the natives were sheep-rustlers and therefore criminals and had to be treated as such. On the other, although alcohol had lured many natives away from any kind of political awakening, contact with Salesian and Anglican missions had led some in-digenous leaders to achieve a certain degree of education and these, in turn, had begun to raise an awareness of land-rights among their tribesmen.

"Thus," writes Borrero, again speaking through the character of the wise old man, "they decided to annihilate them en masse, and they did so, before the civilized world woke up to their odious practices."

Borrero gives an account of one Mister Bond, who worked as an "Indian hunter" and, due to merit, ascended to the rank of captain. "At the beginning he and his companions were paid a pound sterling for each 'pair of ears' they gave in. But as some of the hunters were too soft-hearted and contented themselves with removing the ears without killing the victim... the system was changed and a pound sterling was paid for a head, testicles, breasts or some other vital organ." Mister Bond apparently liked to tell of his exploits during a round of jokes.

THE GOLD RUSH: JULIUS POPPER

Before the Panama Canal opened in 1914, east coast Americans drawn to California could either travel across the Wild West or sail round the Horn and approach their destinations from the Pacific coast. Many chose the latter—and those who made the voyage in the 1880s were delighted to find, only half way through their voyage, that there were rumours of a very Californian dream—a gold rush in southern Patagonia.

The precious metal had been found by chance when black sand and mud were being collected along the eastern coastline. Announcements of a handful of findings were published many times over, generating exaggerated media attention and attracting waves of fortune seekers. The first few years brought numerous mining expeditions into the region, with many making handsome returns. On Lennox and Nueva Islands, over two tons of gold were collected in three short years.

One of the goldhunters was Julius Popper, an engineer, adventurer and explorer born in 1857 in Bucharest. After concluding his studies in Paris he travelled to Constantinople, Egypt, Japan, China, India and Siberia. Then he explored the western hemisphere, passing through New Orleans, Cuba (where he was responsible for the planning of modern Havana), Mexico and Brazil. He ended up in Buenos Aires, where he heard of the riches to be had in the remote south and, in September 1886, he took a team of eighteen prospectors to Tierra del Fuego.

They found gold dust on the beach at El Páramo and Popper duly created the Compañia de Lavaderos de Oro del Sud, realizing significant capital gains at the Argentine stock exchange. He created a private army to protect his interests and franked his own coins and stamps. In an address to the Argentinian Geographical Institute, delivered on 5 March 1887, Popper holds out a land of promise:

> Gold is the great attraction. The smallest particle of the precious metal found on the surface of the earth agitates the minds of people more than thousands of acres of good grazing lands, fertile meads and luxuriant forests. What matters that it requires hours of labor to find a second particle of gold dust? We must have some fixed object in view in this age of steam, electricity and powerful machinery. Do we not hear of enormous quantities of gold extracted from the bowels of the earth even in places where individual labor gives no result whatever; and when the

rumour spreads does it not give rise to all sorts of exaggerations? The gold-hunting epidemic breaks out and before long claims its victims from all classes and ranks of society.

As they travelled, Popper's gang met other prospectors and interviewed them, but they spent days in barren, uncharted areas where food was scarce. The men became hungry, forced to slay one of their mares one day and eat wild celery on other occasions. Attempting to hunt guanaco, they also ran into several groups of natives, not all of them happy to discover white men reconnoitering their territory:

We were pursuing a guanaco, when we suddenly fell in with eighty Indians, with their faces painted red, and in a state of complete nakedness, scattered about behind some short bushes. We had scarcely seen them when a shower of arrows fell upon us, and stuck fast in the ground close to our knees, happily without causing us any loss. We soon alighted, and returned the compliment with our Winchester rifles. It was a strange combat. While we were firing, the Indians lay with their faces to the ground, and left off shooting their arrows; but the moment our shots ceased we again heard the whistling of the missiles.

How strange did this really seem to Popper? Was he expecting the natives to attempt to stand up and fire arrows as they were torn apart by Roca's favourite gun. He describes how, gradually, he and his men were able to withdraw in a windward direction, making the arrows fall short of them. "On this occasion two Indians were left dead on the field," he remarks, adding that such encounters took place "almost daily".

He concludes his lecture with recommendations that Tierra del Fuego be developed through sheep-farming on the one hand and gold-mining on the other. The lecture was later published in English in Buenos Aires, with a cover illustration—based on documentary photographs—showing Popper and his armed men standing tall above the bodies of dead natives.

When the Argentine peso was devalued during the market crash of 1890, Popper's money was highly prized. But the fact was that he had arrived too late. By 1885 gold-rush gains had already slowed significantly (and in 1910 all activity came to a sudden halt). Though many prospectors left as penniless as they had arrived, the influx of people brought vitality to Tierra del Fuego's local economy. *Estancias* were able to profit from supplying goods to the new settlers who provided demand for products where before none had existed. Local stores opened to cater to the influx of immigrants, and the gold rush wave resulted in permanent increases in local populations.

Popper died aged 35 in Buenos Aires. The cause of death remains unclear, but sources suggest he was assassinated by a member of the local gold mafia.

TIERRA DEL FUEGO: THE LOSERS

"For those who exploit him the price of a man is lower than that of a mule, a ram or a horse."

Sociedad Obrera de Río Gallegos, Manifesto, November 1920

Across the road from the Estancia La Anita (which tourists know as an annexe of the ultra-smart Alta Vista hotel) is a small stone monument well hidden in the long grass. A plaque, pinned here in 1998, commemorates the strikers of Santa Cruz, noting: "If there is a history written by those who win, that means there is another history."

La Anita belonged to the Menéndez-Braun clan, which by 1920 controlled dozens of similar establishments, possessing titles to some 3.5 million acres grazed by 1.25 million sheep producing annually five million tons of wool, 250,000 tons of meat and 700 tons of hide.

In 1919 Buenos Aires factory workers marching for shorter working days, free Sundays and wage increases under the banner of the Federación Obrera Regional Argentina (the main workers' federation in Argentina) clashed with the Liga Patriótica paramilitary organization. This quasi-legal body received most of its support and funding from land-owning oligarchs bent on upholding conservative traditions and property rights. For seven days, now known as the *Semana Trágica* (Tragic Week), there were pitched battles in the streets of the San Cristóbal neighbourhood, close to Congress. While many of the workers wielded only the cobblestones they could rip up from the streets and shards of broken glass, the police had rifles. About 700 workers were killed.

Police in Río Gallegos detained members of the local branch of the Sociedad Obrera. Citing the 1902 Law of Residency, which permitted the expulsion of political militants and anarchists, the authorities made moves to have all local socialists and anarchists deported. The union members declared a strike across the whole of Santa Cruz province, demanding their fellow workers be released.

After the men were freed, the union bosses demanded increases in salaries and better working conditions. Negotiations foundered and further strikes ensued. President Hipólito Yrigoyen decided to sends troops south under the command of Lieutenant Colonel Héctor Benigno Varela. The strike was broken up and the governor persuaded both sides to agree to a deal on 22 February 1921. But the landowners subsequently decided that the price of wool was too low to justify any change in terms and reneged on the agreement. They turned, instead, to the Liga Patriótica and on 24 October all the district offices of the Federación Obrera located in Río Gallegos, Puerto Deseado, San Julián and Puerto Santa Cruz were closed down. Union leaders were rounded up and the members declared a strike across the province. On 10 November Varela returned to Río Gallegos with a cavalry detachment. With the support of the provincial governor and the Chilean government, many leaders and other union members were rounded up and summarily placed before firing squads. Between 1,500 and 3,000 men were killed.

In his report to the minister of war Varela observed that: "In general, the impression an Argentinian gets when in the territory of Santa Cruz is that it doesn't belong to the Patria."

Borrero had planned to write a follow-up to his book, which would focus on another series of massacres that took place in 1921. The book, provisionally titled *Orgias de Sangre* (Orgies of Blood), was never written. But in the 1970s Osvaldo Bayer took up Borrero's work with his *Los Vengadores de la Patagonia trágica* (1972-76). Here Bayer views the anarchist uprisings and the massacre of 1922 as a natural development of the earlier programme of ethnic cleansing perpetrated by the landowners.

AFTERMATH

On 27 January 1923 German anarchist Kurt Gustav Wilckens, in a solitary act of resistance, shot Varela dead as he left his home in Palermo, Buenos Aires.

Roca's soldiers and the sheep farmers had won the battle for Patagonia. Between 1876 and 1903, 101,313,000 acres of land were given to just 1,843 landowners, all of them with family or commercial links to government and many connected to Roca himself. Just 66 land barons owned 15 million acres (an area equivalent to three times the size of Wales), and more than six million acres were gifted to the Martínez de Hoz family; the grandson of the grateful head of this household would be minister of finance during the 1976-83 dictatorship.

In Tierra del Fuego a state-supported paramilitary campaign handed all the land to a handful of clans. By the 1960s the Braun-Menéndez empire controlled a fleet of twelve fishing and cargo ships, piers, a shipyard, and a six-plane airline called Austral with routes spanning 2,500 miles. Their La Anónima stores sold everything from tinned food to pick-up trucks and they had 600,000 sheep on their ranches. In a holding company named La Josefina the family had investments in Argentinian banking, insurance and chemical companies. An article in *Time* magazine in 1963 noted that, "Something like a Hudson's Bay Co. of the Southern Hemisphere, 'La Anonima' controls most of the commerce and communications in Patagonia... With all that diversity, they have prospered despite Argentina's continuing financial trouble. By family reckoning, their companies last year had sales of $33 million."

In 2007 the Sociedad Anónima Importadora y Exportadora de la Patagonia had 3,835 employees and recorded sales valuing US$2.1 billion.

Chapter Eleven

TAMING THE WIND:
ANTOINE DE SAINT-EXUPÉRY

"A plane may be just a machine, but what an analytical instrument it is!
It has revealed to us the true face of the earth. Through all the centuries,
in truth, the roads have deceived us."

Saint-Exupéry, *Wind, Sand and Stars* (1939)

Travellers new to Patagonia often encounter more than they expected in
the landscape. They are struck by the way the unpolluted light imbues
everything with a hyper-real glow and by the exhilarating open space that
stretches dizzyingly away into the distance. Such physical perceptions segue
into states of mind: hikers and bikers delight in a new sense of freedom,
which they usually find difficult to define and, once away from the region,
to recover. One traveller who rode a horse across the province of Chubut,
following the hoof-prints of an ancestor, complained that after reading
Bruce Chatwin he had imagined the region as "darker, sadder". He said
that Patagonia was for him an edifying experience, "full of light", and that
the people too were possessed of a quiet energy that could be gleaned from
their manner and they way they looked into your eyes.

The writer who gave shape and detail to these sensations was Antoine
de Saint-Exupéry, whose accounts of flights across Patagonia provide us
with a unique angle on the land and impart a new, modern sense of danger
and drama. In the foreword to his autobiographical work *Wind, Sand and
Stars* (*Terre des Hommes*) he gives an account of Patagonia as seen at moun-
tain-height from a small plane:

> The earth teaches us more about ourselves than all the books in the
> world, because it is resistant to us. Self-discovery comes when man meas-
> ures himself against an obstacle. To attain it, he needs an implement, he
> needs a carpenter's plane, or a plough. Little by little, as he walks behind
> the plough, the farmer forces out a few of nature's secrets, and the truth

which he uncovers is universal. In the same way the aeroplane, the implement of the airline companies, brings man face to face with all the old problems.

In my mind's eye I still have the image of my first night flight in Argentina. It was a dark night, with only occasional scattered lights glittering like stars on the plain.

Each one, in that ocean of shadows, was a sign of the miracle of consciousness. In one home people were reading, or thinking, or sharing confidences. In another, perhaps, they were searching through space, wearying themselves with the mathematics of the Andromeda nebula. In another they were making love. These small flames shone far apart in the landscape, demanding their fuel. Even the most unassuming of them, the flame of the poet, the teacher or the carpenter. But among these living stars, how many closed windows, how many extinct stars, how many sleeping men…

Composed yet yearning, this passage is a classic homage to the sublime, shot through with Saint-Exupéry's particular passion for empathy and self-improvement. Most modern travel writers shy away from this kind of writing for fear of displaying excessive emotion or—as is highly likely—of getting the tone utterly wrong and falling into parody or pretentiousness. But Saint-Ex (as all his colleagues and friends knew him) had little time for petty fears, and his flights of the imagination are always, paradoxically, grounded and rooted in the landscapes he observed, and in his very real, very physical experiences.

Learning to Fly

Antoine Jean-Baptiste Marie Roger de Saint-Exupéry was born on 29 June 1900. The third of five children—but the oldest male and therefore heir—of an old, wealthy French family, Saint-Ex spent his youth in châteaux close to Lyon and St. Tropez. Despite his father's death in 1904, young Antoine had a happy, protected and privileged upbringing. His mother doted on him and he and his brothers and sisters spent long summers filling their private parks and woodlands with fantasy kingdoms and fairytales full of romance and mystery. At the age of nine he was, like all French children, thrilled when Blériot flew across the channel. When a pilot-training school opened close to his home, he went along to watch the aviators and engineers and in 1912 one of the pilots took him on a short flight.

Following the death of his younger brother François in July 1917, Saint-Ex sank into depression, and a period spent as a would-be writer and *flâneur* in aristocratic circles in Paris failed to lift his spirits. After abortive attempts to join the naval academy in Paris, to become an architect and then to join the army (just as the war ended), he was finally, in 1923, recruited by the Latécoère airline company. Shortly after training, he was employed on the service that operated between France and its colonies in North Africa. Though never a model pilot—he was nonchalant about mechanical checks and took too many risks while in the air—Saint-Ex loved his long hours flying over the Western Sahara and spending time with Arab tribesmen while managing the local office, a primitive hut in Cape Juby (now Tarfaya, Morocco). As French scholar and translator William Rees writes, he "found in Latécoère, at last, his true métier and milieu; despite the dangers of the work, and in a sense because of these dangers, the next five years were to be the happiest and most secure of his life after his exile from the magical domain of childhood."

To the Sahara of the Americas

Up until the 1920s Buenos Aires had shown little interest in the remote farms and fishing ports of Chubut and Santa Cruz. But the recent discovery of oil and increasing demand from overseas for lamb's meat and wool meant that small ramshackle settlements were fast becoming bustling towns; the petrochemical industry was clustered around Comodoro Rivadavia, while Río Gallegos and Puerto Deseado were becoming important sheep farming hubs. Even so, communications between central and southern Argentina were very limited, the few roads that existed were poorly surfaced, and horse-drawn vehicles took months to cover the immense distances. To practically and profitably service these small urban centres as well as the larger *estancias*, the government found it necessary to introduce aeroplanes. These could transport public servants and passengers and, most importantly of all, they could deliver the post.

Buenos Aires enjoyed a special relationship with France. Dubbed the "Paris of South America", the capital's grander mansions aped those of the French capital and tango orchestras danced their way between the two great cities of light (and long nights). With the national coffers healthily

stuffed with the gains from meat and grain exports, Argentina often looked to the Old World for specialized industrial and commercial know-how, and it was quite natural that the authorities should grant a concession to run the postal services to a French company.

On 12 October 1929 Saint-Ex was met at the port of Buenos Aires by three of his colleagues at Latécoère (later known as Aéropostale) in South America. Two days later, he flew 400 miles south to Bahía Blanca, the first stop on a proposed Patagonian line, as the passenger of Paul Vachet, then operations manager of the local branch of the firm. From here they continued on, over 800 miles of lonely coastline, to Comodoro Rivadavia. Patagonia was known to the French as the country where the stones fly—motorists were warned not to drive at more than 20 miles per hour lest they suffer a fatal collision with wind-borne stones. Sometimes the winds exceeded 135 mph and flying the fragile airplanes was a dangerous task. This was to be Saint-Ex's workplace until February 1931.

The first work to come out of this experience was Saint-Exupéry's novel *Night Flight* (*Vol de nuit*) published in 1931. Night flying was a key element of the Patagonian operation and essential to the commercial viability of Latécoère's operations. As Rivière, the admirable leader in the book, explains: "For us it's a matter of life and death, since we lost at night the lead we gain each day on the railways and steamships." Though much criticized at the time as being too hazardous to be justified, night flying was proven to be possible by Saint-Ex and his fellow pilots.

This was the heroic age of air travel, and *Night Flight* is an important record of the challenges faced by the pilots as well as a powerful work of fiction. It is the authenticity of the account that draws us in as much as the awe experienced by Fabien, the pilot whose story we follow.

The novel opens with a gorgeous evocation of a pilot's state of mind as he gently cruises above the open plains:

> Already, beneath him, the shadowed hills had dug their furrows in the golden evenings and the plains grown luminous with long-enduring light. For in these lands the ground is slow to yield its sunset gold, just as in the waning winter the whiteness of the snow persists.
>
> Fabien, the pilot who was flying the Patagonia mail from the extreme south to Buenos Aires, could note the onset of night by the same telltale signs as a harbour: by the calm expanse before him, faintly rippled by lazy clouds. He was entering a vast and happy anchorage.
>
> In this calm he could have fancied himself, like a shepherd, going for a quiet walk. Thus the shepherds of Patagonia move, unhurriedly, from one flock to another. He was moving from one city to the next, and the little towns were his sheep. Every two hours he came upon one slaking its thirst by the riverside or browsing off its plain.
>
> Sometimes, after sixty miles of steppes as uninhabited as the sea, he came upon a lonely farm, which seemed to bob backward on its billow of prairie lands, carrying away its cargo of human lives; he then dipped his wings, as though saluting a ship.

W. H. Hudson wrote from a vantage-point that was level with the bare plains, and learned how to observe the tiniest of shifts of colour or form in the Patagonian landscape. From high above, the viewer enjoys a completely different sense of scale. Human settlers have become as organic as the fields themselves; the farms have become sheep. From the minute details of the vision given to the airman, Saint-Ex builds wonder and grandeur.

The raw material of the novel is the daily work of Fabien, a pilot committed to delivering the mail in Patagonia in spite of the great perils involved. We follow his dramatic escapes from storms, experience his sense of timelessness and his solitude and vicariously share his realization that his life depends on the fragile mechanisms of his tiny plane. Parallel to this narrative we hear the thoughts of Rivière, his boss, who is on the ground, waiting for the pilot and the mail. Rivière remains tough and devoted to his duty despite the risks his pilots endure, and even after he has told a wife that her husband is missing in a thunderstorm, he must continue to send other pilots into the night to keep the mail moving.

Night Flight is a celebration of flying as well as an attempt to analyze and explain duty and responsibility. Taken together, Fabien and Rivière embody what for Saint-Exupéry was a sacred canon of behaviour: to follow orders, to confront danger, self-belief, heroism, doing one's duty. For Rivière duty is an "obscure sense" that is "greater than love". Despite this he loves the men he commands, though he never admits as much.

Saint-Ex's earlier 1929 novel, *Southern Mail* (*Courrier sud*), had also provided an inspiring portrait of the heroic airman, but had employed a degree of sentiment and suggested just enough vulnerability to draw the reader in. But *Night Flight* is as clear and coldly thrilling as the Patagonian night. As André Gide writes in a preface to the novel:

> The hero of *Night Flight*, though anything but dehumanized, rises to a super-human virtue. What I like most in this stirring story is, I think, its nobility. We are all too familiar with men's weaknesses, renunciations, and backslidings, and contemporary literature has been only too assiduous in denouncing them; but what we needed was above all this surpassing of oneself which can be obtained through force of will.

There is little doubt that Saint-Ex was driven by a Nietzschean will to self-fulfilment. A few years after publication, with fascism on the rise, *Night Flight* was interpreted as a justification for "doing one's duty" and following orders even though they might be morally wrong. Yet the prose is notable more for its poetry than its politics and while the narrative moves deftly between topography and telling tale, it is in the former that the prose achieves its greater glories:

Now, swallowed up by the night like a watchman, he could see how the night betrays man's secrets: those appeals, those lights, that anxiety. That single star down there in the shadow—a house in isolation. That other star flickering and going out—a house closing its shutters on its love. Or on its boredom. A house that has ceased signaling to the rest of the world. Gathered around their lamp-lit table, those farmers little guessed the true measure of their hopes nor realized how far their yearnings reached in the great night that encompassed them. But Fabien, approaching from six hundred miles away, uncovered them along with the ground-swells that lifted and lowered his breathing plane. Having traversed ten storms, like battlefields, and the moonlit clearings between them, he now picked up these lights, one after another, with a pride of conquest.

Saint-Exupéry dreams up the breathing plane, the living house and the star-like window to forge an imaginative connection between the organic and inorganic worlds, and between the tiny details and the vast universe, which he must have felt to be all around him, expanding and impossibly silent and empty.

LIFE AND ART

Like D. H Lawrence and Ernest Hemingway, Saint-Exupéry belonged to that tiny group of writers for whom work and pleasure, life and art, are inseparable. Consequently his 1939 memoir, *Wind, Sand and Stars*, which provides some of the background to *Night Flight*, is as dramatic as the fictional narrative and conjures an even more powerful bond with the landscape.

Having established an airfield at Río Gallegos, Saint-Ex wanted to extend the service to Punta Arenas. He recalls how his route took him over a range of extinct volcanoes:

Just to the south of Rio Gallegos, the pilot on course for the Magellan Strait flies over an ancient lava-flow, lying seventy feet deep on the plain. Then he encounters a second, and a third, and now every rise in the ground, every even-hundred-foot hummock has its crater within its slopes. No proud Vesuvius here: cannon mouths in the surface of the plain.

But today there is peace. It is a surprising experience in this derelict landscape, where a thousand volcanoes once answered each other with the music of their vast subterranean organs as they spat out fire. Now you fly over a land for ever mute, adorned with glaciers.

Landscape becomes emotion; natural forms give rise to moods, and we get the impression of emotions natural falling and rising with the land. We feel that the author is flying as he writes.

Which is, indeed, exactly what he was doing. Saint-Ex would sometimes cover 1,500 miles in a single day, flying for 18-20 hours straight, stopping only to refuel. When the weather permitted, he would write as the plane flew itself. The cockpit was often littered with papers.

After the bare skin of the young volcanoes came the relative greenness of Tierra del Fuego. Here Saint-Ex is moved by the way grasses and trees have provided the mountains with a luxuriant mantle and is struck by a hope generated solely by nature. He describes this vision of the planet's struggle to be alive in terms of a global well-being:

> Further on, older volcanoes are clad already covered in golden turf... life has taken possession of a new planet, its good earth laid at last over the bare star.
>
> Finally, just before Punta Arenas, the last craters are filled. A smooth lawn clothes the contours of the volcanoes, and all is gentle now, every fissure healed and stitched by the tender flax. The land is silken, the slopes are mild. Their origin is forgotten, its dark sign effaced from the hillsides by the grass.

Peace, gentle, tender, silken, mild: Saint-Ex's prose subverts the common vision of stressed geologies and isolated plains. From his unique, now almost unattainable, perspective—modern airliners are too high and plummet into Punta Arenas too quickly to allow anything like reflection— even pinnacles and glaciers are seen as almost flat; as elements in a divine canvas.

Visions informed by an ordinary magic are at the heart of Saint-Exupéry's work. From the air he sees the rising breath of sheep buried in snow and natives crossing the steppe in threadbare guanaco hides. Even a town like Punta Arenas is "born of the chance presence of a little mud between the timeless lava and the austral ice." The author is as moved by what he calls the "miracle of mankind" as he is by the wonders of creation.

BATTLING THE ELEMENTS

It was not all flights of the imagination. The wind in Comodoro Rivadavia, which can blast at a constant 125 miles per hour for days on end—among the strongest in the world—could knock down herds of cattle and sheep, bowl over cars and trucks and carry away roofs.

Saint-Ex had signed an order prohibiting pilots from landing in the town when the wind speed exceeded 90 mph. The average speed of the Laté 25 or 26, the planes used by Aéropostale Argentina, was roughly the same, so taking off or landing into the wind was akin to revving a car mounted on blocks—though rather more hazardous.

Saint-Exupéry's biographer, Stacy Schiff, describes a typical landing at Comodoro:

> The Argentine government arranged for soldiers to assist the aviators; twelve to fourteen of them were on hand for a Comodoro Rivadavia landing under the most favourable of conditions. They divided into two groups, forming a 150-foot-long, ninety-foot-wide corridor between them, into which the pilot would fly at nearly full throttle. Tail high, the pilot kept his throttle up so that the air speed of the machine remained equal to that of the wind. Several members of the ground crew then rolled a cart under the tail skid of the immobile machine; the aircraft thus remained horizontal, presenting a streamlined profile to the wind. At the same time, the soldiers rushed forward with long bamboo poles, which they hooked through metal eyes installed on the underside of the wings. In this way the aircraft was secured on the ground despite the winds, Slowly, on signal, the pilot then advanced at full throttle into the hangar, guided by his Lilliputian captors on either side, cutting the engine only once he was partially sheltered.

If a sudden gust of wind came down from the nearby mountains, the men holding the wings were thrust several feet above the ground. On one occasion, two men were crushed to death by a wing on the leeward side.

No Going Home

Saint-Exupéry did not like Comodoro Rivadavia. With its oil wells and its complete lack of trees and women, he saw it as a town "in which one traded ten years of one's life for gold... It was a settlement lost amid the winds and rejected by the earth."

Other settlements did impress him, however, and their human element was the souce of their appeal. In Puerto Deseado, then a tiny coastal town of some 200 low-lying houses at the mouth of a turquoise river, Saint-Ex was given a hero's welcome and taken by the mayor on a tour of the town. Schiff rescues a passage from his drafts that never made it into *Wind, Sand and Stars*:

> Nowhere have I encountered a more noble race of men that that of the Argentines of the south. Arrived to build cities on these deserted lands, they built them. A city in their hands became a living thing, to be shaped, to be protected, to be cherished like a child. These men did not dream of exploiting the land to return, enriched, to their paradises. They had come to establish themselves here for good, to found a race of men. It would be difficult to find elsewhere so developed a sense of society, of cooperation, so much serenity. Theirs was the serenity of men who address only the great problems. Once again I had here the opposite sensation of that of Comodoro, a sense of brushing against another era, one in which man settled himself on earth, chose his campsite, and lay the first stone of his new town's fortifications.

Balls were held in his honour in iron shacks. The deepest pleasures of life were long conversations huddled around a fire or a buffet of grilled meat. Schiff comments that the towns were so new that they had built schools for a generation of children not yet conceived, that the cemeteries were empty and local gossip remained almost free of allegations of adultery.

It is highly likely that from this respect and admiration for ordinary heroes—for carpenters, builders, smiths, gardeners and men with a vision of a new home and a new society—came the seeds of the story of *The Little Prince* (*Le petit prince*, 1943). Admirers of Saint-Exupéry also point out that the author's drawings, used in most editions of the book, were inspired by the Patagonian landscape, in particular the peaks of Mount Fitz

Roy and Mount Torre, rendered as vaulting pinnacles on a bare planet. Fittingly, a needle-shaped mountain right beside these is now named after Saint-Exupéry. By 1930 the mail planes were running regularly from Buenos Aires to Rio de Janeiro and to Asunción, with services to Natal on the north-eastern coast and to Bolivia and Chile on the western side of the continent. In March 1950 the Buenos Aires-Río Gallegos route was ready to be opened for a regular service.

But Saint-Exupéry never settled in any homestead like the ordinary heroes he admired. He continued to write and to fly until the beginning of the Second World War. After a brief period in the United States, he returned to Europe to fly with the Free French and fight with the Allies.

His last mission was to gather data on German troop movements in the Rhône. On the night of 31 July 1944 he took off from a base in Corsica and was never seen again. A woman reported having seen a plane crash around noon of 1 August near the Bay of Carqueiranne.

An unidentifiable body wearing a French uniform was found several days later and was buried in Carqueiranne in September—though German records were lacking, there was for many years a romantic assumption that Saint-Exupéry had been shot down by a German fighter pilot. But in 1998 a fisherman found what was reported to be Saint-Exupéry's silver bracelet in the sea, just east of the island of Riou, south of Marseille. Two years later a diver found a crashed Lockheed F-5 photo-reconnaissance plane on the seabed off Marseille. In 2004 a French government laboratory confirmed that the aircraft was, indeed, Saint-Exupéry's. There were no traces of shooting or aerial combat; the crash was probably caused by a technical failure in both engines or in the oxygen supply. Some have speculated that Saint-Ex committed suicide.

Patagonia, like the Sahara, allowed Saint-Exupéry to ponder the meaning of freedom. Landscapes without clutter showed that there was life—nature, beauty, wonder—beyond the strips of gravel, earth or asphalt that men clung to like umbilical cords. True, roads joined people together, but they shied away from topography. They gave a flat, limiting perspective. They drove the spirit in well-travelled directions, hemming it in.

For Saint-Exupéry, the landscape of Patagonia was a reflection of the sky—an exhilarating openness thrown into relief by the solitary stars of homes, isolated on the cosmic plain. If this is an author at ease with the sublime, it is because for him flying and writing were two sides of the same experience. Just as a passage through the blackest southern tempest could be a valuable experience, so a flight of fancy on the page was, in a sense, a moment of risk and of revelation.

Chapter Twelve

RECLAIMING TERRITORY: LATIN AMERICAN NARRATIVES

"Its own extent is the evil from which the Argentinian Republic suffers; the desert encompasses it on every side and penetrates its very heart."
Domingo Faustino Sarmiento, *Facundo* (1845)

"Life takes people to all kinds of faraway places, and generally it winds up taking them to the farthest away of all, to extremes, because there is no reason to break a journey half-way. Beyond, always beyond... until there is no beyond, and then men bounce back and find themselves exposed to a climate, a light..."
César Aira, *La costurera y el viento* (1994)

Francisco Moreno's writings went some way towards spreading the word on Patagonia. But his call for clear initiatives from central government was only a strand of extensive Argentininan and Chilean writings about the geography, wildlife and native peoples of the south. Moreno appealed to scientists, but the first major work of popular journalism to confront the Patagonian question was by socialist author Roberto Jorge Payró.

Born in 1867 in Mercedes, a small town in the province of Buenos Aires, Payró founded the newspaper *La Tribuna* in Bahía Blanca, where he published his first articles. He then moved to Buenos Aires where he worked as an editor at the *La Nación* newspaper, which involved travelling across many of the country's provinces. His *La Australia Argentinas (Excursión periodística a las costas patagónicas)* (*Southern Argentina—a Journalist's Excursion to the Shores of Patagonia*), published in 1898, reflects his ambivalence toward the roles played by the English and French in southern Argentina:

Down the Magellan Straits hundreds of large ships pass every year, and wrecks are a relatively rare thing thanks to our better understanding of

those regions; for, in effect, Sarmiento de Gamboa's wish [to found colonies in Tierra del Fuego] has come true, not because of anything Spaniards or South Americans have done, but because of the indelible trace left by the English and French on the Patagonian and Fuegian coasts.

This is so true that, casting a glance over a map, I find the following place names: Adam, Albermaile, Aymond, Back, Barnewelt, Barren, Beagle, Beauchène, Beaver, Berkley, Bird, Bleaker, Blosom, Brisbane, Bougainville, Bull, Buygle, Byron, Calinford, Camerons, Charmate, Choiseul, Colnet, Cook, Cooper, Coy Inlet, Croosley, Dampier, Deceit, Dotiglas, Driftwood, Dungeness, Edgar, Spinozza, Fairweather, Falkland, Fallows, Fur, Fitz-Roy, Flinders, Fourneaux, Foul, Fox, Franklin, Gay, Grey, Hall, Harriet, Hatily, Herschel, Ilidden, Hope, Katterfeld, Kendall, Lively, Madryn, Meredick, Middle, Moody, Murphy, Murray, Musters, Nassau, Oglander, Oxford, Parry, Pebble, Pembroke, Picton, Pleasant, Purvis, Spencer, Tomasin, Vancouver, Watchman, Webster, Weddel, Winter, Wollaston... all of them quite difficult to pronounce for those who speak a Latin tongue.

Payró notes that even where the Spanish christened places in Patagonia, the English "rebaptized" them and these later names endured because they had been adopted on the maps of the Argentinian navy. As a result, some names went through a shift in meaning, as with Cameron's Bay, named after a British sailor, rendered in Spanish as Bahía Camarones (Shrimps Bay).

Payró reports on the increasing industrial activity along the coast, observing the ships freighting in sheep from the Falkland Islands; port towns where there are barely enough houses for the inhabitants; *estancias* that "advance their conquest" into the interior; axes cutting down trees and the scream of chain-saws. "If a progressive, inspired government should decide to give all this a new push," ponders Payró, "we would in a few years see in these solitary climes another triumph of civilization, a cradle of the strong, dominant races that prosper in cold regions."

We have read this before—in Roca's pre-conquest tracts, in the closing flourishes to Moreno's journals—but in Payró the urge to colonize is shot through with lyricism. His account shifts naturally from this call to action to a contemplation of the blues and greens of the sea, and the way in which the "tame tides bring to my memory the Pampas with their gentle undulations." Thus he links Patagonia to the cattle-raising heartland and, at the same time, imbues his essay with melancholy and a longing for home. The essay closes with a vision of a possible future. Payró imagines settlements all along the Patagonian coast, trains coming and going loaded with produce, steamships plying the river basins between the Andes and the Atlantic, and of a land which "lost… its mysterious, threatening physiognomy" thanks to industry and development. Yet the author gives his tale a twist, claiming that while a great future is assured for the region, it may well lead to a call among the inhabitants of Patagonia for self-government and independence from Argentina. Citing the Welsh settlement in Chubut, Payró argues that the Patagonians feel abandoned by the Argentinian state and are likely to turn to England or Chile for commercial as well as moral support. His warning is directed at the "egotistical" governments of the capital, more concerned with individual progress than nation-building. "Patagonia," he concludes, "is isolated from the rest of the republic more by indifference than by geography."

THE PSYCHOGEOGRAPHY OF EMPTINESS
Payró, like Moreno before him, was ignored. The Argentinian flag continued to wave, but the indifference intensified, and much of the literature that came out of Patagonia during the course of the twentieth century reflected the region's isolation and seeming irrelevance to the national project.

Ezequiel Martínez Estrada (1895-1964) was born in San José de la Esquina, in the province of Santa Fe. He grew up there and in Goyena, a village in the southern reaches of Buenos Aires province. In 1907 he went to live with an aunt in the capital, and after a period working at the central post office began to write poetry and essays.

Martínez Estrada produced admiring monographs on Nietzsche, Montaigne, and Kafka and also felt empathy with his older contemporary Horacio Quiroga, whose short stories about rural life attacked the dehumanization of human affairs that stemmed from technological advances. Writing on W. H. Hudson, Martínez Estrada showed himself to be in sympathy with the back-to-nature ideology. From these influences he forged a passionate, pessimistic style of essay-writing that has had an enduring influence on Argentinian perceptions of self.

In *Radiografía de las Pampas* (X-Ray of the Pampas, 1933) Martínez Estrada portrays the vast, vacant interior as a potential source of most of Argentina's ills. After re-reading *Facundo* (1845) Estrada was struck by the fact that Sarmiento's dialectic of civilization and barbarism and his vision of a pro-European, classicist Argentina had had little impact on the construction of a national identity. Politically, economically, socially and psychologically, Argentina was still an underpopulated wasteland ruled by despotic *caudillos*.

The emptiness of the arid southern steppe is, in Martínez Estrada's view, the ultimate expression of the solitude and hopelessness that beleaguers the inchoate nation. In terms of development, history, potential and promise, Patagonia and all it stands for amount to one great negative. Argentina, in consequence, is an overwhelming *nada* populated by nihilists. Topography, he argues is responsible for the soul of man.

The region that most concerns the author is the humid pampa—the breadbasket of the nation's economy, *ergo* the place where nationhood is forged. But this fertile expanse matches Patagonia for its endless horizons, scant population and unmapped, unindustrialized uselessness. The nothingness, he argues, affects the teeming capital city: "As the evening falls, Buenos Aires is filled with the melancholy of the country... Buenos Aires has no night but that which arrives from the immense pampas." He sees the capital's attempt to generate light and energy as an affront to the natural state of things: "The lights and noises of the centre are not an integral part of the agreeable country night, but rather spasms to break it and cheapen it... Buenos Aires does not have night life; the cabarets and cafés are only keeping watch over the impeccable bourgeois dream."

According to this world-view, the native peoples of the interior are only relevant in so far as they are non-entities, nullifications of the "normal" human condition: "The Indian has no past because he has no future; he occupies merely the space that is taken up by his body, alive or dead, and like an animal, even in society he lives a life that does not extend beyond his senses. He is born and dies in secret."

Radiografía is divided into six sections, the first of which is titled "Trapalanda", a common name for the City of the Caesars, the elusive Patagonian El Dorado. Martínez Estrada argues that a thinly spread population and widespread ignorance were *a priori* conditions for the absence of genuine national unity. But, he says, "The most damaging of dreamers, the builder of images, was Sarmiento. His railway line led to Trapalanda and his telegraph leapt a hundred years into the vacuum." While Martínez Estrada falls short of proposing a non-dualistic alternative to Sarmiento's treatise, there is a sense that Argentinians must embrace their wilderness, or at least accept their Patagonian souls in order to be, if not contented or wise, then at least authentic. The book's final vision is of a vast empty land, where the outposts of civilization are constantly invaded by spectres of fear and amnesia.

Stories from the South

Most writing about Patagonia has been non-fiction prose, usually with an exploratory, adventurous slant. There have, along the way, been fictions by outsiders set in and about Patagonia. Jules Verne set *The Children of Captain Grant* and *The Lighthouse at the End of the World* in the far south. Arthur Conan Doyle used turn-of-the century reports from Patagonia as the basis for his *The Lost World*. James Joyce makes a cursory mention of "the terrible Patagonians" in *Dubliners*. Henry James' story "Patagonia" uses nineteenth-century perceptions of Patagonia to raise questions about exploration and discovery. Generally, though, there have been very few attempts by novelists and poets to tackle Patagonia. Perhaps they have been deterred by the burden of myths contained in non-fiction writings. Only the FitzRoy-Darwin-Jemmy débâcle has inspired anything like a fictional school—and only a tiny one—and most retellings are novelized histories that stick closely to the source material.

But Latin American fiction has its own distinctive roots and evolution. A handful of indigenous writers have employed magic realism to deconstruct the presumed magic of Patagonia. Others have attempted to recover local narratives by writing stories in a social-realist vein. Poetry has been used to articulate the otherworldly beauty the region is often supposed to possess. Most fiction and verse in southern South America is metropolitan in character—itself a very telling fact—but slowly, quietly, Patagonia has come alive as something more than a memory of latter-day conquest or a huge sheep farm run by ruddy expatriates.

For Sarmiento and Martínez Estrada the monotony of the interior was a powerful idea, an attitude. But at the existential level it is, above all, a source of immense boredom. Chilean author Marta Brunet, born in Chillán at the north end of Chile's lake region but writing always with a southward gaze, provides a feminist exploration of emptiness. She was born in 1897, when Chillán was still frontier territory, and her work is written against the backdrop of a nation under construction. A leading intellectual, journalist and diplomat, she was also one of the founders of Chile's *criollista* school which concentrated on portraying rural life and landscapes and plumbing the psychological depths of country people with sympathy and sensitivity.

Her stories are akin to those of Thomas Hardy or D. H. Lawrence, with rustic dialogue hinting at darker motives, though the peculiar folkloric currents that vibrate in southern Chile introduce a supernatural element. In the story "Ave Negra", for instance, the female narrator (women feature prominently in Brunet's work) is a traveller spending the night with a country family. Vultures have been hovering ominously around the volcanoes, and while the family is drinking *mate* a single bird comes close to the house. When it shrieks "like a dog's howl or the rattling laughter of a madman", the hostess invokes "Holy Mary, Mother of God" and chants three times the expression "Salt's tossed, evil's lost." She then tells her guest that the *chonchon*—the local name for a vulture—is a witch:

> "They are witches who can turn into birds on Saturday nights in order to perform evil deeds; they turn into chonchones and screech over the houses they will bring evil down upon. This one has already come several times, but it never catches us off our guard; immediately we chant the incantation, the counterspell, and it is forced to leave."

The visitor is incredulous, but her hostess explains that when she was pregnant a local witch, Doña Bernarda, came to bewitch her as a *chonchon*, and that they were only able to repel the bird by chanting and performing a ritual with a dagger and holy water. Some time later they learned that Doña Bernarda had died. Though their counter spell had been a success, the girl she gave birth was mute. Perhaps, wonders the country woman, this *chonchon* is the witch's daughter. The narrator makes no response and continues sipping *mate*, listening to the crackle of the fire and watching the silver stars shining tremulously in the sky. The tale is left hanging there, the silence resumes and the story finishes without any real sense of closure.

It is in the novel *Maria Nadie* (1957) that Brunet explores most fully the texture and torture of boredom:

> Sometimes solitude weighs down. It is like a mould squeezing a body to the point of oppressing it. Something hurts inside and the numb muscles make no movement that might betray their torpor. These sensations last less than a second, but leave behind the coldness of vertigo in the chest and the flapping of a fallen bird in the heart. That's when someone nearby is sought out, someone to whom a hand can be extended, trembling as it fails to achieve movement and find in the other the certainty of living warmth, some kind of story in which to hide. That solitude of a dank pit that wakes us up at midnight with the dread of being emotionally at the bottom of the pit staring desperately upwards at the unreachable way out.

In her solitude, the author discovers that the freedom of being alone is a sort of prison. The narrator shuns the use of an "I", preferring to present herself as a passive victim of sensations and forces. The language struggles to break out of a circle of negatives; life is a series of gestures, and of dull routines:

> In her life every hour filled a mould. And every hour seemed to be repeating itself. Like those sitting ducks that pass by continually to test the marksmens' accuracy at the summer fair. Like endless lines of sitting ducks, cut out of cardboard, painted in different colours, moving their heads with identical rhythm. The same. One day and the next.

The novel can be read as a purely personal experience of spiritual aridity. But occasionally Brunet moves the argument away from the narrator and considers her as one of many isolated souls attempting to settle the vast spaces.

> We? Who? Us: the country, nations, humanity, we need children, potential men and women, so that at any given moment they can defend the fatherland, defend nation against nation, be heroes, die en masse in obscurity. That's why the atom was split... For death, for death, for all that.

In his novel *Ventana al sur* (Window on the South, 1975), poet and university professor Enrique Valdés—born in 1943 in Río Baker, Aysén, a region cut off from the rest of Chile—analyzes the human imprint of settlement and the hardships faced by communities isolated by political borders, weather and the environment. While Valdés' approach is naturalistic and open to the objective world, his conclusions are in sympathy with those of Brunet. Life is labour from dawn to dusk. Home is the opposite of the imagined rustic idyll—there is just a bed, a fire, a few belongings. The silence is heavy, broken only by the sucking sound of someone drinking *mate*. A condor feasting on rotten horseflesh is something to envy when a long, lonely winter leaves one tiny hamlet near Lago Verde without any stores: "To live here, was to live on the edge of suicide and death. Far from food and remedies. Far from the world, far from everything."

One of the most complex works to explore Patagonian alienation is *La costurera y el viento* (The Seamstress and the Wind, 1994) by César Aira. One afternoon, a child becomes trapped in the trailer of a truck. The truck goes south. His mother, Delia Siffoni, the seamstress of the title, follows him in a taxi, working on a bridal gown as she travels. Her husband follows her. The bride then also goes to Patagonia. The highly improbable becomes the ridiculous when the wind—as the title hints, a central character in the novel—lifts up the truck and causes the bridal dress to lift off like an angel. "Patagonia is the land of wind," writes Aira, and the unpredictable character and inhuman force of this element blows the protagonists and plot of the novel in random directions. The wind bears with it clouds, which "seize and embody all transformations in a single instance, all without exception. That is why the instant, which anywhere else is dry and fixed like a click, is in Patagonian fluid, mysterious, novelesque."

The novel addresses questions of literary creation, memory and madness and exploits (like other works by Aira) structures taken from the cinema to shape its frantic, non-linear plot. Aira subverts the notion of Patagonia as a place beyond history, outside the mainstream. Adapting Bridges, he reminds us: "Patagonia [is] a confine of the world" (*confín* is part of the Spanish title of *Uttermost Part of the Earth*) and then corrects this: "Yes, agreed; but the confine is still of the world." Kindly critics and aficionados of surreal literature embrace Aira's incoherent stories and dream-laced narratives, But *La costurera* is perhaps most interesting if read as a symptom, as the outpouring of a writer who has drunk too deeply on the Patagonian spirit. His work is the fictional counterpoint to Martínez Estrada's essay: the emptiness and the maddening winds seem to deprive the author of any power and control.

MAGELLAN AND THE MOUNTAINS

Chilean author Ariel Dorfman has used the expression *una loca geografía*, a geography gone mad, to describe the extravagance of his country's topography. Long, skinny, seismic and glacial, the country is unlike any other on the planet. South of the Biobío river the land is perhaps even crazier than in the desert north. This has inspired authors born or raised in the southern regions to seek inspiration in their landscape.

Pablo Neruda, raised in Temuco, opens his famous memoir *Confieso que he vivido* (I Confess that I Have Lived, 1974) with this thrilling, impressionistic description of organic birth:

> Under the volcanoes, beside the snow-capped mountains, among the huge lakes, the fragrant, the silent, the tangled Chilean forest… My feet sink down into the dead leaves, a fragile twig crackles, the giant rauli trees rise in all their bristling height, a bird from the cold jungle passes over, flaps its wings, and stops in the sunless branches. And then, from its hideaway, it sings like an oboe… The wild scent of the laurel, the dark scent of the boldo herb, enter my nostrils and flood my whole being… The cypress of the Guaitecas blocks my way… This is a vertical world: a nation of birds, a plenitude of leaves… I stumble over a rock, dig up the uncovered hollow, an enormous spider covered with red hair stares up at me, motionless, as huge as a crab… The piercing interruption of a hidden bird… The vegetable world keeps up its low rustle until a storm churns up all the music of the earth.
>
> Anyone who hasn't been in the Chilean forest doesn't know this planet.
>
> I have come out of that landscape, that mud, that silence, to roam, to go singing through the world.

The title of this rhapsody, in which the ellipses work like the drawing of breath, is "The Chilean Forest". Neruda is, in his litany of living things, summoning into life all the natural wonders of the wild wood. But the passage is also a celebration of language and a personal genesis: Neruda is rooting his lyrical gifts in the rich exuberance of the Valdivian rainforest. The twisted, impenetrable forests that caused John Byron so much grief are here re-imagined as a thriving, fertile Eden. Only the poetic spirit can find a way through the morass and the means to observe it in all its detail.

Elsewhere in his opus, Neruda raises questions about man's role in Patagonia. At the opening of "The Magellan Heart (1519)", from the *Canto General* (1950), he asks:

> Where am I from, where in the devil do I come from,
> I sometimes ask myself, what day is today, what's going on,
> I snore, in the middle of a dream, a tree, a night,
> and a wave is raised like an eyelid, a day
> is born from the wave, a lightning-bolt with a tiger's snout.

Neruda is again concerned with origins, but this time he is thinking as a Chilean, as a child of Magellan. Nature and humanity are at odds, giving rise to a sense of rootlessness. Neruda sets out his poem as a parallel text (prose versus poetry, impulse versus analysis) and allows his mind to drift back to Gondwanaland.

I SUDDENLY
AWAKE IN
THE NIGHT THINKING
OF THE FAR
SOUTH

The day comes and says: "Do you hear
the slow water, the water,
the water
over Patagonia?"
And I answer: "Yes, sir, I'm listening."
The day comes and says: "A wild sheep
Far away, in this region, licks the frozen colour
Of a stone. Aren't you listening to the bleating,
don't you recognize
the blue squall in whose hands
the moon is a goblet, don't you see the drove, the
        rancorous finger of the wind
touching wave and life with its empty ring?"

Neruda is at pains to remind his readers that there is an alternative narrative of Patagonia that is not merely the story of Magellan, mariners,

Pedro de Valdivia and Chile's independence. Shipwrecks and weather and albatrosses are reminders that human endeavour and history are at the mercy of nature, and we should, the poet insists, see the "Magellanic" narrative (of conquest and discovery) as somehow elemental, as only the latest phase in Patagonia's aeon-spanning evolution. But Neruda admits: "At the last, your paradise is lost", and he seems, at the close of the poem, uncertain whether the creation of America has been but a blip in time or a calamity that has changed the land forever.

POSTSCRIPT: THE ANGLO-FUEGIAN

The most intimate autobiography to come out of Tierra del Fuego, *Uttermost Part of the Earth* (1948), was written in English. It deals with the interaction between a tiny Anglican mission on the Beagle Channel and its Fuegian converts. It was first published by Hodder & Stoughton, London. Its writer was the son of Thomas Bridges, the Nottinghamshire-born Anglican missionary who had arrived with his adoptive father, Despard, in 1856.

But Lucas Bridges was born in Ushuaia in 1874, and his book, a huge 558-page memoir spanning almost a century of life and labour on Tierra del Fuego—including the final years of the mission and the Fuegian peoples—is the product of a wholly local experience. Bridges was raised among the native congregations and spent long periods exploring the woodlands and coasts. He and his brother, William, were even formally initiated as members of the Selknam tribe.

In 1869 Thomas Bridges had returned to England, where he was ordained and married Mary Ann Varder from the Devonshire village of Harberton. The following year he founded the first mission station in Tierra del Fuego, at Ushuaia. For his services as a missionary and assisting shipwrecked sailors, and for opening up the territory, Bridges was given a land grant by Roca's government. In 1886 he established the Harberton *estancia* on the Beagle Channel, fifty miles east of Ushuaia. In 1902 the Bridges sons established another ranch, Viamonte, south of Río Grande on the Atlantic coast. The "uttermost part of the earth" is to be found at these two points on the map and in the cool *nothofagus* forests that lie between them.

The book takes its title from Acts 1:8: "But ye shall receive power, after that the Holy Ghost is come upon you: and ye shall be witnesses unto me both in Jerusalem, and in all Judaea, and in Samaria, and unto the uttermost part of the earth." The Bridges believed that they were bringing the good news and protection to the Selknam (called Ona in Bridges' book) and Yahgan natives. But *Uttermost Part of the Earth* records instances of conflict with Selknam poachers and inter-tribal warring, as well as the epidemics that would ultimately wipe out all the Fuegians.

Full of natural history, hunting anecdotes, farming practicalities, domestic details and accounts of skating and other sports, Bridges' book stands out for the range of its interests. The author avoids the Victorian trap of itemizing and classifying—whether dealing with beetles or work units of indigenous individuals—and treats many of his native friends as family members.

Bridges' writing is deceptively plain but it has the force of folklore and myth. Here is a typical episode out in the wilds:

> Many of the mountains of Ona-Land, especially those separated from the main range, were human beings long ago and should be treated with respect. That was the Ona legend. It was considered extremely bad manners to point at any of them. At such rude behaviour, they might wrap themselves in cloud and bring on bad weather. One of them was Heuhupen, the table-land that had once been a witch.
>
> We had cut through a considerable tract of timber-land still wet with winter snow, had carried our track southward along the eastern shore of lake Kami, and were now striking into the great forest of deciduous beech that clothed the northern slopes of the range. Our axes gave out sounds such as had never been heard in those regions before; they were breaking the silence of ages.
>
> Ahead of us, about two miles away, was Heuhupen, her flattish top reaching just above upper tree level. Her steep sides were forest-covered, except where the great slide of rock, which I had noticed during the trip with Slim Jim, had left her bare of trees. Her two daughters, less conspicuous than she, stood out on either side of their mother. I have forgotten their Ona names.
>
> We carried the track past Lake Kami and worked on towards these mountains. After a day or two, the sky becamse overcast and it began to rain. I had my sheet of canvas, and the natives their kowwhi (hide tents)

stretched over sticks planted on the windward side of the fire. In these shelters it was possible to lie or crouch and keep fairly dry, but in a downpour that showed no sign of stopping, it became wearisome after a time. When the rain had continued through the second day, my Ona companions began to voice the suspicion that Heuhupen, objecting to her peace being disturbed by the sound of our axes, had influenced the weather against us.

Everything possible was done to stop the rain. We went outside our windbreaks, one, two or three at a time, brandishing flaming firebrands and shouting in a decisive yet threatening manner at Mohihei and Kowkoshlh, two long-since departed medicine-men who had once had great influence with the fresh westerly breeze, which could blow the rain away.

"Pwrhah, Mohihei! Pwrhah, Kowkoshlh!" was our cry. "Pwrhah!" was a shout of ridicule, often accompanied by laughter; it was used as a jeer when someone had made a particular fool of himself. Mohihei and Kowkoshlh were always invoked in that order—never Kowkoshlh first. When night came the men removed the flint or glass beads from their arrows and inserted specially prepared glowing embers in their places. These were then discharged with full force and a wild, but different, yell of defiance in the direction from which the rain came. As these primitive rockets sped upon their way, the breeze of the flight would cause them to flare up, lighting the glistening foliage overhead with a bright glow that made the surrounding blackness a brief, attractive picture. In response to the entreaties of the Indians, I fired, with the appropriate shouts two or three of my treasured bullets in the required direction, but our united efforts were of no avail.

There is no other book quite like Bridges' masterpiece. Calm and understated, thoughtful and also full of feeling, it is uniquely Anglo-Argentinian in conception. Bridges was probably the first white man to cross Tierra del Fuego on foot, but he took even that in his stride and his spirited sense of adventure smacks of Kipling at his best.

ALTERNATIVE HISTORIES
Authors such as Asensio Abeijón, from Argentina, and Chileans Francisco Coloane and José Miguel Varas, focus in their writings on local detail, life

on the ranches and in small towns, domestic dramas and the influence of the natural world on everyday life for Patagonians. Due to its size, Patagonia is often discussed by politicians, travel writers, and tourists as a single block of territory; these authors strive to show that there is local colour amid the grey steppes, and that microcosms of ordinary town life dot the vastness.

Other authors have sought to give a voice to the native experience. In his novel, *Corazón a contraluz* (1976), Chilean author Patricio Manns fictionalized the life of explorer and gold-hunter Julius Popper during his time at El Páramo. By contrasting the popular myth of an engaging dandy with the facts as related by Selknam Drimys Winteri—whose world Popper is committed to annihilating—Manns corrects the forceful and essentially amoral version of the Popper story.

The most accomplished reworking of a seminal historical encounter in Patagonia is perhaps *Tierra del Fuego* by the Argentinian author Sylvia Iparraguirre. The opening paragraph takes us to the pampas:

> Today, in the middle of this emptiness, something extraordinary happened. So rarely does the plain break its endless monotony that when the dot wavering on the horizon grew until it turned into a rider, and when it was obvious that these poor homes were his goal, our impatience—if watching with a quiet eye stubbornly trained on the horizon can be so called—already had us waiting for him. This was indeed something unusual, and yet watching from my house, separated from the others by a league as he came right toward us, I couldn't even dream of its true importance.

The year is 1865. The narrator is a 53-year-old retired sailor turned gaucho, John William "Jack" Guevara, the illegitimate son of an English sailor, William Scott Mallory, and a native Argentinian woman, Lucía de Guevara. The dot on the horizon brings with it a life-changing letter from a functionary of the British Admiralty in London, requesting that Guevara write up the details of a journey he made years ago on a British ship with Jemmy Button to Tierra del Fuego and Cape Horn, "the continent's southernmost islands, where oceans furiously converge." The report he gives will be used in the trial at which Button is accused of massacring a group of missionaries.

Iparraguirre uses a variety of historical sources, including Darwin's *The Voyage of the Beagle* (Darwin is a character in the novel), Martin Gusinde's anthropological writings and FitzRoy's log, while the colour and detail of the London scenes owe something to Charles Dickens.

She reminds us that Jemmy Button was once named Omuy Lume (Orundellico in other sources), a Yahgan or perhaps Halakwalup boy. But she does not shy away from the gritty reality of how Button would have looked to his European captors. Guevara asks in his journal: "Have you ever been face to face with what the books call a savage, a naked man with ribs exposed, covered with grease, his genitals swollen with disease, his face painted with streaks, and tangled, coarse hair?"

But aboard the ship, and then in London, Guevara and Button become friends. Their lives intertwine as they seek to understand each other. At the age of 53—the present in the novel—Jack corrects his early impressions: "This is how I met Button, but it was through him that, behind such an appearance, I discovered the man I believed did not exist. And behind the man, a people with beliefs and spirit, with respect for life in all its forms, whom I had not known before and would not know again."

Historical detail, carefully wrought dialogue and fine set pieces give *Tierra del Fuego* a vivid immediacy, but there is also an awareness of the broader historical canvas. Button's voyage is contextualized in an age of materialism, colonialism, and imperialism. In an interview Iparraguirre has stated: "The country's project included the price of exterminating the Indians, like what happened in the United States during the conquest of the West. They had to exterminate the owners of these lands in order to establish their own people." For the author this prefigured the "disappearing" of some 30,000 Argentinians during the so-called Dirty War of the 1970s. Like many other artists and writers, Iparraguirre was forced into a state of internal exile, unable to publish her work and earn any kind of income. She and her husband, Aberlardo Castillo, were often broke and suffered further as their friends endured even more terrible fates.

Leopoldo Brizuela's surreal fable *Inglaterra* (1999) also invites a post-dictatorship reading. The author, who was born in 1963, had never been to Patagonia when he wrote three books set there, one of which was *Inglaterra*. The inspiration, he says, came from his father, a sailor, who had visited the southern shores at least once a month for almost thirty years.

He told his young son stories about Ushuaia, Bahía Desolación and "terrible Cape Horn", which awakened the boy's imagination. In an interview Brizuela recalled climbing up into one of his father's huge ships "with the feeling of entering a temple—not a profane temple at all, although its goddess was Patagonia."

From the age of ten Brizuela read Conrad and Melville and other books about the mariners of the South Seas. He wanted, he says, to know what his father had lived through, but discovered only that sailors, whether in novels or logs, "never remember their family."

Brizuela regards Pigafetta's misunderstanding about the big feet of the Tehuelche as a Quixotic folly, but with an ironic twist that, after four centuries, Patagonia—a place born of the imagination—has become real, "an aftermath of the struggle between the... western imagination of the pioneers, and that of the aboriginal peoples... After five centuries, Patagonia is one of the most wonderful kingdoms of literature." The result, he contends, is that any writer who takes on the subject of Patagonia will fail to disentangle the fantasy from the reality.

The novel is set at the beginning of the twentieth century on a mythical island at the southern tip of Tierra del Fuego. Its point of departure is Shakespeare's *The Tempest*, reimagined as the tale of a ship carrying a circus called the Great Will that is wrecked off the Patagonian coast (an idea taken from a report written by Gabriel García Márquez for the *El Espectador* newspaper in Bogotá). This is conflated with a story by Isak Dinesen (Karen Blixen), "Tempests", which tells of a group of actors who gave up their jobs to sail to the end of the world. Brizuela also spins in lyrics from the Doors, elements from Lucas Bridges' memoir, Osvaldo Bayer, Sir John Gielgud, Chatwin and Borges. The characters are equally varied: a child savage; William Shakespeare, who meets a black man possessed of the richest language on earth; and a crazed count who happens to be the teacher of Oscar Wilde.

In this novel the *norte* (north) is everyone else: it is Britain, but it is also Argentina. The last remaining islander, an old native man called Waichai, appears to visitors "to prefer solitude to the company of any 'man from the north'." Yet he serves these visitors—including the narrator—corned beef hash and a bottle of "snap". Patagonia, meanwhile, is italicized throughout *Inglaterra*; it is the ship carrying the circus, which is wrecked at the "Fin del Mundo".

The narrator seens the end of the *Patagonia* as symbolic: "'Because not long after the evening when the shipwreck took place,' we thought, 'the empires died, and the small nations were ruined.'" Falconetti, an anthropologist, is more specific about what is lost: "We had felt that with the *Patagonia*, all dreams were shipwrecked, not only those of Great Will, but those of all England."

Brizuela claims Patagonia was the last corner of the New World: "In the western imagination, deeply and wonderfully shattered by the discovering of America, Patagonia inherited the prestige that Portugal or Iceland once had. After Columbus, Patagonia became the farthest shore man could reach, the last territory to be conquered both by sword and knowledge. And I found in that image of the western fantasy a wonderful metaphor of the work of the poet: we all write on the margins, confronted, like pioneers, with all the things we cannot give a name, that is: with all the impossibilities of our language, and of any human language perhaps."

The novel has a dream-like quality, diving into the subconscious in an attempt to explore this "farthest shore" of the imagination. But Brizuela's Patagonia is also a medium for articulating the unspeakable—unwritable—horrors of contemporary reality. In the interview the author explains how working on a fantastical, historical story allowed his mind to focus on getting the facts right: "Every time I tried to reflect in a realistic way, for instance, the life of the families of the 30,000 *desaparecidos,* disappeared persons, during the dictatorship, I failed. But while I was trying to imagine, in *Inglaterra,* the Indian genocide by the mercenaries of the international trading companies and the Argentine army, at the end of the nineteenth century, I was so concerned about concrete details—colours, sounds, smells, tastes, etc—that my deepest feelings and thoughts and memories came naturally and powerfully into my story."

DEAD ZONES

Brizuela's argument is intriguing: apply magic realist techniques to the fantastical-historical in order to unearth harsh, recent realities. But other contemporary writers have sought to provide a straightforward, realistic account of Patagonia. Leila Guerriero, in *Los Suicidas del fin del mundo* (Suicides at the End of the Earth, 2005), investigates "a wave of suicides" that took place in the tiny town—in Spanish *ciudad*, but for many Europeans this would be a village—of Las Heras, in Santa Cruz.

Between 1997 and 1999, twelve people killed themselves, many of them under the age of 25. Guerriero gives an intimate portrait of the people who died and their families and gives us a plain description of the place where the tragedies took place.

> The route from the hotel to Alberto's house was easy to find. Everything is easy to find in such a small town. Two blocks here, four blocks there, five over there and to the right. However, I wasted a lot of time searching for the precise backstreet where Alberto lived because the streets had no names and there was no one—no one—to ask directions from.
>
> It was my first day in Las Heras. The wind was lifting duststorms, thrashing against the facades of the low-slung houses and all the windows were closed. Later, days later, I realized that behind the shutters were bars and kiosks, stores and markets, a gym, but just then, fighting to make headway against an improbable wind, what I saw was a city that had been blinded and which, thanks to a roadblock was beginning to become, on top of this, a locus outside the world, a lost place.

A degree of poetry seeps in here but Guerriero is stating the facts. Patagonia is full of these almost-places, settlements stripped down to the bare essentials. There is a road, a series of frontages, electric cables, perhaps some street lighting, TV aerials, public space where the locals can sit with their dogs—not always a plaza, but usually some benches and a patch of parched grass—and some place to be taught and another one in which to be buried. It is community in the most basic form, conurbation without colour or recreation.

People's personalities reflect this minimal environment. Life in Las Heras barely reflects any of the customs or pleasures of Argentina. There are no football matches, no convivial barbecues, no busy churches, no sense of being linked to anywhere else. At one stage an interviewee confesses that the people of Santa Cruz "find it hard to be *amoroso* [sweet, loving]." It is as if the Latino-ness of the people has been taken away. Another interviewee blames the divine, or diabolical wind:

> "See! The wind also takes everything away. Psalm 51 in the Bible says 'Wipe away my transgressions, wash away my errors and cleanse me of sin. My sins are before me constantly. Against you, against you, what is

evil in your eyes I have done. Place within me a new spirit, and one that is constant.' God has the capacity to wipe that away, and that makes him speak in this way, so freely, as if I were a whore. Because he already forgave me. He forgot. It's not that he wiped it away. He wiped it in the sense that it doesn't weigh down on me any more. It's there, but it's not there."

Un film de CARLOS SORIN

Historias Mínimas

Chapter Thirteen
MINIMAL STORIES:
FILM AND MUSIC IN PATAGONIA

Until the 1960s Argentinian filmmaking was essentially a Buenos Aires affair. Most of the country's cinemas and studios were in the capital, and directors worked with subjects sure to win approval with local audiences: tango, romance, social manners, farce and the occasional gaucho in traditional garb.

During the last few decades, however, the focus has moved away from the metropolis and many of the themes explored earlier in writings about Patagonia—conquest, anarchy, power and desolation—have been revisited on celluloid. The shift from city to country, from centre to periphery, has been a symbolic and political act for many directors. Patagonia is not only the aesthetic opposite to Buenos Aires, but brings with it a different order of narrative. The historical events that fill school and university textbooks in Argentina unfolded mainly in the centre and north of the country, while Patagonia—leaving aside for a moment the single genocidal sweep that took place between 1880 and the 1920s—was not a major locus of flag-flying or nation-building. A handful of filmmakers looking for alternative history have chosen to recreate other local legends or historical incidents (a crazy French king, sheep-shearing anarchists) and so bring them to a wider audience. But other directors and writers have devised entirely new fictions for the big screen, using Patagonia as an exit from history and from the usual perspectives on current affairs provided by the metropolitan mass media.

The logistical problems of filming in remote, windswept corners of Patagonia are outweighed by the natural drama of the locations. Shooting historical dramas and fantasies is relatively stress-free, as no one is ever likely to drive their car through the backdrop. The pretty lakeside settings are suited to romance and road movies, while the more fearsome Andean peaks are as impressive as any in the Alps or Himalayas and far easier to access. Indeed, one of southern Argentina's most saleable characteristics as both a tourist destination and film set is the juxtaposition of the genteel with the inhospitable.

REALISM: RECOVERING LOST GROUND

In 1942, for the first time in Argentinian cinema history, a collective of directors, actors and writers joined together in a risk enterprise called Artistas Argentinos Asociados (AAA). One of the founder members was Lucas Demare, whose *El Viejo Hucha* (The Old Skinflint, 1942) was the first film to come out of the AAA studio. Demare and his fellow AAA directors went on to make films that pointed towards a cinema capable of drawing large audiences with native themes and an epic treatment of national history, including Alberto de Zavalía's *Malambo* (1942) and Demare's *La guerra gaucha* (The Gaucho War, 1942) and Hugo Fregonese's *Donde mueren las palabras* (Where Words Die, 1946).

By the time he filmed *Plaza Huincul (Pozo Uno)* (1960), one of the first significant films to focus on the grim realities of life for the working classes in Patagonia, Demare was a mature director. His gritty portrayal of oil workers in Neuquén combined folkloric and poetic elements but contained the seeds of a protest movie. While somewhat stilted for a modern audience, the film captures powerfully the landscape of northern Patagonia: aridity, a baking sun and the plundering of the earth to power the cars of the faraway capital. It also put Plaza Huincul, a tiny settlement where life depended on oil, on the map. Interestingly, in 1996 Plaza Huincul would be the scene of dramatic protests against the layoffs following President Menem's privatization of the state oil company, YPF.

Working-class unrest and student radicalism characterized Argentinian metropolitan life in the late 1960s and early 1970s. Juan Domingo Perón was in exile in Madrid, but both political and guerrilla organizations allied to Peronism were on the rise. The return of Perón to Argentina in October 1973 was greeted with euphoria by parties on the left and right, who tailored Perón and Peronism to their own purposes.

These local events, combined with pan-continental cultural and political changes in the wake of the Cuban revolution, gave rise in Argentina to artistic movements that sought to use cultural endeavours for political ends. In Buenos Aires a handful of forward-looking directors, among them Fernando Solanas, Octavio Getino and Gerardo Vallejo, formed a collective called Grupo Cine Liberación. In a manifesto entitled "Towards a

Third Cinema" Solanas and Getino proposed a cinema of decolonization:

> ...countering a cinema of character with one of themes, a cinema of individuals with one of masses, an *auteur* dominated cinema with one created by an operative group, a cinema of neo-colonial misinformation with one of information, a cinema of escape with one that recaptures the truth, a cinema of passivity with one of aggression. To an institutionalized cinema, [the Third Cinema] counterpoises a guerrilla cinema; to movies as spectacles, it promises a film act or action; to a cinema of destruction, it promises a film act or action; to a cinema of destruction, one that is both destructive and constructive, to a cinema made by and for the old kind of human beings, a cinema fit for the new kind of human being, for what each of us has the potential to become.

Héctor Olivera's *La Patagonia rebelde* (Rebelling in Patagonia, 1974), based on Osvaldo Bayer's accounts of the 1920s anarchist movements in the province of Santa Cruz and their suppression by both local and national governments, is a rough-edged, theatrical film set around Río Gallegos and at the La Anita ranch where the events unfolded. Along with Fernando Solanas' *La hora de los hornos* (The Hour of the Furnaces, 1968) and the somewhat less sophisticated *Juan Moreira* (1973) and *Quebracho* (1974), Olivera's film reflected the populist, nationalist sentiments of its time.

In keeping with the anti-*auteur* ideals of the emerging school, *La Patagonia rebelde* is an ensemble piece. Numerous extras—among them one Néstor Kirchner, who would later become Santa Cruz governor and Argentinian president—shadow the rebel leaders to give an impression of a united front. Osvaldo Bayer, not unlike an Argentinian Ken Loach, provided a script full of dialogue that aspires to a raw, naturalistic tone but— at least to the ears of a modern audience—comes over as a series of slogans and thinly disguised agit-prop. As the narrative moves from its opening bomb blast in Buenos Aires to Río Gallegos, the film takes on a frantic pace, employing swift tracking movements, dramatic zooms and deft montage techniques, and incorporating elements of the Western, both directly from Hollywood and as modified by the "gaucho" film genre.

The film crudely reflects Olivera's nostalgia for militancy and trade unionism, all the rebels being presented as heroic, almost flawless victims of social injustice (conversely, the British landowners and their lackeys are portrayed as immoral, whisky-swigging swine). In 1974 Argentina had not yet been fully drawn into the vortex of terror that would lead to the Dirty War and the "disappearing" of thousands of academics, writers, students, left-wing sympathizers and countless innocent families and friends of supposed suspects. Though the return of Perón from Spain the year before had not heralded the era many leftists had hoped for, there was still perhaps room for optimism in the political arena. In his *Film and the Anarchist Imagination*, Richard Porton suggests that the film "could be viewed as an exhortation to return to the glory days of the 1920s." But Porton admits that it ends with a "tragic finality"—the brutal slaughter of some 1,500 strikers and union leaders—that hardly acts as an incentive for a revival of militant anarcho-syndicalism.

Throughout, the landscape looks burned, or bleached. We rarely see the sky, and never see it as the dome of deep blue so often represented in coffee-table photographic books about Patagonia. There is a tangible sense of lawlessness: the landowners can do whatever they like just because they are far from Buenos Aires, ostensibly the fount of the law—though in fact the root of all the corruption.

La Patagonia rebelde was a considerable box office success, a fact that probably led Isabel Perón's government to suppress the film. Internationally, its aggressive, macho style and serious message impressed critics, and Olivera was awarded the Silver Bear at the 1974 Berlin Film Festival. In recent years there has been talk of his collaborating with Bayer on a film about the *conquista del desierto* and he is also taking forward a film called *La bandolera inglesa* (The English Bandit) about Elena Greenhill, a female bandit who lived in Patagonia a century ago.

SURREALISM: RE-IMAGINING LEGENDS

The story of Orllie Antoine de Tounens was always crying out for a film. If Argentina had powerful studios and actors with the address books of Kevin Costner or Mel Gibson, no doubt there would have been a lavish epic featuring blockbuster scenes of the Mapuche crossing the Andes with Gerard Depardieu as the crazy but likeable monarch. But Carlos Sorín's *La película del rey* (A King and His Movie, 1986) takes a step backward and tells the story of an obsessed filmmaker, David Vass (Julio Chávez), who yearns to make a film about the King of Patagonia.

The problem is that Vass cannot find a professional suitable actor to play the king, and so finally chooses an amateur, a hippie who gives him a great deal of trouble. When his financial backing is withdrawn, Vass finds himself with no film at all. After a final walk out by crew and cast, Vass decides to play the role himself, using mannequins as extras.

The film is as much about filmmaking as Orllie Antoine, but the movement of the film's plot, from practical problems and penury to the hauntingly surreal scenes featuring the mannequins, is echoed by Vass taking on the role of Orllie as solitary dreamer and visionary. In Sorín's magic realist universe, local history lives on in the figure of the "mad" director. *La película del rey* scooped awards at film festivals in Venice, Havana, Spain and at home.

Also suffused with surrealism is Ricardo Wullicher's *La nave de los locos* (Ship of Fools, 1995), which explores the myth of the Caleuche—the phantom ship of Chilote legend that carries a drowned crew or, as in the film's title, a cargo of madmen. A young doctor and his wife, Laura, a lawyer, decide to head south in search of a new life (a quest familiar to many urban Argentinians, at least as dinner-table chit-chat). A local couple, Agustín and Julia, give them a warm welcome and offer advice and support. Things fall apart when a Mapuche chief sets fire to the tourist complex that Agustín is building, causing the deaths of Gabriel, his and Julia's son. When arrested and locked up, the chief refuses to defend himself and waits for the arrival of the Caleuche. Laura is appointed by the local judiciary to take on the case. She is helped by a local clairvoyant and together they discover that the Mapuche was in fact reclaiming a sacred burial ground. The legal drama is spliced with fantastical visions of the arrival of the ship, with the surrealist dream-vision serving as a form of political protest.

Alejandro Agresti's *El viento se llevó lo que* (1998) is a film about films in the *Cinema Paradiso* mould, but with a backdrop of desert and dust that means the local village cinema is the sole conduit for experiencing the outside world. The title plays with the Spanish translation of *Gone with the Wind*, and literally means "The Wind Took Away What…", hinting at the way, the Patagonian wind takes away meaning or order.

Soledad, an alienated taxi driver from Buenos Aires, steals a cab and drives to a remote Patagonian village. There she finds a community whose only contact with the rest of the world is through cinema. Its films, however, arrive in terrible condition, with the reels out of order, images upside down and the voices out of synch. As a consequence, the people are also out of kilter, speaking in non-sequiturs and constructing their own notion of reality through random scraps of film.

Among the villagers are three protagonists: a young aspiring film critic who dreams of making his own movie; a projectionist who is tired of changing the rolls; and a hotel manageress desperate for a companion. One day, a French actor arrives, to the general acclaim of the locals—for them he is an idol—and of the hotel owner, who falls in love with him. But all who arrive in this out-of-joint reality are sucked in, and Soledad falls in love with the critic, embracing the general anarchy.

Writing in *La Nación*, respected film critic Adolfo C. Martinez recognized the influence of Argentinian writer Roberto Arlt in the work of Agresti. Like Arlt, he writes, Agresti is a "continual breaker of rules; his characters shift between dreams and reality; they are allowed to knit and then unravel their own joys and pains and he gives them space to slot themselves into the plot in the midst of a sort of chaos, all of which, for periods, threatens to endanger the audience's acceptance of the unfolding stories."

ROADS THROUGH NOWHERE

While there is no great Patagonian road movie to date, almost every director who heads for Patagonia finds at least a few minutes of time in the film for a road-movie scene. Both the inland Ruta 40 and the coastal Ruta 3 might have been made especially for road movies. The former runs from Abra Pampa in Jujuy in the high Andean plain of the north-west to Cabo Vírgenes but, if it is a lonesome highway for most of its 3,000 plus miles, it is during the 400-mile stretch of nothingness that lies between Perito Moreno and El Calafate that it comes into its own. Here, the RN 40 turns into a rough gravel track bordered by a featureless landscape of *coirón* grass. A howling wind is the only sound, except for the occasional pathetic bleat of sheep scratching around for scraps of food miles from the *estancias* that own them.

The Ruta 3, which runs from Buenos Aires to the Parque Nacional de Tierra del Fuego near Ushuaia—with a transporter barge fording the Magellan Strait at Punta Delgada—is mainly paved and dead straight. Its use in films evokes a more abstract ideal of road travel, as used time and again in American films.

Pino Solanas' *El Viaje* (The Voyage, 1991) is about a young man's rite of passage from ignorance to maturity, from cold to heat and from Ushuaia to Mexico. The protagonist, Martín, leaves Tierra del Fuego to go north in search of his father. Along the way, he passes through a flooded Buenos Aires in the thrall of the happily amphibious Presidente Rana (President Frog), while the narrative hops about between a violent collage of cartoons that retell the region's violent martial history and sub-plots that present Patagonian landowners as slightly crazed British thugs (a stereotype that has a kernel of truth to it). A dark film, it is probably Solanas' most ambitious work to date, the wide pans and generally distanced optics indicating his aim of placing Martín in a sweeping historical and global context.

Walter Salles' far lighter movie, *The Motorcycle Diaries* (2004), is imbued with some of the same questions about centres of meaning and revelation: Ernesto "Che" Guevara de la Serna and his companion, Alberto Granado, have to get to Machu Picchu, and then to the Amazon, to make contact with the "real" Latin America.

This is not artistic caprice. European travellers to Latin America and many Latin Americans themselves perceive societies where indigenous populations have survived and persevered as somehow more authentic. But it is striking that a left-wing, highly politicized cineaste such as Solanas should uncritically embrace the idea that Ushuaia is merely a point of departure—a place where Martín has no father, where the lessons of politics and society cannot be learnt, where a sense of self cannot be invented.

In contrast, Marcelo Piñeyro's *Caballos salvajes* (Wild Horses, 1995) takes its characters to the south where they find meaning and self-understanding. The film presents Patagonia and its roads as an escape route—from the city, from the past, and from the police. Veteran Argentinian actor Hector Alterio plays José, a seventy-year-old anarchist who deposited $15,000 in a bank twenty years ago and now wants to withdraw the money. He has no papers to prove the account is his and the bank clerks give him a hard time. So one day he turns up at the bank with a gun and, pointing the pistol at his head, announces that he will blow his brains out if he does not get his *dinero*.

Bored, miserable, twenty-something bank clerk Pedro (Leonardo Sbaraglia) sees this unfolding drama as his opportunity to escape. Spontaneously, he announces that José has taken him hostage and they leave the bank together with half a million dollars. With police and reporters on their trail, José and Pedro travel the back-roads and, as you would expect, begin to bond. They are idealists, so while they also spend some of the money, they also dole out plenty of it to poor people along the way, occasionally sending videotaped messages to the media. Predictably enough, they pick up a beautiful woman named Ana (Cecilia Dopazo), who turns out to be made of tougher stuff than either of them

The film was Piñeyro's debut and is essentially a feel-good comedy with some sentimental references to the idea of freedom. Patagonia—in this case, pretty, temperate northern Patagonia in the summer time—is a metaphor for escape and old-style values of friendship filial love. The final image of the "wild horses" of the film's title is crude, cheesy and beautifully shot—this is Argentinian cinema aping Hollywood and pleasing the middle-class teenage market in Buenos Aires.

Nonetheless the film is interesting, since the year of its production, 1995, was bang in the middle of the period of Carlos Menem's government. A shiny, happy, irrelevant film about a heist—about lucre, easy money and blowing it all on a whim—was just what the audience wanted. *Caballos salvajes* serves as an absolute contrast with the road-type movies of the post-Menem period.

At the other extreme is Gregorio Cramer's *Invierno mala vida* (Winterland, 1997) which turns the road movie clichés around and gives them a twist at once sardonic and surreal. The film follows the slow drives of Valdivia in his beaten-up old Valiant, a solitary figure and sometime petty thief who gets by taking on odd jobs. He wears a threadbare suit and battered shoes and drinks cheap wine, gin and tonic and glasses of Fernet Branca in seedy bars. His only desire in life is the local swimming instructress. Then one day, while trying to steal a car, he meets the mysterious businessman Sr. Ramenfort, who contracts him to collect a golden sheep. It all looks most promising—until hapless Valdivia gets drunk and loses his precious shipment.

The lost sheep, far from being the noble prize of Jason's mythic quest, is a somewhat crude metaphor for the meaning of Valdivia's life. As he contemplates yet another failure, his "nowhere" swallows up the road. As Diego Battle writes in his review in the *La Nación* newspaper: "The director manages to transform... the grotesqueness of certain situations and the pathos of some of its characters into a portrait full of sensitivity and melancholy. He converts Patagonia, with its spectacular, inhospitable vistas, into one more character in the story and not merely a touristy backdrop."

New Routes

In the mid-1990s a breach occurred. Audiences and young directors, getting used to democracy and confronting not death squads but unemployment, family breakdown and growing up, began to tire of overtly political films in the Solanas mode. A new kind of film evinced a subtle approach portraying character, and while *argentinidad* or "Argentineness" was evident, these films were more existential and more universal. The influence of both Italian neo-realism and of French *cinéma vérité* is evident in many of the films of the period, but given the theatricality of much previous Argentinian cinema, the new found understatement and naturalism constituted a powerful aesthetic.

The film that set off a new wave of Argentinian cinema was not set in the wide open spaces of Patagonia but in the closed, claustrophobic back alleys of Buenos Aires, where street kids scratch around for something to do and a few *pesos* to spend. When Adrián Caetano and Bruno Stagnaro's *Pizza, birra, faso* (Pizza, Beer and Cigarettes) was premiered at the International Mar del Plata Film Festival in 1997, it caused a greater stir at home than any Argentine film since Luis Puenzo's *La historia oficial* (The Official Story) won the Oscar for Best Foreign Film in 1986.

The simple story of a gang of poor, street-hardened teenagers trying to turn their lives around with a small-time robbery caught the attention of film critics around the world. In the words of Eduardo "Quintin" Antin, founder of magazine *El Amante Cine*, who spoke at the 42nd Thessaloniki International Film Festival in November 2001: "This new generation [of Argentine filmmakers] has found a more authentic way to present social problems, without considering tradition and the prevailing magic realism as the sine qua non of cinematographic production."

Patagonia, so long associated with a kind of folkloric magic realism for many Argentinians, would feature in several of the most important films to come out of this new school.

Mundo Grua (Crane World, 1999)

Pablo Trapero's gritty and poetic debut follows the changing fortunes of Rulo, a likeable, pot-bellied fifty-year-old who had a brief taste of success as a rock musician during the 1970s. Divorced, down on his luck, with both an elderly mother and a musician son to support, Rulo turns to his best friend Torres, who has connections in the construction industry. He lands a job as a crane operator, but it is work more suited to a younger man and he soon has to move on. Through Torres he gets a job as an excavator driver in Patagonia, where he sleeps at a remote farmhouse with his fellow labourers. These are Argentina's contemporary *golondrinas*—swallows or migrant workers—following in the weary footsteps of the sheep shearers who used to go south every year.

While a certain solidarity keeps up the workers' morale, their relationship with the bosses, always strained, is pushed to the limit one day when their food fails to arrive. In a spontaneous act of protest the workers refuse to work until it does. Their pay is stopped, and everyone's job evaporates. Static shots show abandoned equipment occupying a wasteland against a vast sky. Each worker heads back to wherever he came from.

The themes of the film are quintessentially Argentinian: life is a makeshift project; transience is the norm; Rulo's discovery that making a fresh start at a late age proves nigh-on impossible is familiar to many Argentinians.

Mundo Grua took the Special Jury Prize Award at the 1999 Havana Film Festival. Trapero returned to Patagonia to film *Nacido y criado* (Born and Bred, 2006), about Santi, a successful interior designer who following a personal tragedy, abandons Buenos Aires to take a job in a remote provincial airport where flights are few and days are endless. The boredom provides Santi with the space to consider the ghosts of his past: grief, identity, honesty and love. The moody landscape reflects the trauma of his past. Once again Trapero zooms in on the importance of friendship, in this instance between Santi and his workmates Robert and Cacique.

HISTORIAS MÍNIMAS (MINIMAL STORIES, 2002)

While many American road movies follow a formula in which the road is a gauntlet of obstacles, disasters, crime and cops to be run, Carlos Sorín's driver and passengers encounter nothing but kindness during their quest in southern Patagonia.

The movie tells three interwoven stories. Roberto (expertly played by Javier Lombardo) is a fastidious travelling salesman who hopes to win the love of a young widow by driving miles to deliver a wonderful birthday cake to her son. En route to San Julián he meets the second protagonist, Don Justo, a grandfather on his way to the port city to find his long-lost dog. Meanwhile, Maria is a young mother so desperately bored that the prospect of winning a food processor on a trashy game show leads her to travel 200 miles to be a contestant.

The car—like the film—moves slowly. A camera that refuses to make any judgments and a combination of subtle black humour and social commentary make watching Roberto's passage through Patagonia an engaging experience. Sorín mainly used non-professional actors and they seem at ease in Patagonia; we are aware of the spectacular scenery rolling past the car window, but the protagonists are preoccupied with their dog, cake or food processor. The poverty and isolation of Patagonia come through, but Sorín is at the same time paying homage to small-town life, reminding Buenos Aires audiences that their cosmopolitan self-regard is not relevant to the realities of the far-flung southern provinces. Indeed, by shunning the colour and parochial clutter of urban reality and focusing on Argentina's other worlds—the *pueblo* and the empty spaces—*Minimal Stories* is raised to the level of a universal drama.

Bonbón el perro (Bonbon the Dog, 2004)

Carlos Sorín went "minimal" again in his follow up to *Historias mínimas*. Coco is an unemployed, middle-aged mechanic scratching out a living as a travelling knife salesman. In reward for helping a widow, he is given a pedigree *dogo argentino* (Argentinian mastiff); what is generally regarded as an ugly, notoriously fierce dog turns out for him to be an agent of entirely positive change.

Coco's sister refuses to have the dog at her house, so he has no choice but to hit the road in his truck, with Bonbón riding haughty and upright at his side. Together, man and dog meet a variety of people and Coco's luck begins to change. He is offered work as a security guard, Bonbón proves to be a medal winner at the local kennel show, and soon Coco's life seems to be on the up. Then he meets a dog trainer, who claims that there is money to be made by putting Bonbón out to stud. But while the big white dog can win rosettes in the show tent, seems unimpressed by the bitches in the kennel.

This story of an ordinary man and his dog brings optimism and gentle humour to a breathtaking landscape. Again, Sorín used untrained actors, and again the camera is a fellow passenger and sympathetic, silent observer of the tiny dramas that unfold.

Writing about *Minimal Stories*, Argentinian film critic Sergio Wolf makes a point that is relevant to both of Sorín's Patagonian films: "There was definitely a change. Compared to *La película del rey*, which was Sorín's first film, *Minimal Stories* is a complete inversion. One is a megalomaniacal, gigantic project to create the story of the king of Patagonia and the other is a minimal story about a poor retiree in search of his dog."

GLUE (2006)

Alexis Dos Santos brings a new, youthful plot to Patagonia in his *Glue—Historia adolescente en medio de la nada*, or Teen Story in the Middle of Nowhere. The main character, Lucas, is a gawky fifteen-year-old who kills his time riding a bike around his dusty hometown, sniffing glue and rehearsing in a punk band with best pal Nacho. Like any teen, his body is §a hormonal battlefield and he spends his evenings inspecting every spot, lump, stain and scar. In the warm light of a Patagonian summer, geeky Andrea appears, triggering off new, unexpected tensions and attractions between Lucas and Nacho. To a soundtrack of Violent Femmes songs, feverish kisses are blown dry by the searing hot winds and teen angst is provided with a fittingly barren landscape. Gay media have responded to the film with enthusiasm, and it may well go down in the alternative cultural histories as the first example of a tale set in Queer Patagonia.

These films, in keeping with the style and aesthetics of the new generation of Argentinian directors, seek to revisit a familiar landscape—Patagonia—and use the lens to juxtapose the grandiose, inhuman space with the small, even petty concerns of ordinary people. Solanas and the polemical cineastes of the 1960s and 1970s adopted a frontal approach in their rejection of Hollywood's epic structures and finale-obsessed plots, but the present generation casts an oblique eye over contemporary Argentinian reality in films that are easier on the eye and, in their way, even less concerned with established moviemaking models. Patagonia at once frees the directors from the tango and tourist clichés of Buenos Aires and provides them with a vast screen on which to project their new, precise mythologies.

To date, Patagonia for export—that of tour firms, brochures, guide books and gringo dreamers—has not concerned feature-film makers. But in his feature-length documentary *Fantasmas en la Patagonia* (Ghosts in Patagonia, 1996), Claudio Remedi contrasts the grim reality of unemployment with the pleasurably pointless activities of tourists. The film is set in Sierra Grande, a small town where the government has just closed down the iron mine, the only local source of employment in the region. Lucio and his friends, who have formed a rock band to entertain themselves, wander the streets remembering friends who have already left. There is a Spaniard known as El Gallego, who came to the town following in the footsteps of the anarchists with a dream of building a new land. The other main character is Julio, a mining engineer who roams the empty tunnels of the abandoned mines even as tourists are allowed to explore the ruins of his workplace as an adventurous add-on to their Patagonian holidays.

The film is a depressing reminder that Patagonia is increasingly dependent on tourism as a source of hard currency and that it is subject to the same neo-liberal forces as those towns and villages in the Welsh valleys and Lancashire where mining is already a distant memory and a museum piece. In *Fantasmas en la Patagonia* the region acquires a new generation of ghosts—all those who have left because of unemployment.

SILENCE AND MYSTIQUE

Argentina has a very rich folkloric tradition, both in the city and in the rural hinterland. Country dance forms such as the *vidalita, chacarera, zamba* and *carnabalito*—found in the Andean north-west—are nourished by several strains of music, including indigenous percussive forms, Spanish and creole guitar music and Old World dance rhythms. In the provinces of Misiones and Corrientes, *chamamé* music is a conflation of Brazilian and Spanish styles and the polka brought over by Eastern European immigrants.

Buenos Aires is the home of two legendary beats: on the one hand, tango, with its African, gaucho, Andalucian and Cuban hues and its proud, urban swagger; on the other, Argentinian contemporary rock, which is informed by local politics, jazz, British rock and elements of indigenous folk music.

In contrast, the two main soundtracks of Patagonia are silence and the howl of the wind. Man-made music with roots in the native soil is entirely absent. In the low-life canteens and bars of Comodoro Rivadavia and Río Turbio all you will hear is bastardized salsa and *cumbia*, global pop and an occasional souvenir from Argentina's *rock nacional* archives. The eradication of ethnicities in the period between 1870 and 1930 also wiped out the language and music of the scattered peoples. Anything that remains is, like the anthropological data, third-hand, the memory of a memory.

This means that the resources that do exist are in the form of field recordings. A typical disc, *Caminos Sonoros de la Patagonia*, on the Ülmaru label, brings together dialogues and brief examples of both Mapuche and Tehuelche music recorded in villages in the province of Chubut. The *mestizo* speakers and performers on the recording are almost all very old and, while they claim to be Mapuche or Tehuelche, they struggle to recall even the basic vocabulary of their grandparents' language. The music is played on simple wind instruments forged from cow-horns or bored wood, a kind of Jew's harp called the *trompe*, and the *kultrun* drum, which consists of hide stretched over a wooden bowl. The sounds produced are primitive, echoing the wind or perhaps the plaintive calls of lost or distant animals—which might be guanacos or sheep. Rhythms are repetitive and may well be associated with some kind of trance or incantation, but what we are hearing are the dissonant, unharmonious scraps of an ancient musical tradition. The cow-horn, or *trutruka*, produces a particularly forlorn, plangent single note and when several come together they sound mournful and united in nothing much more than the recognition that life is truly joyless. Above all, this is an alien music, a music whose sadness we cannot quite place. Is it the song of a hope lost in the twentieth century, when the culture was destroyed? Or was there always loss and longing in the music of the Mapuche and Tehuelche?

Notwithstanding the fracturing of traditions, a handful of groups have sought to revive and rework native rhythms. Armazón, a group of musicians from Ancud, Chiloé, mix the sounds of the *kultrun*, *trompe* and the eerie voice of their singer, Neddiel Muñoz, with synthesizers, drum beats and guitar to create a haunting fusion. But the melding of traditions is also a vehicle for an overt, uncompromising political message. The lyrics of "Kachalkura", the first song on the band's 1991 album *Gülkantun*, only the Patagonian version of a work song:

stone axe
stone axe
it cuts nothing
how will I live?
I will freeze to death
No fire, no wood
The pot does not boil
The food will not be cooked.

Beatriz Pichi Malen, a Mapuche singer from Argentina, uses her Mapundungun language in nursery songs, spiritual odes and homages to nature. Born in Los Toldos, a province of Buenos Aires, Pichi Malen is the great, great granddaughter of Coliqueo, a revered nineteenth-century Mapuche chief. Her voice is serene, her message measured, more that of the educator than the rebel, and she uses recordings of nature, such as running streams, and synthesized wind, to drive home the Mapuche connection with nature and the land.

Classical and rock-pop artists have paid tribute to Patagonia. Argentina's much-loved veteran folk rocker León Gieco and the Los Angeles-based producer and composer Gustavo Santaolalla performed a *Buena Vista Social Club* kind of exercise in the early 1980s, recording folk music the length of the country and releasing it as a series of CDs under the title *De Ushuaia a La Quiaca*. Even so, the content is heavily weighted to the north of the country, where Incan traditions have survived in both the instruments used and in many popular folk rhythms.

In the film *El Viaje*, pop star Fito Páez sings "Ushuaia", a breathy ode to the town where the action begins. He tries to recover the magic of the indigenous word, *Ush-oo-ay-ahhhh*, but the overall tone is sentimental rather than sensual.

Ambient-classical composer Bruno Sanfilippo's *Suite Patagonia* is a series of musical postcards recounting myths and legends of the region, including a tribute to the great Mapuche *cacique* Sayhueque, a dedication to Fuegia Basket and Jemmy Button and a suitably glacial piece about the Andes.

All these dedications and homages, exercises and ethnic field studies spring from the void of music in Patagonia. Patagonia adds a kind of mystique to an album, as it does to a clothing label or a travel guide.

EL SUR

If there is a footnote to this absence, it is tango. Argentina's metropolitan folk—Buenos Aires' global soundtrack, the dance of whores and lost *gauchos*—also spares a few silences for Patagonia.

It should not surprise anyone. Tango is shot through with revolutionary nihilism, with the nostalgia evoked by an empty street or a train leaving a trail of whirling dust, and with the loneliness felt by migrant males far from home, from mothers and from lovers. Its genesis occurred when Buenos Aires was a remote suburb of Europe and when the first waves of Europeans were washing up in the capital and in the provincial ports, including those in Patagonia.

To grasp the link between tango and Patagonia, we have to consider the significance of the *sur* (south or southside). The definitive song about the south is Homero Manzi's "Sur", written in 1948:

> South, a large wall and then...
> South, a light from a general store...
> You'll never see me again, as you saw me,
> Sat by the window
> Waiting for you... and now
> I'll never brighten with the stars
> Our undisturbed walk
> Down Pompeya streets.
> The streets and the suburban moons,
> and my love, and your window,
> all's dead, I know...

Jorge Luis Borges took up the notion of *el sur* in his early stories. For him, to go beyond Calle Rivadavia—the traditional frontier between Buenos Aires' rich northern districts and the older, poorer southside—into *el sur* was to enter a quasi-mythical universe of knife-fighters, tango dancers, urban *gauchos* and friendly neighbourhood *putas*. It signified, for him, an earlier, more authentic Buenos Aires, a city that was liminal, and onto which the pampas—and beyond—encroached. In the last two decades of the nineteenth century, following an outbreak of yellow fever in the old neighbourhoods of San Telmo and Balvanera, the middle classes began to relocate to the north of the city. This left the southside with crumbling tenements, abandoned mansions and streets devoid of shoppers, residents, workers and *tangueros*.

Pino Solanas' film *Sur* (*South*, 1988) is a surreal homage to the Pompeya of Manzi's song, with tango ghosts and the myriad phantasms of the military dictatorship meeting at night on the cobbled streets. The past gets drunk and dances with the present. In one scene, the city *sur* and the provincial *sur* are blurred, when the character of María takes a melancholy truck-journey on an endless road down "south" to Patagonia and her longed-for new life. "I wanted to come south," she says, "to find a place where life, where desire, were possible."

Solanas is giving artistic expression to a popular notion. For many Argentinians, the south of the country has remained a vital, mysterious, idealized region. It is otherness, the distant, elsewhere. It is, in a sense, an extension of Buenos Aires' nocturnal, forgotten southside; a counterweight to all-consuming modernity, haste and waste, and the exigencies of the everyday.

Chapter Fourteen

CHATWIN, THEROUX AND THE
TRAVEL WRITERS

"Lady Hunstanton: What did Sir John talk to you about, dear Mrs
Allonby?

Mrs Allonby: About Patagonia.

Lady Hunstanton: Really? What a remote topic! But very improving, I
have no doubt.

Mrs Allonby: He has been most interesting on the subject of Patagonia.
Savages seem to have quite the same views as cultured people on almost
all subjects. They are excessively advanced.

Lady Hunstanton: What do they do?

Mrs Allonby: Apparently everything."

Oscar Wilde, *A Woman of No Importance* (1893)

Travel writers are like literary bulldozers, clearing paths for future generations of guide writers, gap-year students and coach-incarcerated tourists.
Travelogues, like the schematic itineraries dreamed up by tour operators
and—paradoxically—also by hippies and backpackers, create their own
narrow trails and fixed points of encounter. They open up certain routes,
and close others down. When a travel book becomes famous, the literary
pilgrims will set out to pay homage, *Lonely Planet* in one hand and cult
travelogue in the other.

Since the 1970s Patagonia has proved fertile territory for aspiring
writers. Bruce Chatwin kick-started a glittering, if brief, career with a trip
to the region. North-western Patagonia gave Paul Theroux's train odyssey
in *The Old Patagonian Express* (1979) an enigmatic finale. Tom Vernon
and Sara Wheeler made names for themselves with trips to, respectively,
Argentina and Chile, with significant sections on Patagonia in both works.
There are dozens of also-rans too, splicing Patagonia into their travel books
because it provides a vaguely mysterious counterpoint to more mundane
regions, or because it fits in with their holiday plans.

Ships' logs, official reports to heads of state, scientific journals and anthropological writings are all precursors of the modern travelogue. Certainly, by the late nineteenth century, armchair travellers in Europe and the United States would read the works of, say, Darwin and W. H. Hudson purely for pleasure. But travel writing in the second half of the twentieth century is characterized by a heightened degree of self-consciousness. Modern travel writers do not travel and write; they travel *to write*, and feel obliged to impose a narrative of some sort on their journey—by means of a quest, a flight from something, of quirky twist—and, at the same time, place their own character in the forefront of the narrative. They are aware that their readers might have been to the destination being described or may plan a journey on the back of their experience of reading the book. Modern travel writing is, in this sense, a branch of consumer journalism, and rarely a dispatch from some unknowable faraway place.

All this should mean that travel writers refrain from making things up or faking wonder, but, as the controversy over Chatwin's veracity suggests, they are still prone to embellishing their tales or exaggerating certain aspects of a place by omitting others.

Patagonia's appeal is largely due to the layers of literature already available to any writer who chooses to travel through it. Name-checking Magellan, Drake, Darwin and FitzRoy adds some gravity to a story of wanderlust; sneak in a few obscure explorer-adventurers and some unknown Latin Americans and the writer can impress readers with what looks like extensive research. But the region's name hints at a degree of risk or difficulty, a notion of being somewhere on the periphery of modern communications. It has that vague quality that contemporary media pundits might call edginess, and it remains true is that naming Patagonia as part of your travel plans may slightly perturb less well-travelled grandparents. In an essay, "Patagonian Cases", Peter Hulme argues that this was certainly the case when Chatwin and Theroux produced their influential books:

> Pottering around the Andes or island-hopping in the Pacific was in the 1970s simply not difficult enough; but, equally, confronting real danger in the Antarctic or Himalayas was rather too serious: extreme travel (and its writing) was not yet as popular as it would later become. The archetype demanded something like 4.3 on a five point scale of difficulty:

enough in the way of long solitary walks and flooded rivers to induce admiration for endurance, but not the surfeit of risk which might overwhelm the ultimately *social* nature of the travelling experience. As a
"zone of travel" for the late twentieth century, Patagonia rated alongside places like Central Asia, or the highlands of New Guinea, or the
deserts of Australia, as being the right distance away from the metropolitan centres, and with a climate and terrain which promised some
difficulty without real danger.

This is still very much the case. Patagonia has a serviceable transport
infrastructure, hotels and hostels in every town, and people speak Spanish,
and often English and other European languages. Yet it has retained an
"out there" quality, despite heavy marketing as a tourist destination. Tour
operator advertising has played a leading role in protecting and branding
this rather bogus inscrutability. But it has been helped no end by travel
writers, who—notwithstanding Darwin, FitzRoy, Gusinde and all the scientists and anthropologists—have in the main sought to re-mystify the
region and find a means by which Patagonia's natural beauty and mythical heritage might reflect back on them.

CHE GUEVARA: GAP-YEAR GUERRILLA

> "We constitute a single *mestizo* race, which from Mexico to the Magel-
> lan Straits bears notable ethnographic similarities. And so, in an attempt
> to rid myself of the weight of small-minded provincialism, I propose a
> toast to Peru and to a United Latin America."
>
> Che Guevara, *The MotorcycleDiaries*

The notion that Ernesto Guevara de la Serna was ever an ordinary tourist
might not fit the revolutionary profile, but his journey through South
America in 1951-52 definitely belongs to the modern era of travel-as-
leisure. At the time Guevara was a 23-year-old medical student, and his
close friend and companion for the journey, Alberto Granado, who was six
years older, had graduated as a biochemist. Neither of the young men was
certain about his future career, so with the support of their middle-class
families, they took what was essentially a gap year, or year out.

After visiting Guevara's (soon to be ex-) girlfriend and family at the Atlantic resort of Miramar, they drove their 1949 Norton 500cc motorcycle, "La Poderosa", first through the port city of Bahía Blanca on 16 January 1952, and then across the barren plains of northern Río Negro province. They took the Ruta Nacional 22 through Choele Choel to arrive at Piedra del Aguila thirteen days later. From here they travelled on through San Martín de los Andes and Bariloche and then took the lake route through the Andes to Peulla. Once in Chile, they travelled north from Temuco all the way up to the Atacama desert.

Guevara only skirted Patagonian's northern edge but the region is vividly portrayed in *The Motorcycle Diaries*. In part this is due to the lively, personal narrative, much of it dealing with the ruses employed by two young men to cadge free dinners and lodging, and how their beloved bike keeps breaking down. There are also many occasions when the intoxicating freedom of the open road fuels a mutual dream of travelling forever. But being an Argentinian, Guevara renders his accounts of encounters with people and places without the slightest veneer of exoticism, and is, for instance, frank and honest about provincial town planning: San Martín de los Andes, a much-hyped lakeside resort favoured by wealthy, vulgar *porteños*, is "an unattractive, miserable town, surrounded in sharp contrast by magnificent, densely wooded mountains."

There are passages that ring true to the moment of lived experience and, at the same time, query the whole enterprise of unstructured, fly-by-night travel:

> We set off again, passing greatly varying lakes, all surrounded by ancient forest, the scent of wilderness caressing our nostrils. But curiously, the sight of a lake and a forest and a single solitary house with well-tended garden soon begins to grate. Seeing the landscape at this superficial level only captures its boring uniformity, not allowing you to immerse yourself in the spirit of the place; for that you must stop at least several days.

The Times called *The Motorcycle Diaries* "*Easy Rider* meets *Das Kapital*". *The Washington Post* said that Che was a "Latin American James Dean or Jack Kerouac". In fact, the book is more like an earnest young doctor's private diary; Guevara was emotional and excitable at times but he was also a quiet, patient observer, and in this as in other works he prefers to absent himself from the text. Take any modern travelogue set in Latin

America and set it alongside *The Motorcycle Dairies* and the author of the former will appear far more anxious and—as he or she is almost certain to be a non-Latino—alienated.

As with Pino Solanas' film *El Viaje*, the Guevara narrative is based on a south-to-north journey towards illumination. In 2004 Walter Salles' rose-tinted film *The Motorcycle Diaries* popularized the story and the myth of Guevara's awakening. Argentina protects and suffocates the young man; as he moves north to Cuzco—the Incan "navel of the world"—and then onto the steamy tropics, he is awakened to the reality of "his America". On this journey, the early stage, through the scrubland of Río Negro, was a mere preface. Notwithstanding the anarchist uprising of the 1920s, Patagonia was not where guerrillas plied their trade.

BRUCE CHATWIN: TWENTIETH-CENTURY BOY

"By the time I met Bruce Chatwin he had been to Patagonia and had written about what he found there. In doing so, he helped to change the idea of what travel-writing could be. The book that he produced— titled in manuscript At the End: A Journey to Patagonia—was distinguished by the qualities which were to distinguish all his books. It was pungently expressed and delighted in paradox. It hovered teasingly between fact and fiction. It abstained from personal revelation but was full of autobiographical material. Even its central subject was a contradiction: the Patagonians were, it turned out, not one nation but a multinational collection of expatriates and exiles, many of whom felt most at home with themselves when they were abroad. This was a feeling with which Chatwin was in sympathy: in this and in other ways, his first book was a declaration of faith."

Susannah Clapp, *With Chatwin* (1997)

"Think of the word charming... think of the word seduction... He's out to seduce everybody, it doesn't matter if you are male, female, an ocelot or a tea-cosy."

Miranda Rothschild, quoted in Nicholas Shakespeare,
Bruce Chatwin (1999)

It is a pity that Jorge Luis Borges never strayed beyond his beloved Buenos

Aires to tackle the theme of Patagonia in his poetry or in one of the short prose works he described as *ficciones*. But a young British writer made his debut as a travel writer in 1977 with a travelogue that goes some way towards filling the gap. The book is, of course, *In Patagonia*, which refashioned the character of the travelogue and reinvigorated the genre, and became the only travel book that every traveller to Patagonia feels obliged to read—or at least carry around.

Bruce Chatwin, like Borges, forged his literary style through an intricate melding of intertextuality, obscure anecdote, local history and colourful legend. The novice writer had trained as a cataloguer at Sotheby's in London, while the old master had managed the Miguel Cané Library in Buenos Aires, and they shared a passion for inventories and classification. Like Borges, Chatwin adopted a voice that, while purporting elide his persona from the stories he told, in fact threw it into relief. The exotic and arcane appealed to both writers, and where the Argentinian drew on Old World literary sources to enrich his tales of mystery and magic in Buenos Aires' low-life *barrios* and rural hinterland, Chatwin spun stories that moved seamlessly between the English milieus and attitudes of many Patagonians and the bizarre legends and histories of their adopted homeland. It is this conflation of the weird and wonderful on one hand and the familiar and cosy on the other that makes Chatwin's travel writing so accessible, so beguiling and so influential.

In an essay entitled "I Always Wanted to Go to Patagonia", published in the *New York Times Book Review* in August 1983, Chatwin explains how the project came about. Having explained the etymology of his name and summed up his genealogy in the single phrase "descent from a Birmingham button-maker", Chatwin tells us how his mind was peopled by dreamers and adventurers:

> By the time my mother married into them, the Chatwins were "Birmingham worthies", that is to say, professional people, architects and lawyers, who did not go in for trade. There were, however, scattered among my forebears and relatives a number of legendary figures whose names inflamed my imagination.

Number four in a list of seven colourful dead relatives who includes a caber-tosser, a "desert traveller" and a miner, is:

Cousin Charley Milward the Sailor, whose ship was wrecked at the entrance to the Strait of Magellan in 1898. I have written his story in *In Patagonia*. While British Consul in Punta Arenas de Chile, he sent home to my grandmother a fragment of giant sloth's skin which he found, perfectly preserved, in a cave. I called it "the piece of brontosaurus" and set it at the centre of my childhood bestiary.

This story is used to start *In Patagonia*, but "I Always Wanted to Go to Patagonia", subtitled "The Making of a Writer", goes on to tell us how the travelogue actually came about after Chatwin had been struggling to write a more ambitious book on nomadism. After two unsuccessful attempts at completing this great work, Chatwin tells us, he went back to his manuscript one more time:

> Gradually the idea for a book began to take shape. It was to be a wildly ambitious and intolerant work, a kind of "Anatomy of Restlessness" that would enlarge on Pascal's dictum about the man sitting quietly in a room. The argument, roughly, was as follows: that in becoming human, man had acquired, together with his straight legs and striding walk, a migratory "drive" or instinct to walk long distances through the seasons; that this drive was inseparable from his central nervous system; and that, when warped in conditions of settlement, it found outlets in violence, greed, status-seeking or a mania for the new.

The book was too ambitious and gradually "became less and less intelligible to its author". Yet the nomad project does give us an insight into how Chatwin wanted to be perceived. The ex-auctioneer and sometime journalist wanted readers to see him as a visionary, as an academic and a scholar (though he had dropped out of his archaeology course at university, blaming boredom), and also as a champion of nomadism. *In Patagonia* was to be the perfect vehicle for this exercise in self-promotion and reinvention.

IN PATAGONIA

The book opens with a melancholy epigraph taken from *La Prose du Transsibérien et la petite Jehanne de France* (1913) by the French poet Blaise Cendrars. Chatwin leaves it in the original. In translation it reads: "There is now only Patagonia, Patagonia, that can match my immense sadness."

Chatwin's narrative is imbued with this "immense sadness". Perhaps he was consciously, and subconsciously, aware of the political darkness that was spreading across Argentina. He travelled to Patagonia in late December 1974, and remained there for three months. Juan Perón had died on 1 July 1974, a year after returning from exile in Spain, and the country, now governed by his hapless widow Isabel and the Rasputin-like López Vega, was being torn apart by the secretive police-backed Triple A, an authoritarian military command, guerrilla warfare, wildcat strikes and a series of economic disasters.

Chatwin could not have known how these events would soon plunge Argentina into what became known as the *años de plomo* or "leaden years", during which the military government murdered thousands of innocent individuals as part of the so-called "dirty war" waged against left-wing militancy. But he would certainly have seen the newspapers and been aware that his own project—to travel, research and write—was somewhat frivolous given the political and social climate in the country.

By playing on his own loneliness, Chatwin conjures up an empty, desolate Patagonia even while filling it with vignettes, anecdotes and tall tales. Though he rarely uses the first person to express feelings or moods, he places himself at the centre of the narrative as the sorrowful soul. In the following, he portrays himself as the solitary nomad and as a human who seeks hushed communion with the local fauna:

> I followed the fresh spoor of a guanaco. Sometimes I saw him up ahead, bobbing over fallen trunks, and then I came up close. He was a single male, his coat all muddled and his front gashed with scars. He had been in a fight and lost. Now he also was a sterile wanderer.

In the 1970s nuclear war was a constant spectre, and Chatwin alludes to it to reinforce the idea of a stormy beyond. The "sterile wanderer" seeks a place to sleep: "I pictured a low timber house with a shingled roof, caulked against storms, with blazing log fires inside and the walls lined with the best books, somewhere to live when the rest of the world blew up."

There are few direct references to the political crises. On passing through Buenos Aires at the beginning of the book, Chatwin mentions that there would be fewer kidnappings of the rich during the coming summer and that the "guerrillas also rented holiday villas, or went to Switzerland to ski." On the Magellan Strait, an old lady tells Chatwin about the recent coup in Chile: "'Oh it was beautifully done,' she said. 'Of course, we heard rumours before, but nothing happened. And then we saw the planes circling the city. There was a bit of shooting in the morning and by afternoon they had all the Marxists rounded up. It was beautifully done.'"

Yet there is in the book an awakening of sorts, and in tandem with the *faux* quest narrative is the rising curve of the theme of the natives. It is worth quoting a whole chapter to observe Chatwin's style unfold. This is chapter 67:

> In the Plaza de Armas a ceremony was in progress. It was one hundred years since Don José Menéndez set foot in Punta Arenas and a well-heeled party of his descendants had come south to unveil his memorial. The women wore black dresses, pearls, furs and patent shoes. The men had the drawn look that comes of protecting an overextended acreage. Their Chilean lands had vanished in land reform. As yet they clung to their Argentine latifundias but the good old days of English managers and docile peons were gone.
>
> Don José's bronze head was as bald as a bomb. The bust had once adorned the family's estancia at San Gregorio, but under the Allende regime the peons shoved it in an outhouse. Its reconsecration on the plaza symbolized the return of free enterprise, but the family were unlikely to get anything back. Insincere eulogies tolled like funeral bells.
>
> The wind sighed through the municipal araucarias. Ranked round the square were the cathedral, the hotel and the palazzos of the old plutocracy, now mostly officers' clubs. A statue of Magellan pranced over a pair of fallen Indians, which the sculptor had modelled on "The Dying Gaul".
>
> The top brass had lent their presence to the occasion. A band drowned the wind in Sousa marches, as the Intendente, a red-faced General of the Air Force, prepared to unveil the memorial. The Spanish chargé d'affaires stared with the glassy eye of absolute conviction. The American ambassador looked affable. And the crowd, which always turned out for a brass band, shambled round the ceremony with ex-

pressions of stone. Punta Arenas was a leftist town. There were the people who had elected Salvador Allende their deputy.

A block away was the *palais* which Moritz Braun imported piecemeal from Europe when he married Don José's daughter in 1902, its mansard roofs poking above a shroud of black cypresses. Somehow the house had weathered the confiscations and, in a setting of hygienic marble statues and buttoned sofas, the domestic serenity of the Edwardian era survived.

The servants were preparing the dining-room for the evening's reception. The afternoon sun squeezed through velvet draperies and bounced off a runway of white damask, reflecting light over walls of Cordoba leather and a painting of amorous geese by Picasso's father, Ruiz Blasco.

After the ceremony the older generation relaxed in the winter-garden, attended by a maid in black and white, who served some pale tea. The conversation turned to Indians. The "Englishman" of the family said: "All this business of Indian killing is being a bit overstretched. You see, these Indians were a pretty low sort of Indian. I mean they weren't like the Aztecs or the Incas. No civilization or anything. On the whole they were a pretty poor lot."

This passage is classic Chatwin. We are given a lot of disparate information in a very short space, but even more is evoked. Ennui hangs over this urban scene like a battered old crow. Punta Arenas' society is weary—and wearisome—and corrupt, but Chatwin finds the energy to note that the geese are "amorous" and that the painting was by Picasso's father. The scenes shift as they do in a film, from mean visages to fustian furniture to an aside on the massacre of the southern Patagonian tribes.

During the course of *In Patagonia*, as well as vile storms, lonely people and isolated *estancias*, there are recurrent mentions of the exploitation and killing of natives and workers. If, however, the theme of the land-grabbing campaigns at the end of the nineteenth century and the genocide of the native populations of Patagonia serves as a sort of objective correlative for the general sadness, it functions obliquely and eccentrically—a shadow in the text rather than a direct metaphor.

Perhaps the deftest trick of the narrative resides in what is left unsaid. It was this quality—as well as the playing fast and loose with the truth, of which more below—that made the book so attractive to fashionably post-modernist critics when it was published. Paul Theroux complained that the book was "full of gaps" and thought the obliqueness of *In Patagonia* illustrative, even symptomatic, of its author's elusive character. In *Nowhere is a Place*, he describes a conversation he had with Chatwin.

> How had he travelled from there to there? How had he met this or that person?
>
> Life was never so neat as Bruce made out. What of the other, small, telling details, which to me give a book reality.
>
> I used to look for links between the chapters, and between two conversations or pieces of geography. Why hadn't he put them in?
>
> "Why do you think it matters?" he said to me.
>
> "Because it's interesting," I said. "And because I think when you're writing a travel book you have to come clean."
>
> This made him laugh, and then he said something that I have always taken to be a pronouncement that was very near to being his motto, He said—he screeched—"I don't believe in coming clean."

Chatwin's editor, Susannah Clapp, says that she trimmed the book down to 97 loosely chronological mini-chapters, all with a key theme. During editing Chatwin was asked to provide some pointers to help the readers imagine the scene—who was doing what, how he got to a specific place—but not to the extent that it would spoil the author's "cubist" style.

Where the Patagonian adventure narratives of the late nineteenth century—Musters, Guinnard, Dixie, Beerbohm—flow rather blandly like the landscape they are striving to describe, Chatwin (and his editors) turned the unbroken blur of experience into nodal, momentary dramas. *In Patagonia*'s short chapters and its elliptical style, together with the bewildering range of characters and places described, make the work feel modern and impatient, glancing and pithy.

And yet, argues David Taylor in his essay "Bruce Chatwin: Connoisseur of Exile, Exile as Connoisseur", there is sadness and anomie in this very structure: "The melancholy of passage from one fixed moment to the next may be his most outstanding achievement, the post-imperial observer acknowledging irreconcilable distance from what he sees but no longer possesses."

CHATWIN CHASTISED

Chatwin's shining personality and literary output were often confused by his admirers. "Speaking for myself, I fell in love," wrote Salman Rushdie in his memoir about Chatwin. In Chapter One of her book *With Chatwin*, Susannah Clapp writes: "If Bruce Chatwin had been portly, myopic and mouse-haired his life and reputation would have been quite different."

But like all people everyone recognizes as handsome, dashing, brilliant and well connected, Chatwin has his fair share of detractors. Osvaldo Bayer, the political and social historian whose writings Chatwin used in his research into the anarchist uprisings of the 1920s, published a long article in the Buenos Aires magazine *Página 30* in August 1997, in which he berated Chatwin for his manner and mien, and for his abuse of sources in his writings:

> When I met Bruce Chatwin, I took him as an old-school representative of Her Majesty, as yet without the eye-patch. He had an imperial air about him, and in abundance... He was a total gentleman. White gloves, smile, charm, cold blood... The man from the first world let it be known that he didn't have much time. For that reason he is so precise in his questions and in his interests, and in interrupting his interlocutor when the conversation veers away from the theme that concerns him. One shouldn't be prejudiced about the idea "time is money" but in general intellectuals in the third world are talkative and want to tell their guest everything, open up, denude themselves before the Sir...

Bayer complained bitterly about the "fortune" Chatwin had made from his book. The arch-leftist's Anglophobia is rather crude and politically motivated but he writes that he was also incensed by Chatwin's pursuit only of the mythical (for Bayer, read: trivial) stories of the far south: "He wants books, bibliography. No, no, neither anthropology nor ethnology. No prehistory, except for some antediluvian animal that's been found, yes, legends, yes. Ecology, no, no; travellers, legends, episodes, bandits, ranchers. Stories about estancieros yes? Women, Indians, yes, but more adventure too. Strikes? Oh yes strikes! Anarchists? Oh yes, anarchists, wonderful. Cowboys, oh, yes, yes."

Bayer's other main objection was that Chatwin had taken all his research and "cooked" it into a popular account without ever having to do any research—and without fully acknowledging either Bayer's own aca-demic contribution or that of "poor" local historians from the regions. In an interview with the Argentinian writer Adrián Gimenez Hutton, Bayer also claimed that Chatwin ignored the facts in his portrayal of the strikers and in the sequence of events that led to the massacre.

For his part, Chatwin wrote in his diary that "on a cursory glance", Bayer's *La Patagonia trágica* "seemed to me to be the hysterical, doubtless justified, ravings of a poor lawyer, driven to dementia by the greed and drunkenness that surrounded him—the work of a man with persecution mania."

The authors' portraits of each other are obviously emotive and we would be foolhardy to take Bayer at his word. Yet there is little doubt that Chatwin sought only a legendary Patagonia in his investigations or that he happily tailored historical facts to suit his literary style.

The book also suffers from a rather quaint aestheticism. Clapp de-scribes how Chatwin's several flats were decorated pretentiously and exot-ically: a Ming table here, a fragment from a second-century Athenian relief there, and the King of Hawaii's bedsheet thrown lazily over an old dresser. There is a comparable pictorial quality to his books, with colours and forms, impressions and characters—and also words as physical forms—juxtaposed to give an impression of accidental eloquence and busy, even cramped beauty.

According to David Taylor, reading *In Patagonia* is not unlike a stroll through the ex-auctioneer's apartment: "To journey through the temporal and spatial shifts of Chatwin's writing is to confront streams of data—the jostling objects, ideas, and stories carefully recorded by the eye and mind of the former antiques dealer in a dislocated jumble."

Taylor argues that the presentation of history through anecdotes and stories—all laid out artfully yet randomly on the shelves of Chatwin's pages—reduces particular stories and dramas to mere elements in a general vision and is evidence of the author's "refusal to engage with the actuali-ties of human and political contact". When Nicholas Shakespeare asked the subjects of *In Patagonia* what they remembered most about young Bruce, many remarked that he was an incessant chatterbox. The implica-tion is that he was never really listening to anyone he met as he already had a clear idea of where they fitted into his overall scheme.

In *Wanderlust*, her homage to rambling, Rebecca Solnit complains that the walking essay, as a genre, has not moved on much since Hazlitt and R. L. Stevenson. She singles out Chatwin as an anachronistic ambassador for a tired form:

> Bruce Chatwin wrote divinely, but he always declined to distinguish nomadism—a persistent travel by any means, seldom primarily on foot—from walking, which may or may not be travel. Blurring these distinctions by conflating nomadism and his own British walking-tour heritage made nomads Romantics, or at least romantic, and allowed him to fancy himself something of a nomad... None of our revolutionary heroes is worth a thing until he has been on a good walk. Che Guevara spoke of the "nomadic phase" of the Cuban Revolution. Look what the Long March did for Mao Tse-Tung, or Exodus for Moses. Movement is the best cure for melancholy as Robert Burton (the author of *The Anatomy of Melancholy*) understood.
>
> A hundred and fifty years of moralizing! A century and a half of gentlemanly exhortation! Doctors have asserted many times over the centuries that walking is good for you, but medical advice has never been one of the chief attractions of literature.

Chatwin wrote in *In Patagonia*: "My God is the God of Walkers. If you walk hard enough, you probably don't need any other god." Solnit is thinking of this creedal claim and those passages where Chatwin exaggerates the solitude and the simplicity of his travels: "spending nights in the grass, in caves, in peons' huts, and sometimes between the linen sheets of an old-fashioned English estancia. On my back I carried a small leather rucksack containing a sleeping bag, a few clothes... and half a bottle of Vintage Krug to drink at the worst possible moment."

Chatwin portrays himself as an exile or outcast in a land without motels or bars. For Solnit, Chatwin's prose, for all its prettiness, smells of privilege and heritage, of a world full of people—mostly men—who go to Oxford and Cambridge and who walk in wild places because they have nothing better to do. Far from opening landscapes up or unlocking the mind, virtuous walking, she says, is designed only to produce words. You cannot become an aboriginal Australian or a Tehuelche just by following his ancient tracks. As Solnit succinctly puts it, "Bruce Chatwin to the contrary, Bedouins do not go on walking tours."

Peter Hulme concedes Solnit's point, but offers a mitigating argument about Chatwin's literary successes:

> Chatwin's work was taken up by the literary magazine *Granta*, whose first special issue on travel writing, which came out in 1984 and was reprinted thirteen times, did much to rekindle popular interest in the genre. *Granta* has sometimes been seen as peddling a form of gentlemanly English arrogance, but it also helped British travel writing become more international in scope and more culturally self-aware. And it was responsible for reconnecting travel writing with investigative journalism and contemporary political issues.

The most enduring criticism of Chatwin's book has been founded on the discovery that the author made things up. Any straightforward inventions, moreover, were part of a generally liberal handling of the material garnered in Patagonia. As well as noting Bayer's protestations, Nicholas Shakespeare's biography of Chatwin records examples of basic factual errors, names being changed, historical anecdotes fabricated, using others' research material without permission, and revealing the identity of those who had asked to remain anonymous. Chatwin upset local people when he portrayed them as "whiskey-soaked" landowners or hinted that they were homosexuals or asserted that they were Indian killers. Though he never spent very long in any once place—his four days in Gaiman, Chubut, were the longest he lingered anywhere—Chatwin wrote as if he was on intimate terms with most of the individuals who feature in the book.

In the author's defence, Clapp claims that Chatwin's native enthusiasm inclined him to find people interesting: "His inclination was... to be fascinated, beguiled, amused." For her, this excuses any embellishments. Shakespeare makes a similarly convoluted defence: "People who read [*In Patagonia*] to find out something about Patagonia are left behind. The book is largely about interiors, which are elsewheres... Bruce does not subtract the truth so much as add to it. He tells not a half-truth, but a truth-and-a-half. His achievement is not to depict Patagonia as it is, but to create a landscape called Patagonia—a new way of looking, a new aspect of the world."

But he invented Chatwinlandia, not Patagonia. Anyone who picks up Chatwin's other travel book, *The Songlines* (1987), will immediately recognize the style, and the gaze. His only other non-fiction writings were essays and short exercises, and, again, the oblique, apolitical, myth-seeking manner is omnipresent. It is even slightly depressing that new places never fired a new ambition or awakened a new style in the writer, such were his talents.

In Patagonia was a benchmark in travel writing and brought the region to the attention of a generation of British and American readers. The book was described as "a minor classic" by the *Times Literary Supplement*, and, writing in the *Sunday Times*, J. W. Lambert compared it with the writings of Graham Greene and V. S. Naipaul. As a literary model, it is as oppressive a model for aspiring writers as it is a thrilling journey for those who are first reading the book, whether sunk in an armchair in Surrey or on board a coach heading for Bariloche.

PAUL THEROUX: AN AMERICAN IN ESQUEL

In 1901 Paul Theroux's great-grandfather, Francesco Calesa, left Italy for Argentina. He was 52 and miserable, farming in a small village near Piacenza. Argentina meant America, an *estancia*, a better life… His bags were packed, his family—a wife and four children—were ready, and all was set. But he heard about an outbreak of yellow fever in Buenos Aires (this had actually taken place in the 1870s) and decided to go instead to New York. He hated it and lived plotting his escape, but by the time he left America, his marriage had broken down and he no longer had the will to go to Patagonia and start again.

We might infer from this that when Theroux decided to travel by railway from his house in Medford, Massachusetts, to Esquel in Chubut, Argentina, where the line ran out, he was going to complete his great grandfather's dream. But the book of the journey, *The Old Patagonian Express*, starts off with a claim that "I had nothing better to do." Theroux says that he was between books, wasting time and sick of the cold weather. So he took the commuter train and when everyone got off, he stayed on.

Something of this "nothing better to do" spirit runs all the way through Theroux's travel writing. Mentored by V. S. Naipaul (they later fell out in spectacular fashion), Theroux was one of a quartet of writers whose work gave travel writing a new, younger audience; the others were Chatwin, Peter Matthiessen and Robyn Davidson. Theroux had studied his Nabokov and knew the potential of combining a brash, rough-edged

American traveller's persona with that of a more learned, more literary European voice. The truculence and condescension of Theroux's travelling self have often been cited as evidence that "travel narrows", but he remains one of the best-selling travel writers of all time.

In Buenos Aires Theroux seeks refuge in learned conversation and meets up with Jorge Luis Borges, already established as the most eminent writer and best-known Anglophile in Argentina. They chitchat about Mark Twain, the American Civil War, Kipling and Robinson Crusoe, Perón and Videla—the latter the murderous military dictator of the time, whom Borges considers "well-meaning". But when Theroux first mentions that he is heading south, Borges tells him: "I have been there… But I don't know it well. I'll tell you this, though. It's a dreary place."

Later on, after another meeting with Borges (then blind, he liked younger writer to come round to read to him), Theroux is given a short lecture on W. H. Hudson:

> "We don't say Patagonia," said Borges. "We say 'Chubut' or 'Santa Cruz'. We never say Patagonia."
>
> "W H Hudson said Patagonia."
>
> "What did he know? *Idle Days in Patagonia* is not a bad book, but you notice there are no people in it—only birds and flowers. That's the way it is in Patagonia. There are no people there. The trouble with Hudson was that he lied all the time, and soon he couldn't tell the difference between what was true and what was tales". Borges thought a moment, then said, "There is nothing in Patagonia. It's not the Sahara, but it's as close as you can get to it in Argentina. No, there is nothing in Patagonia."

Undeterred, Theroux thinks that this nothing will make a great ending to his book. On the way south he is struck by the relentless scrubland, as viewed from the window of the "Lagos del Sur" express between Buenos Aires and Bariloche. Brown, yellow and pale green dominate, all colours shrouded in dust and seemingly dead, bereft of smell and even of insects. The human habitations are even less inspiring:

> We passed villages; they were named as towns on the map, but in reality no name would do. What were they? Six flat weather-beaten buildings of

which three were latrines; four widely spaced trees, a lame dog, a few chickens, and the wind blowing so hard a pair of ladies' bloomers were flapping horizontal from a clothesline. And sometimes, in the middle of the desert, there were solitary houses, made out of mud blocks or dusty bricks. These were a riddle; they had the starkness of cartoons. The picket fence of branches and sticks—what were they enclosing? what were they shutting out?—was no aid to fathoming the purpose of such huts.

The province of Río Negro looks like an abandoned film set, or a rough sketch of a town to come. Further south it is grimmer still: "The landscape was no longer green, even in that illusory way. It was half-tones of brown and grey and the low ugly thorn bushes were sparser, with fewer leaves... Hudson and other Patagonian travellers mention the bird-life— Hudson goes on for pages about the birdsong in the desert—but I saw nothing but oversize swallows and one hawk all afternoon... It was astonishing how empty a place it was. Borges had called it dreary. It was not dreary. It was hardly anything. There was not enough substance in it for it to have a mood. A desert is an empty canvas; it is you who give it features and mood, who work at creating the mirage and making it live. But I was incurious; the desert was deserted, as empty as I felt."

Is this the honesty of the worn out traveller, the traveller in anti-travel mode? Or the ennui of arrival; the journey, and the book, nearing its weary end? Dust pours into the carriage. People get off the train in small, ugly towns. Theroux laughs witheringly at tourists armed with cameras, bound for the "Tyrolean fantasy" of Bariloche. He sees the landscape as Biblical but bathetic: "dust, withered bushes, blue sky, kitty litter". His fellow passengers, who seem bent on "fumbling with pedigrees", talking about their ancestry and surnames, try his patience, as does a man standing behind him chomping and sucking ice-cubes. When he changes trains at Ingeniero Jacobacci, Theroux moves into classic American paranoia mode, claiming that he "had left a safe place and had journeyed to a dangerous one." (Nonsense, of course, as just about any US town or city, including those in Theroux's beloved Massachusetts, would have had a higher *per capita* murder or mugging count than any Patagonian town.) Lying on a bench, he runs off a litany of landslides, riots, plane crashes, floods and cholera epidemics: his is the fear of the tired, friendless gringo traveller/writer.

Sometimes it seems as if Theroux travels to see how angry he can get, but a few pages on he admits that he only came all this way to prove he is alone, which, "in itself... is like a discovery." An austral angle on the constellations at night and a seemingly "distorted" moon remind him of the distance he has put between his solitary self and his home, and he is energized by that thought. "In the best travel books the word *alone* is implied on every page, as subtle and eradicable as a watermark. The conceit of this, the idea of being able to report it—for I had deliberately set out to write a book, hadn't I?—made up for the discomfort."

A waiter on the Lagos express tells Theroux he is crazy to go all the way to Esquel on a little steam train. The author reflects that across South America he had been warned off Patagonia. It was, everyone had told him, a place where journeys began, not where one ended.

Theroux then prepares us for his final thesis with a claim that he "had no intention of writing about such a place [Patagonia]—that took the skill of a miniaturist. I was more interested in the going and getting there, in the poetry of departures." Of course, this is a ruse. He is desperate to join Pigafetta, Darwin, Hudson and his friend and competitor Chatwin in the ranks of Patagonian philosophers.

Theroux gives us a lesson in observation:

> The landscape taught patience, caution, tenacity. It needed to be studied to be seen. A glimpse of it told nothing.
>
> The Patagonian paradox was this: to be here, it helped to be a miniaturist, or else interested in enormous empty spaces. There was no intermediate zone of study. Either the enormity of the desert space, or the sight of a tiny flower. You had to choose between the tiny or the vast.

Without ever quite losing his urbane, hard-bitten tone, he teases the narrative towards a flourish, towards something akin to a philosophy of life: "I knew I was nowhere, but the most surprising thing of all was that I was still in the world after all this time, on a dot at the lower part of the map. The landscape had a gaunt expression, but I could not deny that it had readable features and that I existed in it. This was a discovery—the look of it. I thought: Nowhere is a place."

Patagonia has shifted from being bland and fatiguing to being interestingly vacant. The "discovery", sincere or not, is tinged with fear. In the final lines of the book Theroux might be contemplating the empty page as much as the drab wastes of Patagonia. His discovery is this: we are, even when creating and imagining and hurrying onward, moving towards nothingness. Literary theorists have made much of the blank page. Gaston Bachelard wrote that it "gives the right to dream." For Jacques Lacan it was the voice of the other, the negation of expression, a death-space. In C. S. Peirce's existential graphs the blank page signified Truth. It would not fit Theroux's train-weary persona to pontificate, but the "nothing" of his discovery coincides with the shift from text to blank page. A philosophy is nascent, and the theme recurs in Theroux's later writings. In *The Mosquito Coast* (1982), a novel, Theroux's crazed protagonist believes: "It's the empty spaces that will save us. No funny bunnies, no cops, no crooks, no muggers, no glue sniffers, no aerosol bombs." In *The Pillars of Hercules* (1995), a travelogue about the Mediterranean shoreline, his narrator is drawn to silent wastes: he enjoys the emptiness of the open sea, the off-season in Nice, the ferry that carries no passengers.

LA TROCHITA REVISITED

Theroux christened a train with a misnomer; the Old Patagonian Express was never an "express", and in the rather timeless context of the station at Ingeniero Jacobacci it would only have seemed "old" in the 1970s to a gringo used to shiny carriages with plastic seats. In recent years the train has gone the way of so many other tourism-thrashed pleasures and become a parody of itself. The 250-mile narrow-gauge line (Argentinians call the train *la trochita* or "little gauge") fell victim to the neo-liberal economic policies introduced during the government of Carlos Menem. The line was privatized—that is, closed down—in 1992.

The partial reopening of the line in 2006 has made trainspotters a little happier. But the service that carries people to it—from Buenos Aires or from the Patagonian coast at San Antonio Oeste—is intermittent, subject to the whims of the state and private enterprises willing to risk a fortune on a scantily subsidized, poorly maintained track. And any latter-day Theroux who chances to alight at the station may find himself waiting forever. In recent years the train has been run as a heritage experience, and only between the stations at Esquel and El Maitén, a hundred miles short of Ingeniero Jacobacci. This journey takes eight hours. Tour groups use minibuses to start or finish their "railway journey". Owing to demand

from some tourists who only want a brief ride on the train, many companies offer a bus pick up service at Nahuel Pan, just sixteen miles from Esquel.

CHATWIN AND THEROUX: LAST TANGO IN PATAGONIA
To promote their books, Bruce Chatwin and Paul Theroux gave a lecture at London's Royal Geographical Society. It was a lively night full of personal anecdotes, storytelling and occasional literary sparring. In 1985 a slim volume called *Patagonia Revisited* was published containing the fruits of this meeting, with illustrations by Kyffin Williams (who had in 1968 been awarded a Winston Churchill Fellowship to record the Welsh in Patagonia).

Chatwin sums up his and Theroux's mission: "Paul and I went to Patagonia for very different reasons. But if we are travellers at all, we are literary travellers. A literary reference or connection is likely to excite us as much as a rare animal or plant." He also reminds us that during the 1970s Patagonia and other remote, unpopulated places—northern Australia, New Zealand, Greenland, though not Siberia—were often mentioned in conversations about the threat of nuclear war and mutually assured destruction: "If the rest of the world blew up tomorrow, you would still find in Patagonia an astonishing cross-section of the world's nationalities."

Chatwin expresses a fascination with "exiles" and especially the "final capes of exile" but seems here to be hinting at a notion that Patagonian was a kind of Noah's Ark, ready to repopulate the world with all its races should the dread buttons be pressed in Moscow and Washington D.C.

Theroux writes that he read Shackleton's *South* at a very young age and, since then, "I associate the word 'south' with freedom." His impulse came from a void: "I had nothing to do, so I decided to go to Patagonia. It was an easy choice. I knew it was the emptiest part of America and one of the least known—consequently a forcing-house of legends, half-truths and misinformation." Patagonia, he says, seemed like a "precinct" of his own country, as people down there were still Americans.

Much of the book is made up of anecdotes familiar from their travelogues or is a straight-forward recapitulation of Pigafetta, Hudson, Darwin's reflections on the melancholy landscape, the saga of Butch and Sundance, the Welsh adventure and all the etymologies of Patagonia and Tierra del Fuego...

Another edition of *Patagonia Revisited* appeared later, with the title *Nowhere is a Place* (after Theroux) and containing colour photographs by Jeff Gnass, marking the arrival of these two literary travel writers in the land of the coffee-table book. Published in 1991, after Chatwin's death, it gave Theroux space to write an introduction by way of tribute to his writer and traveller friend.

Yet Theroux's portrait is of a chattering, impatient, skittish cad, who was in "a state of permanent crisis" as a writer. The Chatwin he knew was a wilful obscurantist with a mind full of half-baked theories. He was "handsome, calculating, and demanding" and a poor listener. The introduction is frank, utterly believable and fascinating, but you would not want a friend like this to draft your obituary.

What binds Theroux to Chatwin, as well as to Patagonia, is the accomplished narrative voice and strident sense of self that runs through both of their books. Both pretend to be utterly alone, Chatwin by physically absenting himself from the text and peopling it with myths, heroes, explorers and anarchists, Theroux by becoming alienated and turning inward and allowing the landscape to provoke ill-tempered observations. But their ultimate ambition was for their names to become synonymous with Patagonia. In this they both triumphed and to a degree that later writers have still not matched.

HANK WANGFORD: PATAGONIA'S COWBOYS

Fascinated by cowboys and eager to explore the roots of the modern myth, country singer Hank Wangford travelled through the Americas "from Patagonia to the Alamo" in 1992. He was drawn to the gaucho ideal, centred in the pampas but present throughout Argentina, and also to the legendary South American escapades of Butch Cassidy and the Sundance Kid.

In 1905 Cassidy and the Sundance Kid, wanted for robberies in the United States, holed up with their ravishing companion Etta Place in a log cabin near the Río Blanco outside Cholila, in Chubut province (the cabin still stands, adorned with *estancia*-style ram's skull) and can be visited. Butch went by the name James Ryan, and Sundance and Etta were Mr. and Mrs. Harry Place. On their twelve acres they kept 300 head of cattle, 1500 sheep and took on a couple of peons to help out. It reminded Cassidy of his beloved Utah, but without the hassle of the cops or the detectives of the Pinkerton Agency, who had vowed to track them down and kill them.

Cassidy sent a letter, dated 10 August 1902, to a friend's family:

> It will probably surprise you to hear from me away down in this country but the US was too small for me the last two years I was there. I was restless. I wanted to see more of the world. I had seen all of the US that I thought was good... This part of the country looked so good that I located, and I think for good, for I like the place better every day... The only thing lacking is a cook, for I am living in single cussidness [sic] and sometimes I feel lonely for I am alone all day, and my neighbours don't amount to anything, besides the only language spoken in this country is Spanish, and I don't speak it well enough to converse on the latest scandals so dear to the hearts of nations...

But Cassidy didn't stop "for good". In 1905 he and Sundance went down to Río Gallegos, where they dressed up as Western gunslingers and rode into town firing their six-shooters into the sky. On the pretext of finding out about land purchasing opportunities in the region, they

strolled into the Bank of London and Tarapaca, where they tied up the manager and made off with 20,000 pesos and £280. It is said that Etta Place shot the telegraph lines down with her pearl-handled Derringer to stop the news of their robbery getting beyond the town.

It is not known whether, after the Gallegos robbery, the trio returned to their northern hideaway or travelled with their cash to Europe. Legend has it that Sundance had become a passionate fan of Wagner while at the Metropolitan Opera in New York and had persuaded the others to join him in attending the Bayreuth Festival in Germany.

On 3 November 1908 two Americans—thought to be Butch and Sundance—robbed a Bolivian mining company's payroll. The pair was tracked to San Vicente, where a shootout between the outlaws and Bolivian troops ensued. The two outlaws were killed—a scene that has become iconic thanks to the 1969 film starring Robert Redford and Paul Newman. In 1991 a team of scientist excavated the San Vicente graves believed to hold Butch and Sundance; the DNA results showed the remains did not belong to either of them.

The Patagonian section of Wangford's book about the journey, *Lost Cowboys* (1995), is in part, a homage to Butch and Sundance. Wangford finds Río Gallegos soulless and centreless, and says that only the memory of Butch and Sundance makes the visit worthwhile. But it prompts him to explore local cowboy culture and iconography: from the horse markets and bronco-busting tournaments to the classic gaucho accessories of beret, *bombachas* (pantaloons), *alpargatas* (espadrilles) and *faja* (cummerbund).

Further north, in Bariloche and across the Andes in Osorno, Wangford shows less interest in the places (an "indoor market full of Indian crap") or local myths, choosing instead to study the character of the South American cowboy. The saddle, he says, was the meeting place of Welsh, Germans, Tehuelche, Irish and Mapuche; the Argentinian gaucho, Chilean *huaso* and Patagonian *baqueano* are often a combination of these bloodlines. Wangford enjoys the hearty country diet of grilled meat and innards and the simple folk music of the Mapuches. Against the backdrop of deracinated European cultures and the often crass version of "the South" sold to tourists, he cannot but admire the "beauty and style" of the cowboys. In a review in the *Irish Times*, veteran journalist Hugh O'Shaughnessy wrote that Wangford "portrays [Patagonia] with a greater warmth and humanity than the often pretentious and self-absorbed Paul Theroux or the late Bruce Chatwin did in their books."

After Patagonia, Wangford rides through the lands of gauchos, *huasos*, *llaneros* and *bandidos*, seeking to prove that "the American cowboy was not the first, but the last cowboy on the continent." As his Latino companion, Jo Tambien, says, "Hollywood owes us an apology."

DOMESTIC TRAVELOGUES

All the memoirs and travel journals of the nineteenth century were equestrian books, but Swiss-born Argentinian adventurer Aimé Félix Tschiffely was the first to make the horse the centre of the story. Better known for his *Tschiffely's Ride* (1933)—about an epic ride on two Argentinian *criollo*-breed horses, Mancha and Gato, from Buenos Aires to Washington, DC— the author made a later journey, mainly by car, from Buenos Aires to Patagonia. The book about the trip, *This Way Southward* (1940), provides first-hand accounts of the last few Tehuelche (drunk most of the time) and a lively journal of travelling along what would later become the Ruta 40. It also features an emotional reunion with his two horses Mancha and Gato, by then retired on the pampas.

Tschiffely aside, Argentinian and Chilean writers have yet to produce a modern travelogue about Patagonia. There are countless photographic essays and guidebooks, most of them richly packed with clichés, but there is no real tradition of travel writing in the contemporary literary culture. Adrian Giménez Hutton's *La Patagonia de Chatwin* (1999) is a thoughtful, sensitive attempt to retrace Chatwin's steps—exactly, page-by-page— and Hutton tracks down many of the people Chatwin met and even re-shoots the photographs that appear in *In Patagonia*. It is an obsessive work, but Hutton seeks to show how Chatwin's supposed exaggerations have been, in turn, exaggerated. Sadly, Hutton died in April 2001 aged 44, in a plane crash .He was on his way to Patagonia to attend a flag-raising ceremony in memory of Francisco "Perito" Moreno's hoisting of the national flag at Punta Bandera on Lago Argentino in 1877.

SECOND-HAND BOOKS

No foreign travel writer has written a truly memorable work about Patagonia since Chatwin. John Pilkington, Sara Wheeler and John Harrison have all written *good* books – but they all seem either Chatwinesque or reactions to Chatwin. Other writers, including Miranda France and Tom Vernon, barely get beneath the surface and seem to have been obliged by publishers to "do something on Patagonia". Is it that *In Patagonia* was a genuine literary landmark—and there is perhaps only one of those per generation—or that its author so subsumed the treasure trove of myths into his narrative that there is nothing new to be unearthed?

Professional travel writers are distinguished by their forced relationship with experience. They travel—and tailor the nature of their experience—in order to write, and they do so in order to be published. Thus they are always editing their journeys, and are noting even when they appear to be at ease and interacting. They are also aware that purely subjective memoirs are hard to sell, so, as Peter Hulme points out in "Patagonian Cases":

> It is one of the paradoxes of travel writing that the ideology of the integrity of the traveller's experience, that supposedly unmediated interface between the traveller and "otherness", is these days almost always mediated in practice by references to earlier travellers, to such an extent that books "in the wake of", or "in the footsteps of" constitute a whole sub-genre in themselves: the "ambulant gloss" as Charles Nicholl calls it.

None of the above writers, one might conclude, had an overriding "reason" to go to Patagonia. Perhaps all wanted to escape something or someone. Some may have sought money and fame. There is also a pioneer/colonist in every travel writer: it is no accident that the two "classics" of modern Patagonian travel writing in English happen to be the two earliest books.

It has happened before: Darwin's *Voyage of the Beagle* was reprinted dozens of times shortly after publication, and the author's reflections on Patagonia's beguiling aridity coloured perceptions of the region for decades after his death and into the late twentieth century. All later writers quote him, often with that reflective melancholy in mind. Chatwin's *In Patagonia* has, in a comparable way, become canonical, unhealthily influential, the subject of academic scrutiny and literary hysteria, and an easy text for all those engaged in analyzing post-colonial discourse. But Chatwin's Patagonia also seems like a closed world, perhaps because the prose—for all its craft and carefully modulated elegance—suffers from a certain stylistic opacity. Somehow, his travelogue is beginning to seem dated and dusty, a remnant of the oddly Victorian 1970s.

Patagonia has not changed as much as some other regions of Argentina over the past thirty and more years, but it *has* changed. Factors include the fragile Argentinian economy, falling wool prices and the erosion of *estancia*-based social networks, as well as the boom in cruises and adventure tourism. Local perceptions have also changed. That travel writers have not caught up with social realities is hardly surprising, since Patagonia offers far more—and far more saleable—riches for those who want to peddle its myths and distant history. It has been easy and convenient to think of Patagonia as somehow not part of Argentina (ergo Latin America and the real world). An imaginative gap has emerged between local artists and filmmakers and visiting writers and photographers, and the more engaging ideas are being generated by the former. Whether there is a great new Patagonian travelogue still to be written is open to question, but certainly all the travel writing currently available has settled down to become either eminently forgettable or, at best, part of the back catalogue.

Postscript

Deconstructing Patagonia:
The Brand, the Brochures and
Jean Baudrillard

"Suddenly the crew sent up a shout—a long ray of light had pierced the darkness."

Jules Verne, *The Lighthouse at the End of the World* (1905)

A search for "Patagonia" on Google gives over 14 million results. The highest ranked is the Patagonia clothing firm, a global retailing operation associated with camping, the outdoors and adventure which incorporates the spiky peak of Mount Fitz Roy in its logo. The company's site explains how "Patagonia" was adopted in the 1970s when it was decided that the original name, Chouinard Equipment, did not quite hit the mark:

> To most people, especially then, Patagonia was a name like Timbuktu or Shangri-La, far-off, interesting, not quite on the map. Patagonia brings to mind, as we once wrote in a catalog introduction, "romantic visions of glaciers tumbling into fjords, jagged windswept peaks, gauchos and condors". It's been a good name for us, and it can be pronounced in every language.

In 1979, on winning the Booker Prize, Iris Murdoch was asked what importance she attached to winning such literary prizes. Her reply was that it mattered as much as if it was raining in Patagonia. She used the same riposte when asked about bad reviews. You can almost here the lofty tone, the superiority in her sense of nationhood and home (Dublin, London, Oxford). Chatwin's *In Patagonia* had been published, but even for literary types the region was exotic, alien, irrelevant.

Ex oriente lux, said the philosophers. Perhaps it is something about the south, and, especially, the south-west. When the 1982 Falklands War

broke out many British people had no idea where the islands were. In 1983 historian Michael Mainwaring observed that Patagonia "is thought by some to be a fictitious country like Ruritania, or somewhere near the Amazon, or next to Mesopotamia, or somewhere off the Hebrides, or a disease... It is the back of beyond, a nowhere place." As recently as 1991, travel writer John Pilkington wrote that "Like Tartary or Siberia, this southernmost tip of South America tantalizingly resisted definition."

But was this true? Is it true now? Or is it not rather that Patagonia's obscurity is merely a useful fiction for writers, artists, generals? It justifies their books, photographs, massacres. Since Magellan's momentous landing, almost five centuries ago, there has been a conspiracy to keep the region distant and empty and inhospitable, at least in the mind. The wind, the tough grasses, and the treeless plains hardly encourage settlement, but harsher climes have been peopled and drawn into the mainstream of nations. London writer Iain Sinclair has argued that Londoners need to conserve wasteland on the edge of the city as a refuge for the soul. Perhaps the margin of the globe is Patagonia. It is the world's poetic refuge, the chthonic hope for all who are forced to live in cramped, man-made spaces.

When remoteness will not suffice, literature will do. The Patagonia clothing website claims that the company's "guiding design principle came from Antoine de Saint-Exupéry, the French aviator" and quotes, at length, a passage from *Wind, Sand and Stars*. Writers also serve those who sell Patagonia as a destination. Brochures offer holiday treks in the footsteps of Charles Darwin, the hoof-prints of Florence Dixie and along the "Lucas Bridges Trail" to Harberton. The literary circuits are part of the general tidying up. *Terra incognita* is now navigable, thanks to "The Seven Lakes Route", "The Southern Highway", "The Old Patagonian Express".

It is the perfect landscape of the imagination: faraway, without form and void, but crisscrossed by storylines and legendary pathways.

WORLD'S END

Ushuaia has become the city at "The End of the World"—and you can get a T-shirt, a fridge magnet and even a passport stamp to prove you have been there. Unlike Punta Arenas, which looks like a city, Ushuaia is little more than a resort town. It feels like a set for a film called *Tourism*. So beautiful is its setting, with the steel-grey, snow-capped mountains draped behind the town, and so clear its air, that the town was always doomed to

look drab and improvised. The prettier A-frame hotels throw into unsightly relief the majority of buildings. A former prison now houses the Museo Maritimo; an old bank is home to the Museo del Fin del Mundo. Most visitors are here to catch cruise ships to Antarctica.

In a typically sardonic essay titled "Tierra del Fuego-New York", published in the French newspaper *Libération* in January 1996, cultural commentator Jean Baudrillard deconstructs Ushuaia and the Fuegian fiction or, as he terms it, "phantasm" of the "end of the world".

Ushuaia, he says, is home to "a chaotic, incoherent, cowboy-film modernity: concrete, dust, duty-free, transistors, petrol, computers and the hubbub of useless traffic—as though the silence of the ends of the earth had to be obliterated. All that is human here is sublime in its natural desolation. All that is human is sordid: civilization's wastes." Ushuaia and New York, for all their obvious differences, he says, share the quality of being constructs. One sells itself as the end of the earth; the other proclaims that it is the centre of the earth.

Baudrillard finds the Fuegian landscape beguiling and repellent: "On every side nothingness, wasteland, sterile horizons, infinite vistas. There is, in fact, neither nature nor culture here, but a savage denial of both—a denial of landscape in the nothingness of the wind, the sooty sky, the Bahía Inútil; a denial of culture in the nothingness of the towns." His main concern is to wrench out of his poetic rapture a classic anti-colonial political protest:

> The Alakaluf [Halakwalup] did not know they were at the ends of the earth. They were where they were and nowhere else—something we shall never be. For the sailors, adventurers and missionaries, it wasn't the end either: they discovered a world entirely unlike their own, but one against which they could pit themselves, a new frontier. We arrive here today with only an imaginary notion of the ends of the earth (to which space travel long since put an end). And while the Fuegians were never parted from their fires (they carried them everywhere, even on their boats in the form of burning embers), we take pains to carry our artificial coldness with us everywhere—even into glacial latitudes.

Whether we are in New York or Ushuaia, the essay argues, we are only ever harbouring our own fictions. Our empty place, our Patagonia, our end of the world, is a fantasy we have tested scientifically, religiously, physically—on horses, ships, airplanes and cars—and always proven it to be illusory. Baudrillard insists that Westerners can never satisfactorily delude themselves with this bogus sense of extremity, as the phantasm shrivels and denies as we continue moving along the "hope-sapping curvature" of the earth. Yet we cling to it. We huddle together in our New Yorks, and yearn to escape to our Ushuaias.

A scintillating, deliciously bad-tempered meditation on extremity as this is, Baudrillard, for all he might strive to reposition Tierra del Fuego in the western imaginary, cannot get away from the poetics of desolation. He writes of Ushuaia's "incoherent" modernity, its concrete, its duty-free shops and its "useless traffic". Yet surely its residents have as much right to these things as those of older, grander cities. The essay purports to be a critique of the European eschatological fantasy of Tierra del Fuego, but it is couched in the classic language of Patagonia as formless void—"wasteland", "silence", "nothingness", "land of disasters"—with its attendant moral slant.

The Patagonian lexicon determines the way we imagine it. The more that is written, the more we travel and the more online searches we make, the more the enduring myths are reinforced. We seem to be equally enthralled by the two dominant, and interdependent, tropes: one of a land that is blank and empty; the other, a land full of unusual lives and improbable legends.

Westerners always want to illuminate their worlds. At the end of the nineteenth century, the San Juan de Salvamento lighthouse was erected on Staten Island, the eastern tip of Argentinian Tierra del Fuego, where the Andes chain finally plunges into the icy ocean. The "Faro del Fin del Mundo", as sailors nicknamed it, was there to guide ships through the tortuous channels and past the false capes. For a short time, the beam of light shone on the prisoners held in the world's remotest penal colony. But the storms raged and the island was deemed unsuitable even for outcasts. In 1899, as they were being transferred to the mainland, the inmates rose up, killed their jailers, and escaped on boats. On 1 October 1902 the light was switched off.

It was only a return to a former state. The Fuegian canoe peoples occasionally took a fire burning with them in the boats—but only for warmth. They were accustomed to living in obscurity and navigating by the stars when the clouds saw fit to clear. For the Tehuelche, the original Patagonians, the big-footed giants seen by Magellan on that fatal shore, night was as familiar as the open plains. Everything in creation came out of the night and all souls were destined to return there. This is the third trope, and the most ancient one: Patagonia as a shadowland, as the final darkness, as absence and death.

Further Reading

ANTHROPOLOGY

Briones, Claudia and Lanata, José Luis (eds), *Archaeological and Anthropological Perspectives on the Native Peoples of Pampa, Patagonia, and Tierra del Fuego to the Nineteenth Century*. London: Bergin and Garvey, 2002.

Bridges, Thomas (Hestermann Ferdinand and Gusinde Martin, eds), *Yamana-English: A Dictionary of the Speech of Tierra del Fuego*. Mödling, Austria: private collection, 1933.

Fernández, César A. (ed), *Cuentan Los Mapuches*. Buenos Aires: Ediciones Nuevo Siglo, 1999.

Gusinde, Martin (Wilbert, Johannes, ed), *Folk Literature of the Selknam Indians: Collection of Selknam Narratives*. Los Angeles: University of California, 1975.

Kirkland Lothrop, Samuel, *The Indians of Tierra del Fuego*. New York: Lancaster Press, 1928.

Martinić, Mateo, *Los Aónikenk. Historia y cultura*. Punta Arenas: Ediciones Universidad de Magellanes, 1995.

McEwan, Colin, Borrero, Luis Alberto and Prieto, Alfredo Prieto, *Natural History, Prehistory and Ethnography at the Uttermost End of the Earth*. London: British Museum Press, 1997.

Wilbert, Johannes and Simoneau, Karin (eds), *Folk Literature of the Tehuelche Indians*. Los Angeles: University of California, 1984.

HISTORY

Bayer, Osvaldo, *La Patagonia Rebelde*. Buenos Aires: Planeta, 2002.

Borrero, José María, *La Patagonia Trágica*. Buenos Aires: Puente Hermanos, 1928.

Boorstin, Daniel J., *The Discoverers*. New York: Phoenix Press, 1983.

Owen, Geraint D., *Crisis in Chubut*. Swansea: Christopher Davies, 1977.

Roca, Julio Argentino, *La Conquista del Desierto*. Buenos Aires: 1881.

Rock, David, *Argentina 1516-1987*. Berkeley: University of California Press, 1987.

Williams, Glyn, *The Welsh in Patagonia. The State and the Ethnic Community*. Cardiff: University of Wales, 1991.

Williams, Glyn, *The Desert and the Dream: A Study of Welsh Colonization in Chubut 1865-1915*. Cardiff: University of Wales Press, Cardiff, 1975.

Williams, R. Bryn, *Gwladfa Patagonia: La Colonia Galesa de Patagonia. The Welsh Colony in Patagonia, 1865-2000*. Llanrwst: Gwasg Carreg Gwalch, 2000.

MEMOIRS, DIARIES, TRAVELOGUES

Agostini, Alberto de, *Andes Patagónicos: Viajes de exploracion a la Cordillera patagonica austral*. Buenos Aires: 1941.

Bridges, Lucas, *Uttermost Part of the Earth*. London: Century, 1987.

Byron, John, *The Narrative of the Honourable John Byron containing an Account of the Great Distresses suffered by himself and his companions on the Coast of Patagonian from the year 1740, till their arrival in England, 1746*. London: S. Baker, G. Leigh and T. Davies, 1769.

Chatwin, Bruce, *Anatomy of Restlessness*. London: Jonathan Cape, 1996.

Chatwin, Bruce, *In Patagonia*. London: Jonathan Cape, 1977.

Chatwin, Bruce and Theroux, Paul, *Patagonia Revisited*. London: Jonathan Cape, 1985.

Clerke, Charles (attributed), *A Voyage round the World in Her Majesty's Ship The Dolphin, Commanded by the Honourable Commodore Byron... By an Officer on Board the said ship*. London: J. Newbery, 1767.

Coronato, Fernando (ed and trans), *Patagonia 1865, Cartas de los colonos galeses*. Comodoro Rivadavia: Editorial Universitaria de la Patagonia, 2000.

Darwin, Charles, *Journal of Researches into the Geology and Natural History of the Various Countries visited by H.M.S. Beagle, under the command of Captain Fitzroy, R.N. from 1832 to 1836*. London: Henry Colburn, 1839.

Drake, Francis Sir, *A discourse of Sir Francis Drakes iorney and exploytes after hee had past ye Straytes of Magellan into Mare del Sur, and through the rest of his voyage afterward till hee arrived in England. 1580 Anno* (known as the "Anonymous Narrative"). Harley MS280, fols 81-90, British Library, London.

Dixie, Lady Florence, *Across Patagonia*. London: Richard Bentley & Son, 1880.

Edwards, Philip (ed), *Last Voyages: Cavendish, Hudson, Raleigh. The Original Narratives*. Oxford: Clarendon Press, 1988.

Falkner, Thomas, *A Description of Patagonia*. London: Hereford 1774.

FitzRoy, Robert, *Narrative of the surveying voyages of His Majesty's Ships Adventure and Beagle between the years 1826 and 1836 describing their exam-*

ination of the southern shores of South America and the Beagle's circumnavigation of the globe. London: Henry Colburn, 1839.

Guevara, Ernesto, *The Motorcycle Diaries: Notes on a Latin American Journey.* London: Fourth Estate, 2004.

Gurney, Alan (ed), *The Loss of the Wager: The Narratives of John Bulkeley and the Hon. John Byron.* Woodbridge, Suffolk: Boydell, 2004.

Hakluyt, Richard, *Hakluyt's Voyages.* London: J. M. Dent, 1927-28.

Hudson, William Henry, *Idle Days in Patagonia.* London: Chapman & Hall, 1893.

Hutton, Adrian Giménez, *La Patagonia de Chatwin.* Buenos Aires: Sudeamericana, 1998.

Jones, Tom, *Patagonian Panorama.* Outspoken Press, 1961.

Keynes, Richard Darwin (ed), *Charles Darwin's Beagle Diary.* Cambridge: University of Cambridge Press, 2001.

King, Philip Parker, *Proceedings of the first expedition (for a survey of the Southern Coasts of America), 1826-30, under the command of P. P. K.* London: Henry Colburn, 1839.

Mainwaring, Michael, *From the Falklands to Patagonia: the Story of a Pioneer Family.* London: Allison & Busby, 1983.

Markham, Clements R. (trans and ed), *Narratives of the Voyages of Pedro Sarmiento de Gamboa to the Straits of Magellan.* London: Hakluyt Society, 1895.

Moreno, Francisco Pascasio, *Viaje a la Patagonia Austral.* Buenos Aires: 1879.

Musters, George Chatworth, *At Home with the Patagonians.* London: John Murray, 1873.

Pigafetta, Antonio (Skelton, R. A. trans and ed), *Magellan's Voyage. A Narrative Account of the First Circumnavigation.* New Haven: Yale University Press, 1969.

Pilkington, John, *An Englishman in Patagonia.* London: Century, 1991.

Quinn, David Beers, *The Last Voyage of Thomas Cavendish 1591-1592.* Chicago: University of Chicago Press, 1975.

Saint-Exupéry, Antoine de (Cate, Curtis trans), *Southern Mail/Night Flight.* London: Penguin, 1976.

Saint-Exupéry, Antoine de (Rees, William trans), *Wind, Sand and Stars.* London: Penguin, 1995.

Theroux, Paul, *The Old Patagonian Express: By Train through the Americas.* London: Hamish Hamilton, 1979.

Tschiffely, Aimé Felix, *This Way Southward*. London: Hodder & Stoughton, 1945.

Vespucci, Amerigo (Northrum, George Tyler trans) *Mundus Novus*. Princeton: Princeton University Press, 1916.

Wangford, Hank, *Lost Cowboys. From Patagonia to the Alamo*. London: Victor Gollancz, 1995.

Wheeler, Sara, *Travels in a Thin Country*. London: Little, Brown, 1994.

Whitehead, Anne, *Bluestocking in Patagonia*. London: Profile, 2003.

Willis, Bailey, *A Yanqui in Patagonia*. Stanford: Stanford University Press, 1947.

Young, John, *An Affecting Narrative of the Unfortunate Voyage and Catastrophe of His Majesty's Ship Wager, One of Commodore Anson's Squadron in the South Sea Expedition*. London: J. Norwood, 1751.

BIOGRAPHY AND OTHER NON-FICTION

Baudrillard, Jean (Turner, Chris trans), *Screened Out*. London: Verso, 2002.

Chesterton, Matt (ed), *Time Out Patagonia*. London: Ebury, 2005.

Clapp, Susannah, *With Chatwin. Portrait of a Writer*. London: Jonathan Cape, 1997.

Clark, Steve (ed), *Travel Writing and Empire*. London: Zed Books, 1999.

Clissold, Stephen, *Conquistador. The Life of Don Pedro Sarmiento de Gamboa*. London: Derek Verschoyle, 1954.

Gribbin, John and Mary, *FitzRoy: the Remarkable Story of Darwin's Captain and the Invention of the Weather Forecast*. London: Headline Review, 2003.

Guerriero, Leila, *Los Suicidas del fin del mundo*. Buenos Aires: Tusquets, 2005.

Harris, Graham, *A Guide to the Birds and Mammals of Coastal Patagonia*. Princeton: Princeton University Press, 1998.

Hulme, Peter and Youngs, Tim, *The Cambridge Companion to Travel Writing*. Cambridge: Cambridge University Press, 2002.

Keynes, Richard, *Fossils, Finches and Fuegians*. London: Harper Collins, 2002.

King, John and Torrents, Nissa (eds), *The Garden of the Forking Paths: Argentine Cinema*. London: British Film Institute, 1988.

Nichols, Peter, *Evolution's Captain*. London: Profile, 2003.

Schiff, Stacy, *Saint-Exupery: a Biography*. London: Chatto & Windus, 1994.

Shakespeare, Nicholas, *Chatwin*. London: Harvill/Cape, 1999.

Tomalin, Ruth, *W. H Hudson: a Biography*. London: Faber & Faber, 1982.

FICTION AND POETRY

Anon, *Primaleon. Los tres libros del cavallero... Primaelon et Polendos*. Venice: J. A de Nicolina de Sabio, 1534.

Brizuela, Leopoldo, *Inglaterra*. Buenos Aires: Clarín Aguilar, 1999.

Alonso de Ercilla (Lerner, Isaías ed), *La Araucana*. Madrid: Ediciones Catedra, 1993.

Iparraguirre, Sylvia (Hardie St. Martin trans), *Tierra del Fuego*. Willimantic: Curbstone Press, 2000.

Neruda, Pablo (Tarn, Nathaniel ed), *Selected Poems: A Bilingual Edition*. London: Jonathan Cape, 1970.

O' Brien, Patrick, *The Unknown Shore*. London: Rupert Hart-Davis, 1959.

Thompson, Harry, *This Thing of Darkness*. London: Hodder, 2005.

Verne, Jules, *The Lighthouse at the End of the World*. London: Sampson Low & Co, 1923.

FURTHER BROWSING

All websites are in English unless otherwise stated:

www.chris-moss.net

Author's own site with links to Patagonian travel stories.

http://darwin-online.org.uk

The complete works of Charles Darwin online.

www.glaniad.com

The most comprehensive site dealing with the Welsh in Patagonia.

www.patbrit.org

Forum and resources related to the history of British settlement in southern Patagonia.

www.saint-exupery.org

Website of the Saint-Exupéry Society in France (in French)

www.mapuche-nation.org

Campaigning on behalf of the Mapuche Nation, with offices in Bristol, UK and Piraeus, Greece.

www.geocities.com/tourtoirac

The colourful site run by the North American Araucanian Royalist Society, which promotes awareness of King Orllie Antoine and the Patagonian royal lineage.

Index of Literary & Historical Names

Index of Places & Landmarks

Printed in the USA/Agawam, MA
July 24, 2017

655737.004